ne

A   vices

VAN NOSTRAND REINHOLD
I⊤P™ A Division of International Thomson Publishing Inc.

New York • Alban   Madrid • Melbourne
Mexico City   )kyo • Toronto

To my bride of 16 years, Lois, and our family,
for patience, encouragement, and enlightenment.

Cover photo courtesy of: Bill Westheimer
Cover design: Paul Costello
Interior design and composition: Benchmark Productions, Inc.

Copyright © 1995 by Van Nostrand Reinhold

I(T)P™ A division of International Thomson Publishing Inc.
The ITP logo is a trademark under license

Printed in the United States of America
For more information, contact:

Van Nostrand Reinhold
115 Fifth Avenue
New York, NY 10003

International Thomson Publishing GmbH
Königswinterer Strasse 418
53227 Bonn
Germany

International Thomson Publishing Europe
Berkshire House 168-173
High Holborn
London WCIV 7AA
England

International Thomson Publishing Asia
221 Henderson Road #05-10
Henderson Building
Singapore 0315

Thomas Nelson Australia
102 Dodds Street
South Melbourne, 3205
Victoria, Australia

International Thomson Publishing Japan
Hirakawacho Kyowa Building, 3F
2-2-1 Hirakawacho
Chiyoda-ku, 102 Tokyo
Japan

Nelson Canada
1120 Birchmount Road
Scarborough, Ontario
Canada M1K 5G4

International Thomson Editores
Campos Eliseos 385, Piso 7
Col. Polanco
11560 Mexico D.F. Mexico

2 3 4 5 6 7 8 9 10   QEB-FF 00 99 98 97 96 95

Library of Congress Cataloging-in-Publication Data
Holleman, Gary
    Food and wine online : a guide to culinary online services / Gary
Holleman.
        p.   cm.
    Includes index.
    ISBN 0-442-02007-4 (pbk.)
    1. Food - - Information Services. 2. Food - - Databases. 3. Wine and
wine making - - Information services. 4. Wine and wine making -
- Databases. 5. Computer bulletin boards. 6. Electronic mail
systems. 7. Internet (Computer network) I. Title.
TX353.H54   1995
025.06'641 - - dc20   95-17184
                                                        CIP

Contents

Acknowledgments

I would like to thank Melissa Rosati, Senior Editor, Van Nostrand Reinhold, for her vision and management of this project. The development team she assembled made *Food and Wine Online* a joy to write. Special thanks to development editors Maxine Effenson Chuck for excellence in detail; Bill Chuck for creativity, humor, and sushi; and Tim Rosa, for technical revisions and encouragement.

Special contributions of many kinds were made to the creation of this book by: Gary Jenanyan, Mary Sue Milliken, Julie Mautner, Jerry Schochenmaier and Indian Harvest, Lois Holleman, Andrea Mulligan and the staff at Benchmark Productions. At Van Nostrand Reinhold: Jackie Martin, Production Director, Amy Shipper, Editorial Assistant, Bill McLaughlin, Marketing Services Manager, Khaled Soliman, Computer Support Specialist, Linda Wetmore, Marketing Manager, Veronica Welsh, Director of Marketing, Culinary Arts, Craig Wolynez, Marketing Assistant, Louise Kurtz, Production Manager, and Mike Suh, Art Director. Kathy Rickard, Leo Anderson, Tron DeLapp, Drager DeLapp, J.T. Salley, Pat Gibson, the members of ChefNet BBS, David Lee, and the subscribers of the Chefs on the Internet Mailing List.

Foreword

I have always been fascinated with the future. Gary Holleman's book *Food and Wine Online* is an incredible tool for explorers like me. I've had a modem for a few years now, however, being a chef, restaurant owner, and mom, I've barely seen a tiny slice of what's out there and interesting to me. Of special benefit are the "Electronic Food for Thought" passages, which profile many food professionals and how they use online services. This guide also highlights some miraculously time saving "Hot Tips" that allow one to move quickly and efficiently through the abundance of information and find what's useful to you.

With my first computer (which had the same size memory as my current palmtop organizer), I thought word processing was a miracle which allowed me to communicate more effectively with employees, customers, and purveyors, and they with me. Via modem, I'm impressed with the incredible arrays of information available to me. In any given day I may need to know the weather in New York, list a job opening, or pickle some vegetables that won't make it until tomorrow. With the resources available to me online, my work can be done quicker and sometimes better than without them. Imagine finding pickled green bean ideas from a farmer in Kentucky with a few keystrokes.

There is a new language to learn and this book teaches it with concise descriptions and concrete examples relating to our industry. Unfamiliar terms and concepts can be found here with ease and not only are they explained but one can't help but be inspired.

Over the past decade that I've been computer literate, I've alternated between loving the time saving machines and despising them. At one point, I even gave up my computer for almost half a year and went back to longhand and calculators.

I've now learned, and Gary concurs, that one must invest time learning these tools in order to receive the benefits. I've also learned that it's worth every minute invested—tenfold. The computer and modem will never replace much of what we do in our hands-on, service-oriented industry, but . . . THEY ARE THE FUTURE and with this guide, you'll be able to use them more fully.

Have fun and send me your favorite pickle recipes—Cookie99@AOL.com

Mary Sue Milliken

Introduction

I vividly remember the first time I went online. Connecting to CompuServe from the frozen, remote, woods of Northern Minnesota, I was astounded at the amount of information that was, all of a sudden, at my fingertips.

It was not long after I first joined CompuServe that I found their cooking forum, Cook's Online. Soon, I began to meet other professional chefs, restaurant owners and culinary students online. However, they were few and far between, and I wondered why more chefs were not using the wonderful resources of online communication.

Today there is a fully developed section on CompuServe for chefs. Moreover, nearly every major online service has an area dedicated to foodservice professionals. It is no longer necessary to wonder where the professionals are. They are online in great numbers.

For the chef knee-deep in emu or foie gras, cyberspace is indeed a confusing place. For the sommelier concerned about new varietals and old vintages, firing up a modem might, at first, seem like a waste of time. *Food and Wine Online* is for the chef who wants clearer vision in cyberspace. It is for the beverage professional who wants time online to be valuable.

My goal, in writing *Food and Wine Online,* is to first demystify the Internet and the rest of the online world. Second, I hope to provide you with the information necessary to get online quickly and efficiently. Lastly, to reduce your discovery time online, I have provided lists of resources that will be of interest to food and beverage professionals.

However, this does not mean that you will not have to work! There is no replacement for investing time, energy and a little money online to learn the basics. Just as you worked your way around the stations in the kitchen or just as you went from drinking a Chablis to enjoying a Pinot blanc, so will you have to grow and learn by doing . . . online.

I am well aware of the inadequacy you may feel when you are trying to "get wired." Take comfort; thousands of other culinarians are experiencing the same emotions during their first time online. Anxiety and misinformation abound. It was not too long ago that I had a colleague convinced that the starfield screen-saver on my computer was actually the live video from the front of a ship travelling in cyberspace!

If you would like a quick analogy to help you get a little more comfortable with exploring cyberspace, consider this:

Cyberspace is a lot like the restaurant industry. The BBS is an online service similar to an independent restaurant. It has a proprietor that will meet and greet you, help you through the menus, and maintain the "property" after you leave.

The large commercial online services, like America Online, CompuServe, DELPHI or PRODIGY, are like the chain restaurants. They serve millions, have a consistent appearance and theme throughout, and are owned by large corporations.

The Internet is sort of like a multi-unit operation where every unit is different, yet everything is connected. It is what I call the Richard Melman approach to online service. However, if Melman owned it (and no one does), it would most likely be called, "Let Us Aggravate and Confuse You!"

Of course, there is much greater detail in this book to explain and direct you through cyberspace.

WHAT IS COVERED IN THIS BOOK

Chapter 1 talks about some very valid reasons for going online. In addition, it will tell you about some other restaurateurs and culinarians who are already online.

Chapter 2 provides an easy to understand discussion of the hardware and software necessary to get connected.

Chapters 3-5 present the three domains of cyberspace—bulletin board systems, commercial online services, and the Internet. You will learn about the uniqueness, strengths and weaknesses of each. These chapters will provide the tools necessary for successful online sessions in each of the three environments.

Chapters 6-13 are guides to resources for foodservice professionals such as chefs, restaurant managers and owners, hospitality executives, and even culinary students. These chapters contain the information needed to find and connect to each of the resources.

Chapters 14-17 are for beverage professionals or restaurateurs concerned about beverage service for wine, beer, spirits and even coffee. These chapters point you to the resources in each of the domains of cyberspace and help you decide which will be most appropriate for your situation.

CONVENTIONS USED IN THIS BOOK

Electronic Food for Thought are vignettes of food and beverage professionals who are already online. You will hear about what they find valuable, where they spend their time, and how they leverage the technology.

Hot Tips are short and simple items that will help make life online a little easier. Some of the tips point you to more information online concerning a specific topic.

Key Terms/Key Ingredients are definitions of important words and concepts that may be new to the reader. They are not words common to the kitchen or the wine cellar.

Mise en Place is a convention that will be familiar to many culinarians. It literally means "to put in place" and is used here to indicate items that must be in order before taking the first step in a procedure. Mise en place is often used in food recipes to point to items of preparation and readiness that must be done before the recipe can be executed. In this text, mise en place is presented as a check list at the beginning of a procedure. The Culinary Institute of America's *New Professional Chef* states, the mise en place is more "a state of mind." I concur and have used the term in the fullest sense of the word.

Commands that are entered by the reader are indicated by a bold font or typeface. Text that is generated by a remote computer online is indicated by a typeface that looks like this:

```
This is an example of computer text.
```

HOW TO USE THIS BOOK

You do not need to read this book like a novel. I recommend you read it like a cookbook. However, if you read cookbooks from beginning to end, you will not be disappointed.

If you are taking your maiden voyage into cyberspace, take the time to read Chapters 1-5, they will give you a good foundation upon which you can build. If you are an experienced cyberchef, you may wish to browse the first 5 chapters, reading about your friends and peers online in the features called **Electronic Food for Thought**. Then continue into Chapters 6-17, browsing for new and interesting resources to explore.

The book is written and designed to sit on your desk next to your computer. After you read the narrative, keep *Food and Wine Online* nearby as a resource and reference.

NOW, GO GET WIRED!

Chapter 1 will introduce you to others who are already online. As you read their stories and then go online yourself, let me know how it goes. Send an e-mail message with your victories and discoveries to **holleman@chefnet.com.**

Key you later.

Hospitality Online and in the Know

"Chefs don't belong in front of computers, they belong in front of a broiler!" The boss believed that my priorities were in dire need of reevaluation. So off I went, toque in tow, to work the line in the kitchen. This was 1990.

As the executive chef in an upscale restaurant with a shiny new **point of sale (POS) system**, I saw the potential for food cost control and recipe management and yearned for free time to learn the use of this new tool. However, each time I was directed away from the computer I secretly suspected that the owner simply wanted more time to **upload** the sales data to the personal computer, so he could try to make sense of it by himself.

Who should operate a computer? Professionals in administration and management? Line employees? In today's competitive environment both the chef and the owner should make use of the computer and related functions for the same purpose: fast and accurate access to information. This chapter will outline five important reasons why one should investigate,

A **point of sales system** is a business machine, usually computerized, that tracks sales transactions. In a restaurant, it generally tracks the sales of individual menu items. Often, such machines are connected to personal computers for sales analysis.

Uploading is the process of transferring information from your computer to another.

Downloading, on the other hand, is the exchange of information from another computer to your own. Uploading sends data outbound; downloading brings data inbound.

Online services are computer-based information and communication resources that are accessed with a modem.

Computer-aided communication is the exchange of information between computers. It includes not only file and data exchange, but also text-based conversations between two individuals using computers.

learn about, and use **online services** in the hospitality industry.

The five reasons are these:

1. First of all, online services provide instantaneous connection to information.

2. Using a computer to connect to information enables and empowers the user.

3. The most accurate and current information available is increasingly found only online.

4. Professional relationships are greatly improved by **computer-aided communication (CAC).**

5. Online services provide a powerful opportunity for customer acquisition.

FIVE REASONS TO COMMUNICATE ONLINE

What is it about electronic communication that motivates food and beverage professionals to look into online services? What are the key benefits they stand to gain?

1. Electronic Communication Provides Instantaneous Connectivity.

Waiting until the office or the library opens to start research is no longer necessary. Receiving information online is not contingent on business hours in any respect. Even the wait for a fax from a coworker often can be eliminated with online access to the proper information.

Instantaneous connection is not limited to just information. With the expansion of the **Internet** and the proliferation of **chat services,** professionals separated by continents can visit via computer with the speed and ease of a local phone call.

ELECTRONIC FOOD FOR THOUGHT

The term "chat" implies a casual conversation, but the chat mode on **bulletin board services** (**BBS**s) and the Internet can also be used to conduct business economically and efficiently.

Jo Lynne Lockley is the owner of the San Francisco search firm, Professional Chefs Agency. She uses the Internet to conduct business each day, and "chat" is just one of the tools she employs. Here is an account of a recent chat session on the Internet.

"The Internet not only lets us reach out to potential candidates and provide extensive industry insights," says Lockley, "but we are also beginning to use it as a communications tool. Recently, we had an IRC (Internet Relay Chat) chat with a candidate in the Midwest, an associated agency in Switzerland, and a client in Japan. (An IRC is the Internet's tool for live chats via the keyboard.) At the end each of us possessed a written record of the communication after generating a log of the session."

Quick retrieval of information and around-the-clock communication are becoming necessities in the 1990s. Historically, these abilities allowed users to be leaders. What is the cost of delays and unnecessary effort in communicating information? Time, money and the loss of your competitive edge.

ELECTRONIC FOOD FOR THOUGHT

Foodservice sales representatives spend large amounts of time "on the road" meeting with foodservice chefs and buyers. For the consultative sales person, information is critical to selling success and often difficult to obtain while traveling. Ken Harkins services only contracted foodservice accounts for distributor Thoms

The **Internet** is a vast, worldwide network of computer networks. Growing at an unimaginable rate, the Internet's actual size is not really known. It is a tool for education, research, and, more recently, business and recreation.

Chat services allow users to connect online with each other, instead of a database or message board. This allows for *real-time* communication as opposed to the delayed response from, say, electronic mail.

A **BBS** is a dedicated computer that accepts dial-in access for the purpose of leaving private and public messages, transferring files, and chatting with other members.

Proestler. When he goes online to access information from company headquarters, he knows the response will be immediate. Harkins says, "With the computer and modem I get that instant gratification we have all come to know and love." The information that he wants is literally at his fingertips.

2. Electronic Communication Has Become a Tremendous Tool for Empowerment.

Jerry Schochenmaier, general manager of Indian Harvest Specialtifoods, calls computer-aided communication (CAC) the "ultimate tool for democracy," where individuals have equal opportunity to express opinions, publish views, and become a catalyst for action. Small companies have the same opportunity online as multinational corporations. A marketing manager in Wyoming has the same leverage in the electronic community as a vice president of marketing in New York City.

Much of this empowerment comes from the interesting "broadcast" abilities available through computer-aided communication. Broadcasting messages online may happen in several different ways. For instance, copies of messages can easily be sent to a large group of individuals on an electronic mailing list with no more effort than that required for sending a single message. Any individual on the Internet can send a message to thousands of other individuals on the Internet. The same ability exists in many other online environments. It is significant that for the first time in the history of mankind, a single individual with relatively modest resources can connect so quickly and communicate so effectively with such a huge audience.

ELECTRONIC FOOD FOR THOUGHT

Richard Z. Hexter, executive chef at Schumpert Medical Center in Shreveport, Louisiana, recently enrolled in a business management class. While working on a research paper examining employee theft, Hexter went online looking for industry examples. Broadcasting via electronic mail, he asked an easily identifiable group of more than 200 chefs online for assistance. The response was immediate and authoritative. Responses reflecting all manner of trust and violation, and spanning the industry, came in.

With only a couple of weeks to complete the project on a limited budget, using postal mail or industry advertising would have been too slow and too expensive. But by broadcasting his plea, Chef Hexter successfully completed the paper. In the same manner, shortly thereafter, he announced his graduation from college and sent a "thank you" to his peers.

Information retrieval can be as empowering as broadcasting. Informed managers and employees are better equipped to accommodate the daily needs of a business in the 1990s. Edwards W. Demming, quality assurance guru to the Japanese, correctly pointed to the improvement in quality and profits when workers were given the information needed to make decisions. Online services provide access to information as never before. Smart employers are responding in new and innovative ways.

A former general manager of the Sheraton Suites Hotel in Plantation, Florida, provides access to a basic CompuServe account for business applications. He recognized that enabling employees to access and respond to information is pivotal in empowering workers. Hotel employees quickly found a valuable use for the CompuServe information service.

ELECTRONIC FOOD FOR THOUGHT

Banquet and Catering Manager Michael Hewes, at the Sheraton Suites Hotel, Plantation, Florida, consults the weather maps on CompuServe to make sure no severe weather conditions are predicted before he sets up for outdoor events.

"Recently, we had a large wedding reception planned for the outdoor rotunda. The reception was scheduled to take place at 6 p.m.," says Hewes. "I checked the CompuServe weather forecast and saw that storms were moving in off the coast and began to plan to move the reception indoors. I called our contact people for the reception and told them about the change of plans and the approaching storms. They were quite disappointed. When the storms arrived, and the reception was underway inside, our guests saw that the celebration would have been ruined. They were very grateful and showed their appreciation for the extra effort to protect the wedding reception."

As weather forecasting becomes far more detailed and accurate, few catering professionals can afford to ignore such important information. This is particularly true in Florida where the weather can quickly turn violent. Few professionals would have taken this extra step to go online and check the weather, but it made Michael Hewes a hero.

3. The Most Accurate and Up-To-Date Information Available is Online Information.

Current issues of gourmet food and beverage publications are available online. Class descriptions for the famous cooking school, Le Cordon Bleu, can be found on the Internet. New product announcements can be found on CompuServe in an article abstract for New Product News. Many industries are certainly more aggressive than foodservice in posting information online, but few are growing more rapidly in online content.

The isolation of American foodservice from international culinary professionals is quickly deteriorating as food and beverage professionals worldwide discover computer-aided communication. Professional culinary information is now appearing online from as far away as Australia, New Zealand, and the United Kingdom. In many cases, this information is *only* available online.

ELECTRONIC FOOD FOR THOUGHT

Jo Lynne Lockley is a "toque hunter" and an avid online visitor. As the owner of Professional Chefs Agency, a search firm placing chefs in new positions worldwide from her office in San Francisco, California, Lockley carefully guards her "network" of contacts and clients. But she quickly identifies online resources as an important asset in the servicing of that network.

A **mailing list** is an automated mail distribution tool on the Internet for electronic mail.

"The Internet is helping me extend my own long-term network," says Lockley. "I initially viewed the Net as an immediate resource for standing job orders. Instead, it has become a much more valuable resource, providing me with insights and contacts across the country and the world."

The current status of any job opening is a vital and fluid statistic. In foodservice, where chefs often change jobs as frequently as once every two years, accurate and up-to-date employment information is a valuable commodity. When trade publications often work with 60-day lead times and most newspapers are only regional, computer-assisted communication offers unique solutions to age-old problems.

Recently, Lockley posted an urgent request for help when a client lost a baker just two weeks before opening a new European style, all-natural bakery. By posting messages on the **Chefs on the Internet Mailing List** and several other online hang-outs for food professionals, Lockley got quick replies for the bakery to consider.

Messages sent to a "list server" are redistributed to all list members. **Chefs on the Internet** is exclusively for food professionals, culinary students, and culinary educators.

4. Electronic Communication Encourages and Enhances the Development of Professional Relationships in the Hospitality Industry.

Today, computers do more than crunch numbers and process words in the back office. They connect people and build relationships.

By nature, the hospitality industry is a people-oriented business. Building relationships is its cornerstone. Restaurateurs value relationships with each and every customer. The interaction between the sales representative and the chef is vital to a kitchen's success. Even the relationship between the chef and the customer has become important to the success of a restaurant.

Janos Wilder, chef and owner of Janos Restaurant, Tucson, Arizona, finds it increasingly difficult to spend time in the kitchen.

"My guests insist on seeing me, the owner, out front meeting and greeting," says Wilder. Janos Wilder understands the "people" side of the business as well as the culinary side and spends a great deal of time maintaining a visible presence in the restaurant.

In contrast, other chefs turn to the computer to enhance either customer or professional relationships. Robert Weyandt is marketing chef for Guest Services Inc.(GSI), Fairfax, Virginia. GSI is a contract foodservice company with accounts such as school, business, and industry cafeterias; it also serves museums such as the Smithsonian Institution's National Air and Space Museum. Weyandt has found that electronic communication can enhance professional peer relationships. Weyandt is a member of ChefNet, a bulletin board service (BBS) for chefs. Online, Chef Weyandt has met others in his industry, obtained product samples, and acquired new suppliers for some of the GSI units.

As more food and beverage professionals go online, professionally rewarding relationships will be enhanced and will multiply.

When electronic relationships multiply and flourish, an exciting phenomenon begins to take place. Professional users of online services find they are becoming members of a **virtual community.** They are communities in the sense that relationships become interconnected and complex; they live

The term virtual is often used in describing aspects of electronically created environments. It refers to the existence of something in effect but not in actual form. A **virtual community** is one that has many of the attributes of a community as we know it in the day-to-day world; however, it exists and expands electronically.

and die based on the personal energies of individual participants. Citizens of a virtual community learn to trust and distrust based on their experiences. They learn to depend on one another, to discipline and police themselves based on both written or unwritten rules.

In **cyberspace** professional relationships are born hundreds of times a day. It is easy to understand how important such a community, formed around electronic communication in cyberspace, becomes to its members. Consider how important other communities have become to the hospitality industry. The American Culinary Federation is a global force in culinary education. Members share a camaraderie that is strong and vital. Uniting the lodging industry are many state hotel and motel associations that permit members to network with their peers.

These unique communities are the foundation of professional networking. A limiting factor with these organizations, however, is that communication is often difficult due to the restrictions of time and distance. Attendance at meetings of professional organizations is almost imperative to "feel" like a member and obtain the most valuable benefits of membership.

Electronic or virtual communities are often more flexible and less demanding than more traditional communities. While many culinary organizations have existed in a traditional manner for many years, some new organizations have invested in cyberspace as a way to develop their community.

The International Association of Women Chefs and Restaurateurs (IAWCR) is the first culinary association to homestead in cyberspace. The IAWCR exists to further the advancement of women in culinary and foodservice careers. Mary Gaylord, executive director of IAWCR, places a great deal of value on developing a sense of community online. Gaylord believes that being online offers a unique opportunity to conncct to, and develop relationships with, women who are foodservice professionals.

When the term cyber is used it often implies the electronic transfer of information. Thus, **cyberspace** becomes the vast, almost tangible region of the online world where electronic communication takes place.

5. Customers Can Be Acquired Online.

So you think that just because you can't upload an herb-crusted lamb chop or a bottle of Jordan Cabernet that there are no customers online? Think again.

ELECTRONIC FOOD FOR THOUGHT

Terry "Burk" Burkhardt is the chef/owner of Burk's Cafe in Seattle, Washington. Burk's Cafe is one of only a handful of restaurants with a Web page on the Internet. While the cafe draws mostly from the local neighborhood for clientele, the international exposure of the Net has had its impact.

"Several customers a week come in and let me know they have seen the Web page," says Burkhardt. Burk's Web site features the menu, hours of operation, a map, and more. In addition to the customers who mention the page, Burkhartd says that over 350 people view his Web site each month. An added promotional bonus came when a local newspaper featured Burk's Cafe in an article on commerce on the Net. It has all added up to a considerable amount of exposure and new business.

Burkhardt was inspired to publish the Web page by two events. First, he visited and admired the Web page published by Mark Miller and the Red Sage restaurant. Then, when his Internet provider offered the Web server for use by clients at no cost, Burkhardt seized the opportunity. "I am computer literate yet I don't know anything about programming. But I found that the language needed to create a Web page was not difficult," says Burkhardt "I did it for the experience of doing it . . . for the fun of it."

Burkhardt is optimistic about the Web and its future. "The nature of it is such that the larger it gets, the better it gets. Restaurants are prime territory for the Net because they must continuously get the message out."

In keeping with Internet philosophy, Burkhardt tries to give something back to the Net by including his list of favorite culinary links on the Web. He intends to continue to upgrade his page by including some photos of the restaurant.

___

There are many ways to attract paying customers to the doors of your restaurant or bar. In fact, the most creative customer acquisition techniques have yet to be explored. Cyberspace is still a new and untamed frontier that begs to be settled and developed by the food and beverage industry. With literally millions of eating and drinking customers online, who can argue that a business presence online doesn't make sense?

It is commonly, but inaccurately, believed that nothing is sold on the Internet, that advertising is verboten. In fact, the Internet, all the commercial online services, and many BBSs are teeming with life from the entrepreneurial species. Some are even your competitors!

ELECTRONIC FOOD FOR THOUGHT

Mark Miller's restaurant in Washington, D.C., Red Sage, is at the forefront of leveraging online technology to create relationships, reduce costs, and attract customers. The Red Sage has created a **World Wide Web (WWW) page** for advertising its daily specials. In the highly networked, highly computerized District of Columbia, an online presence can be quite valuable. *USA Today* reports that guests in the restaurant have even recognized the voice of their waiter as that of the narrator of the Web audio for Red Sage.

CONCLUSION

There are five key reasons why hospitality professionals benefit from being online. First, it provides instantaneous access to information that is essential for conducting business. It is no longer a matter of being *better* informed than competitors; it is a matter of being informed first!

The **World Wide Web** is the fastest growing and most exciting aspect of the Internet. Able to display full-color graphics and photos in an easy-to-navigate manner, the Web has become a mecca for entrepreneurs. Some Web sites even provide sound and video clips for downloading.

___

A Web document is called a **page**. It often includes not only multimedia but also links to other pages. By "clicking" on a link the Web user is effortlessly and transparently connected to another specified page on an entirely different computer, possibly on another continent!

The second key that results from being online is empowerment. Employees can receive the exact information that will enable them to make more informed decisions with confidence.

Accuracy is the third reason that communication technology is valuable. New computer-aided communication tools improve the ability of a business to acquire more *accurate* information. This ensures reduced risks, improved quality, and lower costs.

The fourth advantage to communicating online is that it fosters professional relationships. Communities have become an important part of doing business in today's environment. Establishing relationships is a key factor in professional networking, industry coalitions, and consultative selling. The sense of community can be enhanced and cultivated online. Information on demand and the immediacy of online communication serve to encourage the development of a community.

Last, online communications can help food and beverage companies acquire new customers. Online resources include advertising opportunities, efficient communication, and order placement.

C H A P T E R 2

Launching into Cyberspace

Connecting one computer to another computer, whether on the other side of town or the other side of the planet, is truly a marvel to behold. The experience is like the first solo drive you take in a car as a teenager. You feel a sense of power, freedom, and mobility. But before you could know the joy of driving, you needed your parents to lend you the car—and you needed to learn how to drive. In cyberspace, the computer is your steering wheel and the modem is your vehicle. Once online, you begin to understand what draws people by the millions to venture into cyberspace.

Getting online requires a computer and a **modem.** You also need a telephone line, the appropriate software, and a little tenacity. This chapter will provide you with information and helpful tips on how to work with your computer, modem, and software to take your first journey. You are encouraged to summon the fourth item, tenacity.

THE MODEM: A NEW ADDITION TO THE CHEF'S PANTRY

A modem takes information in a **digital** form, transmits it as an audible signal over a telephone line, where the receiving modem and computer transform it back to digital. Figure 2.1 shows how the modem connects to the computer.

A **modem** is a device that converts (*modu*lates and de*mod*ulates) electronic signals from one form to another form.

A computer stores information in the **digital** form of a series of 0s and 1s.

13

FIGURE 2.1
HOW THE MODEM CONNECTS TO THE COMPUTER

Computer offering online services, such as a BBS

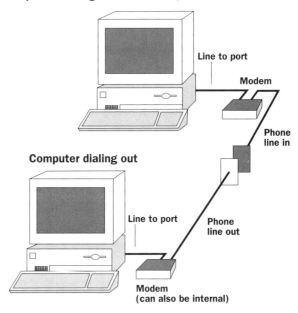

The 0s and 1s that the computer uses to store information are known as **bits**. They are generally transmitted in groups that include eight data bits plus a start bit and a stop bit.

A **kilobit** is a unit of 1000 bits.

Modems are rated by speed. Early in the history of computer-assisted communication 300 **bits** per second (bps) was the top speed. Take a minute to check the manual for your modem. What is the maximum speed your modem can run? Is the maximum speed specified for data transmission or facsimile (fax) transmission? Many modems operate at a lower speed for data transmission. When you set your modem to run at a specific speed, the modem will transmit data at the maximum rate you have set. If the receiving modem is slower than your transmitting modem, your modem will slow down to the speed of the modem at the other end. Today, speeds of 14,400 bps, or 14.4 **kilobits** per second (kbps), are common. The speeds on the most advanced modems are as high as 28.8 kbps over standard telephone lines.

ELECTRONIC FOOD FOR THOUGHT

Wendy Straub is a chef/consultant in New York City. Her first venture into culinary cyberspace occurred in June 1994, when she became a member of CompuServe. Straub remembers her thoughts as she browsed through the CompuServe Forum, Cooks Online, for the first time.

"I thought it was the most amazing thing in the world," she recalls. "It was thrilling."

As Chef Straub began to explore her computer equipment in addition to the online service, she discovered there was a lot she didn't know. Even the help manuals were difficult to understand!

"I opened my modem manual one day and found it was mostly numbers and words I didn't understand. I thought 'What are these bits? What is this? What is that?' says Straub.

But Straub didn't despair. In fact, she used CompuServe to help her figure out the answers to her questions.

"I dialed CompuServe with my modem and posted a message for help in one of the technical assistance forums. They have a lot of helpful people there," says Straub.

She even finds that other chefs assist with the answers to technical questions.

"I met a chef from the West coast and he was my first online friend. We can talk about computers and setting up databases." Because they are both restaurant consultants, they have a great deal in common.

"It's very special," says Straub.

Chef Wendy Straub finds help understanding the jargon and complexities of the online world by using help forums online. She also develops friendships with other professional chefs that she meets

An **initialization string** is a set of pre-defined commands that your modem uses to send and receive data over telephone lines.

Once you determine how your data communications software lets you enter initialization strings, you can modify the configuration to your personal preferences. For example, to set your speaker volume, enter L0, L1, L2, or L3 into the initialization string. (L0 is the lowest and L3 is the loudest.) Consult your modem manual for more commands.

in cyberspace. Together they solve the problems and answer the questions.

Each modem can be customized to function in a specific way. This means that the operation of a modem is changed to suit specific circumstances. This is done by sending a series of letters and numbers called an **initialization string,** or "init string," to the modem.

Telephone Lines

Phone lines are the figurative pavement on the information superhighway. Be aware: Extension telephones on a data line can disrupt communication during an online session if they are used.

HOT TIPS

If you find yourself spending a large amount of time online, obtaining a dedicated data line can be very convenient.

Linking Your Computer to Your Modem

Modem software is the link between the computer and the modem. The modem software makes it possible to send instructions to the modem. The software can be very basic or quite powerful and complex. However, most modem software lets you customize a few basic options:

- Dialing methods
- Dialing directories
- Modem speed settings
- Port settings
- Terminal emulation settings

Dialing Methods

The most basic feature of any modem software is the ability to dial a phone number. Most software allows either tone or pulse dialing. Although tone dialing is used most often, pulse dialing may be necessary at times. Check your modem software manual for specific instructions on dialing methods. Examining the init string for your modem will tell you what dialing method the modem is currently using. The first characters of the init string are AT, which tells the modem to wake up and pay (AT)tention. The second pair of characters are probably DT or DP. DT indicates Dial Tone; DP indicates Dial Pulse. DT is usually faster than DP.

Dialing Directories

Modem software lets you create **dialing directories** for automatic dialing. Each phone number links to a record that holds setting preferences for dialing a specific number. If you choose not to customize the settings, default settings are most likely provided. These default settings are listed in your software documentation.

Modem software also lets you store other settings through the dialing directory. For instance, if you have call waiting, inbound calls will be a hindrance; the sound that indicates there is another call interferes with data transmission. You can eliminate this interference, however, by manipulating the dialing code sequence.

If you are on an office phone system, you may need to precede the phone number with a 9 to get an outside line. Spaces and dashes can be included in the number, but they are not necessary. When a comma is included, however, it causes the dialing process to pause. This is helpful if your phone system delays slightly before connecting you to an outside line. For example, to include a pause for a connection to an outside line before dialing ChefNet BBS, enter the dialing number like this: 9,1-218-751-5149.

Port Settings

Most modem software will connect to the correct **port** based on information you supply during installation. Each port has a name, address, and interrupt or **IRQ.**

A **dialing directory** is a set of phone numbers that can be stored by modem software and accessed for later use.

A **port** is the point at which a modem connects to a computer.

An **IRQ** or interrupt number is a line the port uses to tell the computer that there is information to process. Each device *must* use a unique IRQ.

Terminal Emulation Settings

When connecting to another system it is often necessary for your computer to **emulate** a specific terminal type. This lets incompatible computers communicate. A little experimenting with emulation on various systems will be helpful in understanding the differences in emulation from terminal to terminal. Descriptions of emulation options follow.

The American National Standards Institute (ANSI) is the best emulation choice when connecting to a BBS. It will usually yield colors, bold, and blinking fonts and generally provide a pleasant online experience. Additionally, these graphics are intended to help users navigate and make the BBS easier and more pleasant to use.

Remote Image Protocol (RIP) is the newest and fastest growing emulation for use on BBSs. RIP provides colorful screens that have easy-to-understand graphics. More importantly, RIP provides a way to use a mouse to click on buttons that help you move from screen to screen. In order to use RIP you must have modem software called **RIP***term.* RIP*term* is available from BBS operators who use RIP graphics on their bulletin boards such as Steve Adams' HotelNet or Indian Harvest's ChefNet. It is available only for IBM-compatible computers. However, even though a BBS uses RIP graphics, you can still use ANSI emulation to log in. Culinary artists appreciate RIP graphics for their stunning visual appeal. New releases of RIP allow the display of photos and the generation of sound online. Because RIP is the most advanced of all BBS interfaces it is destined to grow quickly and become the interface of choice not only for culinary professionals but for all BBS users.

Teletype (TTY) is the most basic terminal emulation available. It can be used when you do not know the type of the system to which you're connecting.

Digital Equipment Corporation VAX Terminal 100 and 102 (DEC VT-100, VT-102) emulations are used by some Internet providers who do not have graphical screens. Using these emulations can sometimes cause your keyboard

When one type of computer terminal simulates the operation of another type of terminal it **emulates** the other terminal.

ANSI is an acronym that indicates a specific standard for communication.

Remote Image Protocol (RIP) lets you see graphical images and use your mouse to navigate through a BBS.

The special modem software that lets you see the RIP screens on a BBS is called **RIP***term*.

TTY is an emulation of a typewriter or teletype style keyboard. It is effective and sufficient for basic text communication.

to act differently than you expect. For instance, the backspace and the delete key may not work properly. However, these emulations will let you successfully connect to some Internet services.

Here are few rules of thumb to get you started:

- ANSI emulation is best for most BBSs.
- RIP graphics are the leading edge of new emulations, but they are only available with RIP*term*.
- TTY emulation is best when the correct emulation is uncertain.
- VT-100 and VT-102 are often the best choice for a basic Internet connection that does not offer graphical screens.

The emulations called **VT-100** and **VT-102** do not allow you to view graphics online. They are text-only emulations used by some Internet providers.

CYBERSKILLS FOR ONLINE NAVIGATION

At the beginning of the chapter we compared your first trip into cyberspace to your first solo drive in a car. Just as the modem and computer are analogous to the automobile on a trip, you too must acquire a few skills online to travel successfully.

For instance, moving a file from one computer to another is a fundamental activity online. Downloading means moving a file from a remote computer to your own. Uploading is exactly the opposite. The file is transferred from your computer to a remote computer. When you download or upload a file you are actually copying it because the original version of the file remains in its initial location.

File transfers have brought to light a problem that has plagued some computer users in recent years. **Computer viruses** can be transmitted from online sources as a result of file transfers. Some types of file transfers are more risky than others.

Text file transfers rarely put a computer at risk for viral infection. Because they are simply text it is difficult to store computer language that might cause viral infection in the file. You can identify text files by the extensions .txt, .doc, or .asc added to the filename. Another type of text file transfer,

When special computer language that will cause harm to hardware, software, or data is hidden in a computer file, it is called a **computer virus**.

When you capture in a file the content of screens you see online, you create a **log file**. A log file serves as a record of an online session.

When a computer file is a software program, it is considered to be an **executable file**. That is, it will execute commands as directed.

Software programs are written in special non-readable language called **binary code**.

A computer program that can examine the contents of a file and identify viral contamination is **viral detection software**.

called a **log file,** is equally harmless. You can create a log file that will record the content of the text screens you access online by using your modem software.

HOT TIPS

If you are reading messages online that you would like to save, making a log file is a good idea. Read your modem software manual to find out how your specific software starts a log file.

ELECTRONIC FOOD FOR THOUGHT

Remember Jo Lynne Lockley, the owner of a culinary search firm mentioned in Chapter 1? Lockley sent a transcript of a job placement negotiation that took place on the Internet to participants. The negotiation was "live"; each participant used a keyboard to communicate. The transcript was created using the text from a log file.

This is a creative and powerful use of the log file option. The text is a verbatim record of an important discussion. It is much more reliable and accurate than simply summarizing the online meeting.

Transferring a computer program instead of simple text can put a computer at risk for catching a computer virus. An **executable file,** graphics file, or other **binary code** is the more likely carrier of a viral infection. Binary files can be identified by extensions like .exe, .bin, .gif, and .tif. Scanning binary files with **viral detection software** before running them is a good, safe computing practice.

FILE TRANSFER PROTOCOLS

There are a number of different conventions, or **file transfer protocols (FTPs)**. FTP is a fixed set of rules that determines how data is transmitted over a phone line. For a file transfer to be successful, the selected FTP must be used by both your computer and the remote computer; the same FTP must be agreeable to both ends of the transfer.

FTPs have names such as **ZMODEM** (pronounced "zee modem"), **XMODEM,** and **YMODEM.** Each method has specific strengths and weaknesses. To determine which protocol your communications software supports, check your software documentation.

An **FTP**, or file transfer protocol, is a fixed set of rules that determine how data is transmitted over a phone line.

ZMODEM, XMODEM, and **YMODEM** are the most common sets of rules, or file transfer protocols, for uploading and downloading files online.

ELECTRONIC FOOD FOR THOUGHT

Purveyors to the foodservice industry find opportunities to profit online. Doug Garn is a case in point. To hear him talk, you would imagine you're visiting with a technoid from Silicon Valley and not a distributor sales representative (DSR). But Garn is, in fact, a DSR on the Eastern Upper Peninsula of Michigan for Reinhart Foods, one of the largest independent food service distributors in the nation.

"I'm on a California BBS daily to download RIME packets for 30 to 35 different conferences," says Garn. (Translation: I use my computer and modem to call another computer in California every day. The computer I call is an electronic bulletin board system (BBS) that allows the public posting of messages. It is actually part of an echo network that bounces messages from computer to computer all over the country. I download the messages from many discussion groups that I find interesting, mostly groups that deal with computers and food.)

Is this just an abnormal fascination with technology for DSR Doug Garn? Not at all.

You need to create each entry in a dialing directory only once. After you set up the entry, you only need to access the number in the directory and tell the modem to dial the number.

"If a customer has a computer problem they look to me as a resource. It helps me serve my customers more professionally, and that translates to more sales."

If a modem is connected to a port with the same IRQ as another device, such as a mouse, an IRQ conflict occurs. If you have an IRQ conflict, one or more of the devices will not work properly. You must then consult your modem software manual to change the IRQs to unique interrupt numbers.

When you view an ANSI screen while emulating another terminal you may see useless or distracting characters, called control characters, on the screen.

ZMODEM is the FTP of choice in the mid-1990s. It is easy to use and fast, and it has great error-correcting capabilities. As data is transmitted across telephone lines, line noise can cause transmission errors. ZMODEM is very good at finding and correcting these errors. For this reason, this FTP is considered robust and flexible. It also handles multiple file transfers without reinvoking the protocol.

XMODEM is the most widely used FTP despite ZMODEM's strengths. First used in 1978, it is the oldest of all the FTPs. XMODEM can transfer only one file at a time and needs to be reinvoked to download each new file. XMODEM (checksum version) is the most basic version. XMODEM (CRC version) is recommended for downloading files using Microsoft Windows Terminal.

YMODEM is a version of XMODEM that lets you transfer more than one file at a time. It also marks the files with a date stamp.

FILE TRANSFERS:
KEEP THOSE FILES a' MOVIN'...
Transferring files is not difficult, but it tends to be intimidating and confusing for those new to cyberspace. To start, it is best to take a deep breath, relax, and prepare for your journey.

Downloading files is the most important method for obtaining files for your own use. Here are the general instructions for downloading files. In this example, you will learn how to download a help file from ChefNet BBS.

MISE EN PLACE
Download
✓ First, read your modem software manual to find out how to tell your modem that you are going to transfer a file.

✓ Read your manual to determine which file transfer protocols are supported by your software.

✓ Identify a file online to download.

PROCEDURE

1. CHOOSE A FILE TO DOWNLOAD.

```
File "BBSUSER.DOC" is attached to this message
(it is 105387 bytes long)!
Would you like to display or download the file now
(Y/N)? y
```

2. SELECT A PROTOCOL WHEN PROMPTED BY THE REMOTE COMPUTER.

```
L ... Listing (a screen at a time)      B ... YMODEM Batch
A ... ASCII (continuous dump)           G ... YMODEM-g
M ... XMODEM-Checksum                   Z ... ZMODEM
C ... XMODEM-CRC
ZR... ZMODEM (resume after abort)
1 ... XMODEM-1K
K ... Kermit / Super Kermit
T ... Tag file(s) for later download
Choose a download option (or 'X' to exit): z
```

3. IF YOU ARE USING A PROTOCOL OTHER THAN ZMODEM, TELL YOUR MODEM TO RECEIVE THE FILE.

```
(Hit Ctrl-X a few times to abort)
Beginning ZMODEM download of the file attached to
message #95583 from Sysop
rz
*** DOWNLOAD COMPLETE ***
```

HOT TIPS

To upload a file, follow steps that are similar to those for downloading. Just select UPLOAD on your modem software instead of DOWNLOAD, then tell your computer to SEND a file instead of RECEIVE.

Most regions of the country accept the *70 string to disable call waiting code. If you are dialing a BBS and the number is, say, 555-1212, the number to dial and disable call waiting is *70 555-1212.

Should you get online and find yourself unable to disconnect, there is a simple remedy. Unplug the phone line! It may not be rocket science, but it works.

A great many viral detection software programs can be downloaded from online services and the Internet with no charge.

CONCLUSION

In this chapter we compared a trip into cyberspace to your first solo drive in a car. The simple analogy draws a correlation between the automobile and the combination of a modem and a computer. Together they become our vehicle.

The modem is rated by speed, in terms of bits per second, and is controlled by the modem software. The modem software lets you customize the initialization string, dialing, speed, terminal emulation, and many other settings.

File transfer is just one of the skills we must learn online. The protocols most often used online for file transfers are ZMODEM, XMODEM, and YMODEM. It is important that FTPs be done correctly and checked to be virus-free.

Finding a BBS in Cyberspace

Imagine you have just moved to a foreign land, into a new community you know very little about. Your furniture has arrived, your boxes are finally unpacked, and you can now settle into your favorite easy chair. Although the house is comfortable, you have an uneasy feeling in the pit of your stomach. You look out the window at a cafe across the street. The clothing of the patrons is different. The language and gestures are strange. Worse, everyone seems to know one another. You are most definitely a stranger in a very strange land—much like your first visit to cyberspace.

Your modem is working, the settings are correct, and the phone line is clear, but questions flood your mind. Where do I go? What do I do? How do I behave? Who will help me figure all this out?

With a pocket guide in hand (this book!), you venture out into your new community, and your first stop might very well be the neighborhood cafe. In cyberspace, it will very likely be the online equivalent of a cafe—the electronic bulletin board service, or BBS.

A BBS's online manager, host, and sometimes bouncer is called a **sysop.**

THE CYBER WELCOME WAGON

On a BBS, just like most actual cafes, there is a person who will make you feel at home, show you around, and offer guidance through the menu. That person is a system operator (**sysop**). If this sounds a lot like hospitality, it is.

Most hospitality professionals would be surprised to find that there are more than 60,000 BBSs in the United States. Most of these boards exist in relative obscurity, known mostly to a subculture that comes together only in cyberspace.

CORKBOARDS REINVENTED

Like the corkboards that hang in schools and offices, BBSs are public message areas accessed with a modem and a computer. Whether you choose to post a message or retrieve one, you will find this to be an extremely useful tool.

A BBS may have only a few users or several thousand active participants. Some BBSs have a subject focus, such as HotelNet, which is for hospitality industry professionals; others are just social boards, an open gathering place for anyone interested. Because BBSs are relatively inexpensive to set up, they are often owned and operated by one person. However, many corporations create upscale, high-end BBSs for marketing or product support. Table 3.1 lists some BBSs of interest to food and beverage professionals.

TABLE 3.1
BBSS FOR FOOD AND BEVERAGE PROFESSIONALS

BBS NAME	DESCRIPTION
FoodTrak BBS	Support for FoodTrak recipe and food cost management software
HotelNet	For hospitality professionals in lodging management and hotel foodservice
ChefNet	A service for culinary professionals
Nutrient Data Bank Bulletin Board	USDA BBS for information on food and nutrition issues
Murray Hill BBS— The Virtual Tasting Room	For wine professionals and serious wine enthusiasts

COMMUNITY LIFE

As Table 3.1 illustrates, there is a BBS devoted to nearly every discipline in the hospitality industry. In many cases, BBSs are more than just electronic focal points for public messages on a particular subject—they are *communities*. Individuals choose to spend time, money, and creative energies in the electronic presence of others. Relationships are formed. Trust and mistrust develop among citizens of the virtual community, based on their experiences online.

Professional communities form in cyberspace and create opportunities for new partnerships, joint ventures, and other profitable pursuits. The *virtual corporation* of the 1990s exists, in part, because of the proliferation of electronic communities. However, finding a BBS to meet your needs is similar to trying to find that special restaurant, bar, school, or place of worship in a new community. You want to find a place that you will want to return to again and again.

ELECTRONIC FOOD FOR THOUGHT

Culinary Institute of America Chef/Instructor David St. John-Grubb is a strong proponent of online communities. Recently, he posted the following message online exhorting chefs to become more active in the virtual community:

"This is a phenomenon for chefs to be able to communicate nationwide, let alone worldwide, with the affordability of the link into the Internet system via ChefNet BBS. The ability with which we can communicate our thoughts, questions, and feedback to each other is beyond even the wildest of dreams.

Think of the possibilities that we are about to encounter through this process in the electronic age. The ability to throw out a question on a particular subject or focus that we are involved in and to have the response of our colleagues from some far distant corner of the world is very exciting. This is like having a library at our

Many professional BBSs will ask for real names; others will accept a pseudonym. A pseudonym is a name that is different from the name you use offline. In a professional online environment, your real name is most appropriate. On a social BBS, you may prefer to use a handle for reasons of security and privacy.

fingertips and not having to thumb through volumes, swamped by unnecessary introductions and peripherals, before getting to the answer; to have an employment exchange on tap; to have a conference facility without having to move out of the house or office. I personally travel many thousands of miles a year in the name of the Culinary Institute of America, facilitating other people's needs. Now I have this great system to tap into with my laptop computer.

To all of you who have formed your careers in the foodservice industry: Use this great system, this is what we have been waiting for. We need it. The system itself is still young; become part of its growth ... Communication results in feedback, which is the breakfast of successful champions. BE ONE OF THEM. JOIN US.

Sincerely,

Chef David St. John-Grubb"

A certain chemistry must take place between the BBS, other users, and yourself. Be patient if the first BBS you dial isn't exactly what you had in mind. Each BBS is different and attracts a different type of user.

When you find a BBS that meets your needs, your return visits will become more frequent and friendships will develop. In many cases, you will find that some small level of social risk taking is necessary to become a member of the community. For example, if you want some information from a certain person or source, leave a message. Ask a question. Upload a file. Be a participant!

ORIENTATION FOR THE, YES, DISORIENTED

When you first get online with a BBS, you will need to perform a few basic tasks. In the process of performing these tasks, you may find that you feel lost as you move from screen to screen. Because many BBSs use hierarchies of menus, it is not unusual for a new user to become disoriented after making his or her way deep into the submenus.

Finding a BBS in Cyberspace

To minimize feeling lost, keep in mind that each BBS has a **main menu,** which is the navigational focus of the board. It is a place you return to often, to get reoriented and start off in a new direction through the BBS.

As a new user you will need to create a user ID and a password. Write both the user ID and password down somewhere so you don't forget them. Next you may be asked to answer a few questions about yourself, including your address and phone number. In a professional BBS environment these questions are used to qualify you for access based on your **off-line** work.

After you complete the new user information, most BBSs show you a menu for navigation purposes. While each menu is different, many elements are typical. Figure 3.1 shows the menu from ChefNet BBS as it appears when viewed using RIP*term.*

The **main menu** on a BBS is a screen that serves as the primary menu of services. It is from this menu that each service on the BBS can be reached. The main menu is the top of the BBS.

When the computer and modem are not transmitting data over the telephone lines, you are **off-line**.

FIGURE 3.1
CHEFNET BBS—MAIN MENU

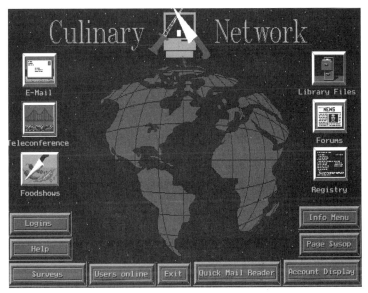

29

TABLE 3.2
CONTACTING A BBS

It is important to know how to exit a particular screen or area. Common exit commands include X to E(x)it from screen to screen, J to (J)ump to another section, and M for (M)ain menu. On BBSs that offer RIP, an EXIT button is provided. Common keys for disconnecting are G for (G)oodbye, B for (B)ye, and X for E(x)it.

BBS Name	Subject	Dial Number	Emulation
ChefNet	Culinary	218-751-5149	ANSI
HotelNet	Lodging	303-296-1300	ANSI
MHBBS	Wine	212-683-1448	ANSI or TTY

The menu is fairly typical in many respects. First, it presents various areas that can be accessed with a few keystrokes or the click of a mouse. On most BBSs, the Library Files, E-Mail, and Forum discussions are the most frequently used features. Most main menus will give you an opportunity to find out who else is online, as well as provide you with more information about other users from a registry.

Are you are ready to take your maiden voyage into cyberspace? Your mission is to log in, set up your account (all of these BBSs allow a free trial), find a public message, read it, and log off. Try one of these BBSs listed in Table 3.2.

MISE EN PLACE
BBS Message Reading

✓ Choose a BBS to dial.
✓ Create a dialing directory entry for the BBS, making sure all the correct settings are made including terminal emulation, modem speed, and phone number entry.
✓ Select and write down a password next to your name exactly as you are going to enter it when you log in.
✓ Check to make sure the phone line is connected to the modem.

PROCEDURE

Once you have completed the sign-up procedure, you will be presented with the main menu. To get to the public message boards on each of these BBSs, use the following guide.

ChefNet

1. FROM THE MAIN MENU, CHOOSE CHEFNET AND INTERNET FORUMS (F).

```
Welcome to ChefNet!

            "Culinary Center of Cyberspace"
                  Favorite Areas:
            [F]... ChefNet & Internet Forums
            [E]... Electronic Mail
            [M]... Electronic Food Show
            (Some material deleted to save space)

Make your selection
(F,E,M,L,T,Q,R,A,I,P, ? for help, or X to exit): f
```

2. CHOOSE CHEFNET FORUMS (C).

```
Please select one of the following:
C ... ChefNet Forums
I ... Internet/UseNet Forums
Q ... Configure Quick Scan
S ... Standard MBBS msg interface

Forums Select menu (FORUMS)

Make your selection (C,I,Q,S,? for help, or X to exit): c
```

3. PICK A FORUM AND ENTER THE NUMBER OR LETTER.

```
Welcome to the ChefNet Forums, Sysop.
1 = The Breakroom (Misc.)        A = C.I.A. Forum
2 = Student's Forum              B = Private Club Chefs
3 = Culinary Arts                C = Help / Work Wanted
4 = Computers & Software         D = IBM Chefs
5 = Professional Chef's Forum    E = Macintosh Chefs
6 = Catering Forum <New          F = Int. Assoc. of Women
7 = Research Chefs                   Chefs &
    Affiliates(RCA)                  Restaurateurs(IAWCR)
8 = Restaurant Menus             G = Pastry Chefs
9 = Environmental Issues         H = Foodservice Sales Reps.
0 = Buy & Sell Classifieds       I = Internet Chefs
                                 (alt.food.professionals)


Select a number from this list or type X to Exit:  5
```

4. SELECT READ MESSAGES (R).

```
Please select one of the following:
R ... Read Messages
W ... Write a message
Q ... QuickScan Menu
F ... Filescan
T ... Teleconference
M ... goto Main (top) menu
G ... Goodbye (Logoff)

Make your selection
(R,W,Q,F,T,M,G,? for help, or X to exit): r
```

5. SELECT SCAN MESSAGES (S).

```
You can select the messages you wish to read in the fol-
lowing ways:
S ... scan through messages one at a time
L ... list messages non-stop
K ... keyword-search for specific messages

Enter your choice
(just hit RETURN to "scan", or ? for help): s
```

6. STRIKE THE ENTER KEY TO READ THE FIRST MESSAGE.

```
Enter message number to start scanning at, or ? for help
(Also, just hit RETURN for new messages, F for first, or
L for last): l


Date: Saturday, December 24, 1994  4:55am   /Cyber
From: INTERNET: baaki@halcyon.com
Msg#: 108749
To: ** ALL **
```

HotelNet
1. FROM THE MAIN MENU, CHOOSE HOSPITALITY SERVICE MENU (H).

```
              HotelNet
      Hospitality Industry Online Services
              The Digital Inn
   Online Services for the Hospitality Industry
         [H]ospitality Service Menus
         [E]mail - Local,Internet,Fidonet
         [M]essage Areas
```

```
        [V]irtual Community Center
        [F]ile Libraries
        [O]nline Conferencing
        [D]igital Marketplace
        [B]ulletins, Info & Online Help
        [I]nteractive Entertainment
        [S]ubscribe To This System
        [P]ublications Online
        [U]ser Settings & Utilities

[W]ho's Online      [T]ime        [-]Prev      [G]oodbye
```

2. CHOOSE HOSPITALITY INDUSTRY FORUM (3).

```
           Hospitality Industry Services

        [1] Job Search Employment Service
        [2] HotelNet Marketplace
        [3] Hospitality Industry Forums
        [4] Hospitality Publications
        [5] Hotel & Restaurant File Areas
[E]-Mail   [P]ub's   [W]ho's Online     [-]Prev     [T]ime
[M]essage Base   [F]ile Base [O]nline Conference [O]Top
Menu [G]oodbye
```

3. SELECT THE FRONTDESK (1180).

```
         Individual Message Board Selection
   1180 FrontDesk       Hotel discussions from
                        the front desk point of view

Enter #, <CR> Restart Listing, <G>o To, <S>earch,
<C>hange Display, <Q>uit
```

4. CHOOSE NEW MESSAGES (N).

```
<F>orward or <R>everse Multiple <N>ew Messages <M>arked
Messages <S>elective Retrieval <I>ndividual Message(s)
<A>bort Retrieve

Which One? N
```

5. ANSWER YES TO "PAUSE AFTER EACH MSG?" (Y).

```
Pause after each msg(Y/N)? Y
```

Murray Hill BBS

1. FROM THE MAIN MENU, CHOOSE THE VIRTUAL TASTING ROOM (V).

```
        MAIN:           B)ulletins       C)hange Setup
F)ile Areas             G)oodbye (log off)   ?)help
I)nfo on MHBBS          M)essage Areas   O)ff-line reader
U)serList               V)irtual Tasting R Y)our Stats
Select: v
```

2. CHOOSE JUMP TO MESSAGES (J).

```
Virtual Tasting Room:
A)uctions           C)hange Setup     F)ile Areas
G)oodbye (log off) J)ump to Messages  M)ain (1st) Menu
O)ff-line reader    R)evealed Wine God T)astings
V)TR—About It       W)ineWise

Select: j
```

3. CHOOSE BROWSE MESSAGES (B).

(Some material deleted to save space)
```
MESSAGE:
A)rea change        N)ext message       P)revious message
E)nter message      R)eply to a messag B)rowse messages
C)hange current ms =)ReadNonStop

Select: b
```

4. CHOOSE CURRENT AREA (C).

```
Which areas:
C)urrent area T)agged areas (selected through T)ag com-
mand - default) A)ll areas Q)uit
Select: c
```

5. CHOOSE NEW MESSAGES (N).

```
Type of messages to show:
A)ll messages N)ew messages (everything since last read
- default) Y)our mail (messages addressed to YOU)
S)earch (specify to/from/subj/body and keywords) F)rom a
specified msg# to the last message Q)uit ?)help
Select: n
```

Welcome back! How was your first venture? Exciting? Frightening? Overwhelming? Informative? Don't worry, there's more to come.

CREATING MESSAGES ONLINE

If you don't know anyone on a particular board, public message areas are the best place to begin establishing relationships with other users. These public message areas are called by different names on different BBSs. For instance, on HotelNet they are called forums. On the In Heaven There is No Beer BBS, they are called conferences. On other BBSs the public message areas may be called topics, discussion groups, or even just plain message areas. Regardless of what they are called, public messages have a few basic components that are always used in message construction.

In an online message, there are several designated areas that are either manually or automatically filled with specific information. These designated areas are called **fields**.

ELECTRONIC FOOD FOR THOUGHT

"I was nearly computer illiterate when I first went online," says Scott Monfils. Monfils is the executive chef for two restaurants in Washington D.C., Tom Tom and Roxanne.

Monfils is a frequent visitor to ChefNet.

"The thing that has impressed me most is the helpfulness and responsiveness of those I meet online," says Monfils. "With the help of others online around the country I can research food products, equipment, menus, and even jobs online."

Scott Monfils is just one of nearly 400 chefs who have connected with ChefNet.

Public Messages

Messages that can be viewed by anyone online have a unique attraction and power. They combine a sense of self-publishing with a form of voyeurism. The content may be valuable or mundane. Whatever the content, public messages all have common attributes or **fields**. Table 3.3 describes standard message fields.

TABLE 3.3
STANDARD MESSAGE FIELDS

The **From:** and the **Date:** fields are often filled in automatically by the online service so you do not need to enter them manually.

Field Name	Description
To	Contains name(s) of people who are to receive the message
From	Contains the e-mail address of the person who wrote the message
Subject	Contains a one-line summary of content
Date	Contains the date the message was sent
Time	Contains the time of day message was sent
Body	The message itself

The To: field can direct a message to a specific person or to the board users in general. If the message is general then the To: field should contain the word "All" to signal an open invitation to everyone interested to respond. Here is an example of a message that is addressed to everyone on ChefNet BBS:

```
From: Norman Myshok
To: ALL
Subj: performance appraisal
Date: 11-03-94                                    19:51
Message: I am currently involved in evaluating and
improving the performance appraisal process used in my
organization. I am interested in learning:
a) How many other chefs are using a formal performance...
```

Norman Myshok is a Canadian chef at a YMCA resort and conference facility. His message requests information on what other chefs do for staff performance evaluations.

Replies to this message will not be directed to "ALL." Instead, they will be sent to the person who posted the original message, Norman Myshok. Richard Z. Hexter, executive chef at Schumpert Medical Center in Shreveport, Louisiana, replies:

```
From: Richard Z. Hexter
To: Norman Myshok
Subj: performance appraisal
```

Finding a BBS in Cyberspace

Date: 11-15-94   15:55
Message: NORMAN, I am sorry to be so long in answering
your request for information on performance appraisals.
It has taken me some time...

There are now two messages in the **thread** related to performance appraisals. As others reply, the message base on this subject grows. Note that even though the reply is addressed to Norman Myshok, it is still a public message and anyone is free to reply to it at any time. A message on a BBS or online service is directed to a specific individual, but it is not a private message. Private messages are sent by electronic mail, not posted on public message boards!

Messages that are related by a common subject are part of a message **thread**. Threads are an important way to group and organize messages online.

The From: field has the sender's name. It also contains the e-mail address of the person who wrote the message.

The Subject: field reveals the message's overall content. When creating the Subject: field you should try to choose your words carefully; try to make the subject descriptive so that others will know what to expect if they choose to read the message. The subject may also contain information about the origin of the message. It may indicate that the message is a copy of one sent previously (cc:), a forwarded message, or a reply to a previous message. Replies to a message become part of the message thread.

The Date: and Time: fields are reference points that help you determine the context and age of a message you receive. If you are sending a message, these fields are created and filled automatically.

The Body: field is the content of the electronic posting. If the message is a reply to a previous message it may contain some **quoting** from the original text. The quote may be indicated by symbols such as >>, <<, or simply > at the beginning of each line. Quoting is used as an electronic method of reminding the recipient of the message's content. This is especially helpful when the BBS posting is not being read in the threaded order. Here is an example of a message reply that uses quoting. A chef from CT's restaurant, New York City, Timothy Oltmans, is replying to a message posted

When a section of the original message is included in a reply, it is called **quoting**. Many BBSs let you quote a message automatically so that you don't have to retype the original message.

by chef/consultant Wendy Straub. Oltmans quotes Straub's original message in his reply. The quoted message is preceded by the initials for Internet Wendy (IW). Timothy Oltmans's comments are preceded by his initials (TO).

The **Subject**: field provides a way to group messages by content. Many online services let you search for messages by the thread. The first message in a thread is called a "parent" message. If you need to find messages that are related to a parent, check the online service's manual for thread searching capabilities.

```
Date: 11-21-94  13:28
From: Timothy Oltmans
To: Wendy Straub
Subj: Re: Daniel Boulud ****
Quoting Internet: Wendys@chefnet.com to Timothy Oltmans
IW> Tim- can you send me that file from AOL? The Daniel
IW> review? A very good friend, my former sous/mentor at
IW> Les Halles, is sous chef there.
TO> Sorry, Wendy, I can't send you the review e-mail.
TO> For those who are connected to America Online
TO> I think it is available through their arts and
TO> entertainment guide that they call @times (as are
TO> hundreds of NY Times restaurant reviews).I also
TO> have a hard copy that has not been recycled yet if
TO> you are interested.
TO> Also note that Daniel placed a nice thank you in the
TO> Times this week
TO> listing his staff names and thanking them.
TO> Very classy,
TO> Timothy
```

Creating Private Messages—

Using Electronic Mail

Electronic mail (e-mail) is the *private* equivalent of the public message. E-mail is a very powerful form of communication. The reader, or receiver, will always access the message when he or she has a desire to read it! Unlike a phone call, the electronic message can be read later, at a more convenient time.

The private messages that are sent from one computer to another are called **electronic mail,** or **e-mail**.

A private e-mail message has the same fields as a public message. It identifies the sender, receiver, subject, date, and time. The body of an e-mail message may also contain quoting from another message. The fundamental difference is that e-mail is a private message, not a public one. On most BBSs, e-mail is sent only to the other members of the BBS. This is done by addressing the message with the user ID exactly as it is used online. If the user ID is Richard T. Jones, don't try to e-mail Rich Jones. The address must be spelled exactly the same as the ID used online.

Some BBSs, such as HotelNet and ChefNet, offer Internet e-mail services; this means that messages can be sent to individuals outside the BBS itself, as long as the receiver has an Internet e-mail address. Special rules apply for sending Internet e-mail from a BBS; it is best to consult the BBS documentation or sysop for assistance. The process is not difficult, but the instructions are very specific.

ELECTRONIC FOOD FOR THOUGHT

The Wood Company, Allentown, Pennsylvania, is a progressive contract foodservice management company, and Tim Mott is the Manager of Personal Computer Support.

"Anybody can do this," says Mott. He is referring to the Wood Company's e-mail system. With more than 300 users in the company, he may be right. "We discussed installing something more complex than e-mail but decided against it." Mott wanted to make sure that the chefs and managers in the field were not overwhelmed by the technology.

"The chief benefits are having paperless communication, savings on postage, and quick, efficient memo distribution."

Mott doesn't hesitate to point to the reason for the success of the three-year-old e-mail system. Just putting personal computers with modems in the foodservice units doesn't guarantee that employees will use e-mail. Besides making it simple, says Mott, "Management in each unit made it happen."

When new technology is simple to use, saves time and money, and has the support of management, it can transform a company.

The conventional advice for those new to a BBS or online service is to "read only" for a while. This gives you the opportunity to become familiar with the board's tone and content. This level of activity is called "lurking" for obvious reasons. Some people lurk for months before leaving a message.

If you choose to reply to a message on a BBS you will usually be prompted to use quoting. It is aggravating to have to read great volumes of long quotes, so be sure to limit the quote to the relevant section of the message by deleting extraneous portions.

Now that you have briefly explored exchanging messages, go back to the BBS you logged into earlier. Post a message, public or private, to the sysop and introduce yourself. See if

Chat and teleconference are two terms that are often used interchangeably to indicate a conversation between users that is typed on a keyboard instead of spoken. In some online environments they may be two distinct forms of communication.

Internet Relay Chat (IRC) is the most popular chat facility on the Internet. It is comprised of hundreds of "channels" that are open only as long as a user is present. Each channel allows multiple users to chat simultaneously.

you can leave a message for the sysop using e-mail or a public message that introduces yourself and your professional ties.

Once again, we must gather some courage and social fortitude and venture online!

LIVE FROM CYBERSPACE! IT'S TELECONFERENCE ...

Many people enjoy the **chat/teleconference** available on many BBSs. In fact, BBSs often use chat as a primary *raison d'être*. They are known as chat or social boards. The Internet features its own style of chat known as **Internet Relay Chat (IRC)**. Chat or teleconference is a "live" conversation that takes place in **real time** for all participants. Two or more individuals log in from remote terminals and choose to "talk" to one another. Each can see the text generated by the others as well as the name or ID of the contributor. The text appears on the screen after the writer presses the <Enter> key at the end of his or her comment. As the conversation progresses, the comments scroll off the top of the screen.

This form of communication has both strengths and weaknesses. If you have your disk capture or session log turned on, then you can make a permanent record of the chat. In a professional setting this is quite helpful. Additionally, many people can join in a chat session, thus creating some interesting dynamics. The number of participants is limited only by the number of inbound lines to the BBS or online service.

There are several opportunities for online chat with other food and beverage professionals. ProVisions Online, a Prodigy service for industry professionals, often features afternoon chat sessions for members. Chef members of AOL get together on Monday nights in a special event of Chat Room called "The Back of the House." Spontaneous chat sessions take place on ChefNet BBS.

On the other hand, the more individuals involved in a chat, the more disjointed a session can become. A delay occurs between one comment and another as the messages are being typed. When many people are involved, even as few as four or five, several subject lines or threads can develop, causing some confusion. During a recent chat session, I was asked by an exasperated user, "How do I get this **** thing back in synch?"

Some BBSs actually have two different modes of communications, the chat described above and an even more direct form where each keystroke appears on the screen as the writer types it. This helps alleviate the lag between messages; on the other hand, it also eliminates the ability to edit the message with any finesse. All the errors and wrong key strokes appear on the screen. In the case of the frustrated user mentioned above, we went to a chat mode that allowed us to see each other typing; this way we could see that we were in "synch."

For people who are very verbal and type fast, chat mode can be fruitful. For mouse-clicking, two-finger typists over a long-distance line, chat mode can be quite frustrating.

The actual time in which a process under computer control occurs is called **real time**. When users communicate simultaneously online, the communication takes place in real time. When, as in e-mail, communication takes place in a delayed fashion, it takes place outside of real time.

HARVESTING FILES

Downloading files is probably the most common activity on most BBSs. Finding a file online and taking possession of it on your own computer for personal use can be alluring. There are lots of reasons to download files:

- Obtaining free or demo versions of recipe management software from online software libraries

- Receiving text files such as foodie newsletters, food product specifications, and wine tasting notes that can be printed out for review

- Acquiring recipe files that can be manipulated by word processing software

- Obtaining help manuals that can be printed for assistance on various online activities

- Receiving food images and graphics such as rare wine labels that cannot be viewed online

PERIODICALS ONLINE

Another common online pursuit is reading electronic journals, newspapers, or magazines. Reading a periodical online is sometimes difficult because text formatting is cumbersome, and, with smaller computer monitors, screen resolution may be poor. In many cases, online periodicals do not have photographs or graphics to accompany the text. However, the ability to search for subjects or specific text while browsing compensates for the difficulties of reading online.

Hospitality magazines can be found in several places online. For example, the European version of the Penton publication *Lodging Hospitality* is online with HotelNet. *Restaurant Hospitality* can be found on America Online. Back issues of Indian Harvest's *Plate Coverage* newsletter can be found on ChefNet. *Decanter* magazine is archived on Internet resources.

COMMERCE ONLINE

An area of increasing growth for many BBSs is online purchasing. Common on many boards is a Classified Ads section. Classified ads online work just as they do in a newspaper or magazine. You place a short description of what you are buying or selling in the appropriate place online, and others who read the ads respond if they are interested. In the case of online services that cater to the hospitality industry, the ads are more focused and usually involve selling or buying equipment or food supplies. The classified ads are also a good place to post job openings or availability.

Electronic malls are a new shopping experience destined to be around for a long time. In an electronic mall, catalogs and order-processing centers sell goods and charge your credit card number for their cost. However, some interesting experiments exploring the use of electronic cash are being conducted.

One form of electronic cash is net-cash. This fairly simple currency is generated by an online transaction processor in exchange for a debit on a credit card. The holder of this "pocket change"—electronic coupons, in effect—can send the electronic coupon to anyone accepting net-cash. The merchant receiving net-cash may redeem the electronic coupon at the net-bank. The net-cash model is the first attempt at creating a virtual economy.

Food and beverage professionals may find items of interest in electronic malls. Bonding Corporation markets its high-quality pastry creams and sauces to pastry chefs online. Coffee supplies are often found in electronic malls, and brewing kits are a standard on many of the beer BBSs. Computer supplies are a natural fit for electronic malls, and hospitality-related BBSs often offer foodservice software. Many services, including chef consulting and employment search firms, are also offered in electronic malls.

FLAMING

As in any community where people must coexist there are some basic ways to "fit in" and avoid offending others. Most of the rules of etiquette are unique to online life, but they have a parallel to behavior in our more traditional communities.

Flaming is universally condemned, yet is omnipresent in the online world. Flaming is an online attack using hostile language directed at another user.

Flaming is full of name calling, demeaning language, and often serves no other purpose than to ridicule and anger the one who is flamed. Often a flame attack can erupt into a flame war with many participants. An informal rule in cyberspace is this: Don't be quick to offend and don't be easily offended.

An **electronic mall** is an overtly commercial online service that seeks to match buyers and sellers.

When a person attacks another person online with abusive and condemning language it is called **flaming**.

A graphical symbol used to convey emotion and facial expression that is designed from keyboard letters and symbols is called an **emoticon**.

EMOTICONS

In daily conversation we constantly use facial expression, inflection, and tone of voice along with body language to communicate deeper meaning. In cyberspace **emoticons** help serve this purpose. Emoticons are text symbols that quickly convey hints about the tone of a comment or message. The emoticon is viewed correctly by turning the page 90 degrees clockwise. With the page in its portrait position the emoticon is on its side. Consider the following emoticons:

:‑) A standard "smile" to convey humor or happiness

8‑) A smile with glasses

:‑(A sad face

;‑) A wink

:<) A smile with a mustache

The design of an emoticon involves creativity and can be very telling when conveying the tone of a message.

ELECTRONIC FOOD FOR THOUGHT

Chef Ann Cooper of the Putney Inn, Putney, Vermont, is an ardent user and creator of emoticons. The day she discovered the little sideways smiley faces and all their variations she sent the following e-mail message:

"I've got my computer at my desk—We've done over 1,000 meals today—We've got a dinner banquet in a few minutes & as I was reading your message I started giggling—One of my sous chefs walked by & couldn't believe that in the midst of all this I'm grabbing a bite & giggling over your e-mail—Thx for the laugh I needed it—I love the cute smiley faces [==]:-}"

Here are some of the culinary emoticons that Chef Cooper uses on her communications:

```
  ||
[==](:*                    Exploding brain of overloaded cyberchef
  ||
[==]:-)                    A chef smiling
```

Jo Lynne Lockley, Chef's Professional Agency, has also created some emoticons:

@=:{>	Chef Pierre Mustache
$=|:^)	Wolfgang Puck
@#%'Q	"That's the worst sauce I ever tasted"
q;!)	Chef of the chefs-don't-wear-toques school of chef dress
S==l:{.\>*..	Master chef
S#;(	Sous chef who didn't get the promotion
[=|:-]>>>>....||	Techno chef
*-<#;'?	First day culinary student (with freshman beanie)
@=};(>	What do you mean, you want food cost reduced by 15%?

More smilies can be found on the Internet and many BBSs. For a list of smilies look for the Smiley Dictionary. Using Internet FTP you can find a copy at:

`ftp://ftp.gsfc.nasa.gov/pub/smiley-dictionary`

SHORTCUTS

Another communication tool is the less graphic, more verbal version of the emoticon. These shortcuts to common expressions appear often in cyber-communication.

FYI	For your information
IMHO	In my humble opinion
PMFJI	Pardon me for jumping in
BTW	By the way
GD&R	Grinning, ducking, and running

Last, there is a method of posturing that can be easily conveyed. These are words indicating actions contained within < > marks. For instance:

Copies of a free guide to etiquette online can be found in the Netiquette Guide. You can obtain it on the Internet at:

`FTP://ftp.sura. net/pub/nic/ internet. literature/ netiquette.txt`

<grin> indicates, well, a grin!

<g> also indicates a grin

<laughing hysterically until eyes water>

<hands clasped behind back, whistling, and
    trying to look inconspicuous>

These all tend to lighten the conversation, convey meaning, and avoid conflict. Sarcasm is not always detected and understood without body language.

All keyboards contain upper and lowercase characters for writing. It is very difficult to read all uppercase letters in a message, especially if you do a lot of online reading. Uppercase typing is reserved for those who need to shout a portion of a message. THIS IS CONSIDERED SHOUTING! This is not shouting. BE CAREFUL HOW YOU USE THE CAPS LOCK KEY . . . If you have difficulty pressing the Shift key, LEARN! It is a skill that needs to be developed.

CONCLUSION

Venturing into cyberspace through a BBS is a lot like moving to a new city in a foreign land. The terrain is unfamiliar, and the customs are new. The sysop is the person who will help you acquaint yourself with the new environment.

There are BBSs for nearly every interest and several exclusively for hospitality professionals. Each BBS is a unique community, so take some extra time to get to know the information content and personality of each BBS. This will help you find one that suits your own needs and personality.

The public message area of a BBS is the best place to meet new friends and learn from your peers. The basic components of a message include To, From, Time, Date, Subject, and the message itself.

1. The To: field identifies the receiver of the message.

2. The From: field identifies the sender.

3. The Time: and Date: fields indicate the time and day the message was sent.

4. The Subject: field reveals the contents of the message.

5. The message is contained in the message field.

E-mail is a powerful form of private communication. E-mail messages have the same basic fields as public messages.

Chat/teleconference is another way to communicate online. It differs from e-mail and public messages because it takes place in real time. During chat you carry on a live conversation with another user online by typing instead of speaking. Log files enable you to keep a record of a chat or teleconference.

Obtaining files online is a common activity for most BBS users. Hospitality professionals will find numerous files of interest on the industry BBSs, including free trial software and product information.

There are many periodicals online of interest to hospitality professionals. Online periodicals can be read online or searched by using online tools to find information.

Buying and selling online are becoming commonplace. BBSs often provide a classified ad section, and electronic malls are gaining acceptance. Hospitality professionals will find purveyors and service providers occupying space in electronic malls or virtual food shows.

There are a number of ways to convey emotions online. Flaming is a negative way to express anger and dissatisfaction. Attacking other online users with insults and name calling is called flaming. Correctly communicating feelings, facial expressions, and voice inflection is difficult in cyberspace. Emoticons and other shortcuts have been created to assist in expressing yourself online.

Cruising the Big Boards

The commercial online services are actually huge BBSs that facilitate e-mail, encourage file transfers, offer chat and tele-conferencing, and permit access to a wide variety of information sources. Sheer magnitude, depth, and breadth separate the Big Boards from smaller, simpler BBSs. The Big Boards offer a large number of options for information and entertainment. Some are unique to a specific online service, and others are nearly ubiquitous in cyberspace. However, each of the Big Boards has its own personality, strengths, and weaknesses. For the hospitality professional, they offer a wealth of information needed to meet daily challenges.

This chapter provides an overview of the four largest commercial online services:

- America Online
- CompuServe Information Service
- DELPHI
- PRODIGY Service

To help you decide which service is right for you, let's review six critical areas for each. Everyone has different reasons for going online, as we discussed in Chapter 1. Some need information, others have unique communication needs, and still others want to be part of a community. As a hospitality professional you need to prioritize both your time and your money. This chapter will allow you to spend your time and money more wisely by helping you to identify the service that will meet your needs. Each service will be discussed in terms of the following factors:

• A general description of the service

• Features of interest to hospitality professionals (For a more in-depth analysis of food and beverage resources see Chapters 13 and 17.)

• General directions on how to navigate through various departments and sections

• Costs for using the service

• Benefits and strengths of the service

• The downside or weaknesses of the service

On AOL, **screen names** are used for identification online and resemble CB "handles" or pseudonyms.

When a computer program requires that uppercase and lowercase letters be used in specific instances, it is said to be **case sensitive**.

AMERICA ONLINE

There's no doubt about it. America Online (AOL) is friendly. From the monthly letters to members by AOL President Steve Case to non-stop, around-the-clock talk on the chat lines, America Online exudes friendliness. The menus are easy to read and understand. Pointers offering help are everywhere.

One of the first things you will notice on AOL is that members have **screen names** instead of numbers or real names. In fact, any one user can have several names! If you are a chef and a wine connoisseur you might have two screen names—one to reflect each passion. Then as you meet with chefs online, your name will reflect your occupation; when you hang out in a wine-related area your interests will also be evident. For instance, I have ChefGaryH and ChefNet as screen names. I use them at different times and for different reasons. Screen names are not **case sensitive**—my name could be spelled chefgaryh or even ChEfGaRyH, but neither would be as effective.

FIGURE 4.1
SAMPLE AMERICA ONLINE SCREENS

A.

THE AOL PRIMARY DEPARTMENTS.

B.

THE WINE AND DINE ONLINE SCREEN.

FIGURE 4.1 CONTINUED
SAMPLE AMERICA ONLINE SCREENS

```
America Online - [Restaurant Hospitality magazine]
File   Edit   Go To   Mail   Members   Window   Help
```

What you need to know about the restaurant trade.

Topics: 20   Postings: 94   Created   Latest

Job Opportunities	4	12/21/94	12/27/94
Cooking Equipment	6	12/19/94	12/26/94
Ads & Offers	5	12/19/94	12/28/94
MESSAGES *FROM* YOUR HOSTS	4	12/18/94	12/19/94
Management, Etc.	6	12/14/94	12/27/94
Non-Commercial Foodservice	1	12/14/94	12/14/94
ABOUT RESTAURANT HOSPITALITY	1	12/10/94	12/15/94
MESSAGES *TO* YOUR HOSTS	16	12/10/94	12/24/94
Subscribe to RH	6	12/10/94	12/28/94
In This Month's Issue	3	12/10/94	12/16/94
Letters to the Editors	1	12/10/94	12/15/94
Contests	6	12/10/94	12/22/94
Your Staff	3	12/10/94	12/27/94
Computers & Communications	10	12/10/94	12/26/94
Expanding Your Business	1	12/10/94	12/15/94
Cooking Equipment	2	12/09/94	12/16/94
Laws & Politics	2	12/09/94	12/23/94
Cooking Tipsheet	6	12/09/94	12/20/94
Health & Nutrition	2	12/09/94	12/21/94

Date of Last Visit: This area is new to you.

List Messages	Read 1st Message	Find New	Find Since...	Create Topic	Help & Info

---

C.
FOLDERS IN THE RESTAURANT HOSPITALITY SECTION OF WINE AND DINE ONLINE.

A **message board** is an area where members can post public messages on a specific topic.

On AOL, a **guide** is a specially designated helper identified by the word guide somewhere in his or her screen name.

Primary Departments

Members Online Support

AOL gives members a lot of support. Most notably, it offers Customer Service Online, a service in which human beings answer questions live and in cyberspace. The online support is located in a special chat room reserved for helping lost, confused, and misguided travelers. I spend my share of time there . . . There is also a Members Helping Members **message board,** which provides offline help within AOL; there are even online **guides** who spend time in various departments on AOL and offer assistance when needed. They can be easily recognized because they have the word "guide" somewhere in their screen names. For example, the screen name GuideSue indicates the presence of a guide.

Entertainment

There are plenty of entertaining hot spots in the Entertainment Department. While these are mostly recreational pastimes, there is material of use to hospitality professionals. If trivia is a priority in your bar, the Trivia Club is a great source for material.

News & Finance

The News & Finance Department is online 24 hours a day. Check out the headlines, visit StockLink for market quotes on your publicly traded restaurant competitors, or just read the Market News. If you aren't interested in the news about the multi-unit chains, the Microsoft Small Business Center is also located in this department. It offers a wealth of information valuable to independent restaurant owners as well as small business owners. Chicago Online has restaurant reviews for businesses operating in the Windy City. Restaurateurs in the Mt. Prospect area might want to check out what members are saying in the Good North Shore Restaurants section! Chefs will find contemporary recipes in the Chicago Tribune Cookbook online.

ELECTRONIC FOOD FOR THOUGHT

AOL has a lot to offer professionals from all segments of the foodservice industry. Just ask Gary Egel, a distributor sales representative (DSR) in Peoria, Illinois. Egel is a DSR for Thoms Proestler Company, a large broad-line foodservice distributor.

"I use America Online (AOL) extensively," says Egel. "I check out restaurant reviews with Chicago Online, keeping a watch for specialties I can share with my customers."

But Gary Egel doesn't stop with just menu suggestions.

"I also keep my eye on the futures market through AOL. Coffee, shrimp, and soybean oil for instance." With such valuable information

Gary can notify customers of potential price changes without depending on the TPC buyer to alert him first. Foodservice professionals with a little creative effort can find many new applications for online services such as AOL.

Lifestyles & Interests

The Lifestyles & Interests Department has several dozen forums. One of the most active is Wine & Dine Online, which features the Culinary BBS as well as a Wine Dictionary and even *Restaurant Hospitality* magazine.

Other areas of interest are as diverse as Gay & Lesbian Forum, which might be of interest to operators who service large percentages of patrons with alternative lifestyles, and Real Estate Online, which is helpful if you are looking for locations to build a new hotel or restaurant. This is one of the most rapidly growing departments on AOL.

Computing & Software

This department boasts some interesting features including computer news and many forums for product support and discussion. Busy hospitality executives can find the latest information on Personal Digital Assistants such as Newton. You will also find an extensive library of files to download.

Travel & Shopping

The Travel & Shopping department has much to offer the food and beverage professional. Chefs who travel often will find EAASY Sabre airline reservations system for arranging travel a benefit. Bed and breakfast operators will find this department very informative. There are B&B recipes and a B&B database for the United States and Canada. B&B operators interested in quality control should read the candid thoughts from travelers regarding the many B&Bs in which they have spent the night.

Learning & Reference

Every restaurant and hotel operator needs to do research occasionally. Chefs can research the culture representing a particular cuisine, and hotel operators can research a specific industry to prepare for an upcoming convention. Maybe you just want to find the definition of a term used in your modem manual so you can upload to the corporate offices; it's here in the Dictionary of Computer Terms.

ELECTRONIC FOOD FOR THOUGHT

Carl E. Nordberg, a chef at Interlachen Country Club in suburban Minneapolis, has spent considerable time on AOL.

"I value the opportunity to communicate with other chefs coast to coast," he says. "I am not restricted to Minneapolis if I have a problem with a recipe, employment issue, or equipment." As to how quickly the number of chefs online might grow, Nordberg says, "Chefs are already using modem-based ordering technology. They have the ability to go online immediately and don't even know it!"

People Connection
The People Connection Department consists of private and public **Chat Rooms** and **Event Rooms**. Any hospitality segment can set up a chat room and invite peers and coworkers online for a conference. Multi-unit chain operators or food-service management companies can bring more than 20 employees online in a private chat room to discuss company business.

The Newsstand
One of the newest departments on AOL is The Newsstand. America Online has done more than any other service to bring periodicals and magazines to regular members. Members can browse through 45 (at press time) different periodicals and newspapers at no extra cost to membership.

When a group of members forms a regularly scheduled **Chat Room**, it may become an **Event Room** where discussions are more focused and have hosts. The schedule for Event Rooms is posted in the PC Studio.

A **folder** on AOL is a menu selection that contains text files for reading. The folder is identified by an icon that looks like a file folder.

To increase your participation in the online community, create an Online Profile. By selecting the Members menu from the menu bar and choosing Edit Your Online Profile, you can create a profile of yourself that others can refer to if they meet you online.

The offering is broad and includes *Restaurant Hospitality* (RH) magazine. You can subscribe, write a letter to the editors, and even correspond with other restaurant professionals in the RH section.

The @times section is produced by the *New York Times* and includes a Food and Wine **folder** that lets you respond to reviews of restaurants.

Of Interest to Hospitality Professionals

Back of the House Chat

This is an Event Room for culinary professionals only. Each Monday night at 10:00 p.m. ET, culinary educator Rick Vermillon hosts this event from Erie Community College.

Wine & Dine Forum

Wine & Dine Forum offers a broad selection of online databases, reference materials, message boards, library, files and columns, and online newsletters. Featured within the Wine & Dine Forum is Chef/Instructor Abby Nash, who teaches a course in Matching Food and Wine at Cornell University.

Culinary BBS

This obscure message area on AOL is difficult to find, but it is the online home of many culinary professionals. Located in the Cooking Club Forum, it is expressly for chefs and restaurateurs. The message area gives professionals an opportunity for networking.

Restaurant Hospitality

This important resource offers items of use to the hands-on operator. Not only can you find out what is in the newest issue of *RH*, but you can review jobs offered, discuss equipment features and benefits, stay up to date on upcoming food shows, and much more.

@times Message Board

The @times Message Board is a service provided by the *New York Times*, one of the periodicals offered by AOL. The message board features a Food & Wine folder that contains articles on dining and restaurant reviews. The message board offers an opportunity to post public messages in regard to *Times* food and wine articles.

Internet Resources for Food and Beverage Professionals
AOL offers limited access to the Internet. Many of the resources discussed in the Internet chapters of this book are available on America Online. Included in the AOL Internet offering are the Chefs on the Internet mailing list and the Usenet newsgroup, alt.food.professionals.

ELECTRONIC FOOD FOR THOUGHT

John Lawn, Penton Publishing, is the editor of *Foodservice Distributor Magazine*. John has been a long-time advocate of the professional use of online services. In fact, he was one of the first foodservice editors to publish an e-mail address for industry communication—an America Online e-mail address.

"I was involved with computers when they used to fill entire rooms," says Lawn. But he has stuck with them right into the 1990s as they have grown smaller, more powerful, and into communication tools.

"I like America Online. There are a number of foodservice distributor sales representatives online, and they are our readers. I get responses to articles via my e-mail box," says Lawn. He has even searched the Member Directory for profiles that list foodservice distribution as part of the listing in the directory. The results now comprise an industry e-mail list he can access for professional needs.

Navigation
Connecting to AOL requires the use of special software. AOL supplies the special software for Microsoft Windows, DOS, or Macintosh format. The software is sent free when you request it by calling AOL's toll-free number. Getting

FIGURE 4.2
EXAMPLES OF AOL ICONS

GET MAIL   COMPOSE MAIL   TRAVEL   CHAT
(Flag on mailbox goes
up when you have mail)

MEMBER   GO TO   PRINT   SAVE TO
SERVICES-   KEYWORD   FILE
SUPPORT

AOL names depart-
ments with words
that can be entered
with the keyboard.
These words are
called **keywords**,
and their use gives
quick access to vari-
ous departments
and services.

around on AOL is most easily done with **keywords**. Many services on AOL can be accessed by choosing Keywords from the drop-down Go To menu and entering the appropriate keyword.

Each keyword will produce a myriad of choices once you have navigated to your chosen department area. AOL uses small icons to represent the type of information accessed with each choice; see Figure 4.2. These icons can represent several levels of screens before getting to the area you want so, even when you use keywords, you still need to go to various menus and select a number of icons to get where you are going.

If you don't use keywords to navigate your way through AOL, you could browse. You may prefer to choose items from the Departments screen and work your way through successive screens. This allows you to discover new areas of interest in each department you visit.

The Costs of AOL

AOL's 10 hours of online time for $9.95 per month is one of the best bargains in cyberspace. Only a few areas require additional fees, so the costs are quite predictable and affordable.

Strengths of AOL

Some of AOL's strengths include the People Connection, its straightforward billing system, and the partial access to the Internet.

The People Connection is the heart and soul of the AOL community and one of its greatest strengths. There are rooms for spontaneous chat as well as Event Rooms, which are more focused and regularly scheduled. From the daily conversation in private Chat Rooms to mega-events with rock stars on Center Stage, this is an exciting area for those looking for real-time communication. Entry into the People Connection starts in the Lobby. If you are looking for a particular room, a guide is on duty from 12:00 noon to 6:00 a.m. to help orient members. Clicking the Rooms icon can reveal all rooms available. (Don't forget the More Rooms button, though!) Also available are Private Chat Rooms. The only way to enter one of these is to create one or to get invited into one.

The Monday night "Back of the House" chat takes place in The People Connection. If you find a group of hospitality professionals online with a slightly different focus, such as restaurant owners or beverage managers, you may want to organize a similar chat group one night a week.

AOL's straightforward billing system makes the service very attractive. When I log in, I know exactly what it costs me because I know precisely how much time I have spent online each month. I can go almost anywhere on AOL and not incur extra fees.

The partial access to the Internet, available on AOL, is another of AOL's strengths. That AOL has provided an economical, easy-to-use interface for the Internet is significant. However, it is somewhat difficult to find. The best way to get access to it is to use the Go To Keyword **Internet**.

The Internet area on AOL not only provides limited access to some Internet resources, but it also provides information about the Internet such as the classic online publication,

Zen and the Art of the Internet, magazines such as *Wired,* and many other help documents.

Weaknesses of AOL

Although AOL is an excellent resource for networking and for accessing a variety of information sources, it is not the source of choice for information that has depth and technical sophistication. Most of the information resources are geared toward pop-culture and basic consumer information. However, the deeper and more narrow information resources are not available here.

The message boards on AOL are decentralized and difficult to find. For example, the Culinary BBS, one of the message boards for food professionals, is in the Cupboard section of the Cooking Club, in the Cookbook and Software Review folder! This is not where one would expect to find a discussion among professionals.

COMPUSERVE

CompuServe markets itself as "the world's most diverse information service." And, in fact, it has the most resources for professionals, business owners, and researchers. The databases available online are the most extensive of all the online services and can offer a great deal to hospitality professionals. While CompuServe offers food- and wine-related resources that are similar to America Online and PRODIGY, the research and business tools available make this a unique resource for hospitality professionals.

To introduce you to CompuServe, Figure 4.3 shows the opening screen as you would see it from the Microsoft Windows version of **CIM,** the **CompuServe Information Manager.** CIM is also available for IBM-compatible computers without Microsoft Windows (DOS CIM) and for Macintosh users (Mac CIM).

The Culinary Pro/Schools is where the food professionals gather on CompuServe. The posts are diverse yet focused on professional and educational issues.

CIM is the CompuServe Information Manager software that lets you access and explore CompuServe.

FIGURE 4.3
SAMPLE COMPUSERVE SCREENS

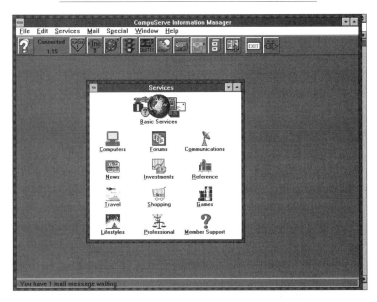

A.
COMPUSERVE MAIN MENU.

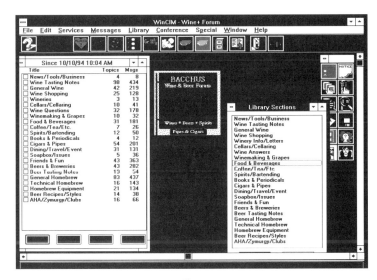

B.
THE BACCHUS WINE AND BEER FORUM.

FIGURE 4.3 CONTINUED
SAMPLE COMPUSERVE SCREENS

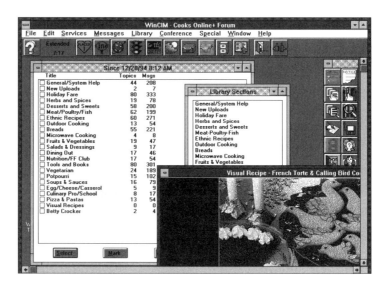

C.
THE COOKS ONLINE FORUM.

Basic Services are those areas of interest on CompuServe that are included in the basic fee for membership. CompuServe offers unlimited access to Basic Services.

Extended Services are offered to CompuServe members for an additional cost.

CompuServe provides unlimited access to **Basic Services** to all members. These include sending about 60 three-page electronic mail messages and receiving as many mail messages as you can get your friends and professional contacts to write. You also have unlimited access to the Electronic Mall for shopping, a few games, membership support, some news, weather, and sports. With Basic Services you also get unlimited access to *Grolier's Academic American Encyclopedia,* a few investment reports, and some travel services.

Extended Services are where the more specialized information assets of CompuServe are located. Hospitality professionals will find culinary professionals in the forum Cooks Online. Wine enthusiasts can be found in the Bacchus Wine and Beer Forum. Among the extended services are hundreds of special interest forums, chat services, games, special news sources, and research databases. Hospitality professionals will find an array of databases of interest. These databases include health-related information on nutrition, diet and AIDS, periodicals such as *Nation's Restaurant News,* and information on publicly traded restaurant and hotel companies.

For the business executive CompuServe offers an Executive option. The Executive option lets you set up folders that will automatically collect news from several wire sources, "clip" them, and store them—all based on keywords that you supply.

The Primary Services

Members will find AP Online, PA News Online (UK), weather maps and forecasts, and even *U.S. News & World Report* included with their Basic Services. The weather maps and forecasts located here are the services that Banquet and Catering Manager Michael Hughes used to predict the storm that would have destroyed the outdoor wedding reception at the Sheraton Suites, Plantation, Florida.

Reference Library

The Basic Reference Library offers members unlimited access to the *Academic American Encyclopedia,* which can be used for researching such diverse subjects of interest to hospitality professionals as ethnic cultures or the history of special events such as Mardi Gras.

The Extended Reference area is the most extensive among the commercial online services. A quick electronic search of the Business Database Plus turned up 375 articles on wine and over 750 articles on the wine industry. Just enter a word to search by, and in seconds you can begin to

There are numerous hospitality applications for the Executive option. For example, a chef watching the price of a commodity like pork or beef may electronically clip any news wire reports containing relevant information. Better-known chefs might even choose to monitor the wires for any mention of their own names! Beverage professionals can receive the very first reports of the Beaujolais Nouveau in the fall of each year.

read the selected articles. This is just the tip of the iceberg of information available in this service.

ELECTRONIC FOOD FOR THOUGHT

Nickolas Ramus is Executive Chef for the catering division of Professional Foodservices Management, San Marcos, Texas. Ramus has been online with CompuServe for more than 5 years and has successfully used his computer and modem for researching various issues related to his profession.

"When we are catering an event for a visiting scholar or dignitary here at Southwest Texas State University I use CompuServe as an information source. For instance, if we have a guest who is respected for his work in ancient Roman history I will search online for ideas and information about food, cuisine, etc., that will help me produce a set piece or menu. Not only will I find the information in online encyclopedias and articles, but I have often met the authors of the articles online and corresponded via e-mail."

Ramus is quite emphatic about the importance of the computer and modem in his professional career. "I would never have been able to accomplish what I have had I not been computerized and online."

Health

Extended Health includes nutritional information, such as the Health Database Plus, which is of interest to concerned restaurant operators adding low-fat and healthy items to their menus.

Home/Leisure

Basic Services offers the Zagat Restaurant Survey. This survey can be an integral part of a restaurant's quality control program if used creatively. A new service called Premier Dining offers discount dining at more than 9,000 restaurants nationwide in exchange for an annual membership fee. Interested operators might want to participate. There is also a UK Restaurant Guide called AA Restaurants in case you are considering operating a restaurant abroad.

Magazines

Only a few magazines are offered under the Basic Services but the Extended Service options are numerous; computer, consumer, business, and financial magazines abound. Busy restaurant executives might prefer to search electronically for business information instead of buying the hard copy and browsing.

Sports

Sports resources at the Basic level are minimal—Lanier Golf Database and AP Online. The Extended Service offers AP Sports Wire, fantasy sports forums, and the NCAA Collegiate Sports Network. If sports trivia is important in your bar or restaurant, this is a great way to find new trivia.

Education

The Peterson College Guide is offered with unlimited access. A search of the guide for listings of colleges with culinary programs yielded 144 schools that have culinary studies. Members can research each one online with the Peterson College Guide. Most of the hospitality industry disciplines can be found in the guide.

Fun & Games

Members can spend hours with trivia or other games if they choose. If your operation profits from trivia other than just sports, the Science Trivia section will be of interest.

Communication

Basic Communication options include e-mail, unlimited access to classified ads, and even a Practice Forum to help novice chefs and restaurateurs develop basic online skills such as posting public messages and downloading files. The Extended Communications include a CB Simulator, which is CompuServe's chat area. Instead of creating a "room" to chat in, CompuServe provides a simulated CB radio where various channels can be accessed for chat. Hospitality professionals with coworkers in the United Kingdom or Asia will find this an efficient communication tool.

Professional

The Extended Services menu is full of appropriate items for food and beverage professionals. In an industry where managers wear many hats, a variety of professional resources is welcome. Highlights are the Marketing Forum, Entrepreneur's Forum, and even an Office Automation Forum for the technologically advanced restaurant.

Travel

Basic Travel information online offers restaurant guides as well as some air, hotel, and rental car material. The Extended Services include the more valuable airline reservation systems such as WORLDSPAN, EAASY SABRE, and the OAG Guide. Celebrity chefs constantly boarding jets can plan their own itinerary from the hotel room. Reserve a hotel room, book a flight, and rent a car, all on CompuServe.

Entertainment

When you finally get a day off, if you aren't up to date on the new movies, check out the movie reviews by Roger Ebert. Chefs with artistic interests other than cooking will find there are several discussion forums on art, music, and other performing arts.

Computers

The Basic Services Computers area consists of a directory of computer support services online. The Extended Services offering in Computers is the heart of CompuServe. Over 425 hardware, software, and **shareware** companies are online in the forums to answer questions, supply parts, and download new programs. If your restaurant is computerized this is a valuable area to access for support and upgrades. If you are just exploring the possibility of obtaining a

Software that is offered on a "try before you buy" basis is called **shareware**. The user is obligated to pay a registration fee after a trial period if use of the software continues.

computer for your restaurant office, this area has experts who offer advice in abundance.

Finance

CompuServe is strong in the financial information area. Basic Services offers Basic Quotes and a Loan Analyzer, among other services. Publicly traded companies are analyzed online; the analysis can provide valuable insights for the savvy competitor of a publicly owned restaurant. For those considering refinancing, the Loan Analyzer is online 24 hours per day.

Shopping

The Electronic Mall is open 24 hours a day, and you can stay as long as you like for your basic membership fee. Buy new CDs online for your bar or restaurant or even browse the New Car Showroom for a new company catering vehicle.

Member Services

Member Services are available for all Basic Services members. Important resources such as how to find people and services, rate and pricing information, new features, and access numbers for CompuServe are resident in the Member Services area.

Of Interest to Hospitality Professionals

Food and beverage professionals have specific ways to profit from using CompuServe. Here is a quick summary of areas that will interest students and professionals in the food and beverage industry.

Cooks Online

Cooks Online is a bulletin board that offers more than 20 sections of culinary discussion. One in particular, Culinary Pro/Students, is specifically for professionals. Gary Jenanyan, executive chef for the Mondavi Great Chefs School, is the section leader for the professional section. He provides valuable insights gained from nearly 20 years on the job with the world's greatest chefs.

Food and Wine Online

ELECTRONIC FOOD FOR THOUGHT

When I was called upon to cater an English-style dinner for a local literary group discussing the work of English writer C.S. Lewis, CompuServe was a great asset. With the active community in Cooks Online and the service's strong presence in the United Kingdom it was a perfect resource.

I posted a message online, explaining the theme of the dinner and the plight I faced as one who is ignorant of the cuisine of the United Kingdom. Soon, menu suggestions from culinarians in the United States and abroad began to flood my e-mail box. I also received beverage suggestions, quotes from C.S. Lewis and lessons in food history.

The dinner was a huge success. Not because I prepared a gastronomic spectacle, but because of a diary I produced for the guests. Each page consisted of an e-mail message with a suggestion or a comment from around the world. They were delighted to find their small town event had become the subject of international discussion!

Each section of the Cooks Online forum has a file library associated with it. When you are in the Cooks Online forum, just select LIBRARY from the menu bar or click on the library icon, choose BROWSE, and then pick a section from the forum that interests you. Browsing will turn up thousands of files of interest to both professionals and amateurs.

Bacchus Wine Forum

Professionals will find an extensive message base from members on wine-related subjects. Also online are issues of *The Informed Enophile*. Brew pub owners will be interested in the brewing topics.

Knowledge Index

The Knowledge Index lets you access over 50,000 journals through more than 100 databases. Included in the databases are journals and periodicals from the foodservice industry such as *Nation's Restaurant News.*

Computer Resources

The computer resources on CompuServe are outstanding. With hundreds of computer-related manufacturers online,

CompuServe provides the food and beverage professional interested in computers an unparalleled opportunity.

Marketing, Small Business, and Entrepreneurial Forums
Given the increased emphasis on the business skill of both culinary and beverage professionals, these forums are a wonderful resource. Professionals from each area congregate in these forums to offer advice and ask questions.

The Executive News Service (ENS)
The ENS is part of the Executive option. With it you can electronically clip stories from several news wires and periodicals. The service will examine stories as they appear on the wires and look for matches with keywords you supply. Restaurant operators might have the service clip any stories on e coli during an outbreak, or a competitor's expansion could be captured in a file by searching by company name. Keywords can be any words of interest from the restaurant, hospitality, or general business world. ENS is a tremendous time saver and an easy way to stay on top of breaking stories.

Navigation
The best way to access CompuServe is to use the CIM, which is available in most computer stores for about $35. The software is often packaged with an online credit for nearly the amount of the purchase price. If you have never been online before, CIM offers a cost-effective, easily learned way of connecting. One aspect of navigation on CompuServe that is not available on some other services is the ability to create a list called Favorite Places. When visiting a forum or area of interest you can use the pull-down menu to select Favorite Places and include it in the list. Then, for future visits, you need only to access Favorite Places and choose the area you wish to visit. Figure 4.4 shows CompuServe icons.

The Costs of CompuServe
CompuServe offers Basic Services for a flat rate each month of $8.95.

Food and Wine Online

FIGURE 4.4
COMPUSERVE ICONS

CONTEXT-
SENSITIVE
HELP

USER-DEFINED
FAVORITE
PLACES

SEARCH
AND FIND

GO TO

FILING AREA
FOR
MESSAGES

EXIT ROOM

DISCONNECT

To control your online costs with CompuServe, carefully monitor your CompuServe billing to get a feel for the costs associated with various areas of interest.

When you create an account with CompuServe you will be offered the Executive option for an extra $3.00 per month. This option is particularly useful for professionals who are managers or have executive and administrative responsibilities. Members pay extra for Extended Services, with the charges varying from a few dollars an hour to more than $20 an hour, depending on the service. Hospitality professionals will find culinary professionals in the forum Cooks Online and wine enthusiasts in the Bacchus Wine and Beer Forum. These are both Extended Services. Nearly all of the databases online are Extended Services as well.

The charges for Extended Services are not easily deciphered because they tend to be layered. To help you understand these costs, keep in mind the following information:

• Everybody pays the Basic fee.

• Some services carry an hourly charge plus the Basic fee.

• Some services include the Basic fee, hourly charge, and a surcharge.

• Still other services include the Basic fee, hourly surcharge, and a membership fee such as the Executive Option.

Strengths of CompuServe

CompuServe is the oldest of the commercial online services. The strengths of this service include the computer-related resources, Cooks Online, the international community, and CompuServe's monthly magazine. The large number of computer-related offerings set CompuServe apart from the other services. It provides, by far, the most extensive contact with support organizations from more than 425 computer software and hardware companies. Members can obtain the following items in the extensive support areas: product upgrades, patches and programs, macros to make completing repeated tasks more efficient, answers to technical questions, and information on new products.

Most major companies represented on CompuServe monitor their own forums to answer technical questions, and they respond within 24 hours in most cases. If you are struggling with a Microsoft or Lotus program, for example, you can post a question in their respective forums at any time of the day or night. The next day, when you log in, you are likely to have an authoritative and complete answer to your question.

The **Cooks Online forum** is another great strength of CompuServe. The recent addition of a section designed specifically for professionals has brought the professionals online so that they are now more visible and accessible.

CompuServe Magazine is another strength. This magazine, free with membership, has a special focus each month, such as shareware or small business management. Each monthly focus is enhanced with many related side-bars that highlight what members do online, where the best files are located, and listings of tips for using CompuServe.

Weaknesses of CompuServe

Certainly, if you are on a limited budget CompuServe may not be for you. While CompuServe is a good value, the actual cost can be far greater than the $8.95 per month. Watch the expenses carefully. Not only do the charges add up quickly, it's often difficult to estimate what various activities will cost.

Like other online services, some of the forums are quite large; as a result, it is easy to get lost in the crowd. In a well-managed forum, this won't happen. Some of the forums are better managed than others. Cooks Online is run well, but others are either too large or poorly managed.

DELPHI

The public message areas on DELPHI, defined by subject, are called **Special Interest Groups (SIGs).**

While DELPHI is different from the other online services in terms of its installation and graphics, it does have similarities to the other services. For instance, **Special Interest Groups (SIGs)** are DELPHI's public message areas and serve as forums for public discussion. The Internet is offered as a secondary and limited service on other Big Boards, but the Internet is a primary feature on DELPHI. It provides members with many of the most valuable Internet tools. Figure 4.5 shows some sample DELPHI screens.

ELECTRONIC FOOD FOR THOUGHT

Nik Bushell is a DSR for Lady Baltimore Foods. He started in foodservice at 14 as a salad boy and made his way up the ranks so that when he left the back of the house he had been sous chef at a convention hotel in St. Louis, Missouri. "Lady Baltimore Foods went online with laptops about three months ago. After the initial shock (I was computer illiterate) I started looking for things that could advance the computer into a more sales-oriented tool rather than just taking orders with it," says Bushell. His first stop was DELPHI.

"I first went online with DELPHI on my laptop, then with a PC at home. DELPHI has a few food and recipe SIGs and also access to the Internet and gophers (an Internet tool discussed in Chapter 6)

Cruising the Big Boards

FIGURE 4.5
SAMPLE DELPHI SCREENS

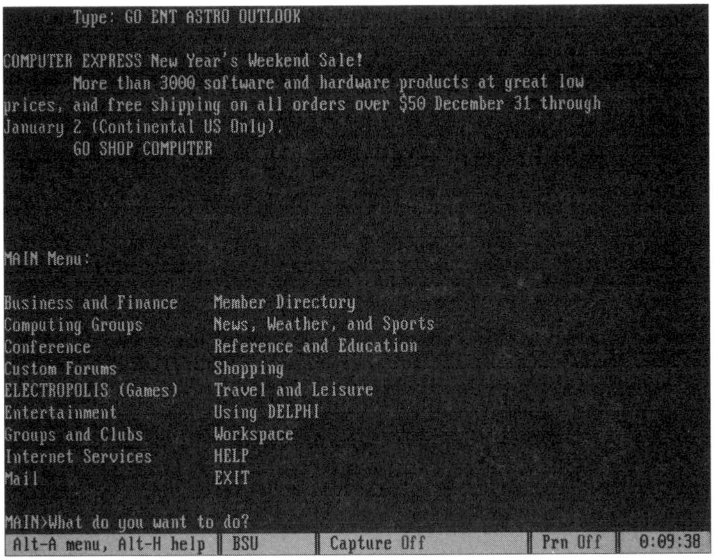

```
     Type: GO ENT ASTRO OUTLOOK

COMPUTER EXPRESS New Year's Weekend Sale!
        More than 3000 software and hardware products at great low
prices, and free shipping on all orders over $50 December 31 through
January 2 (Continental US Only).
        GO SHOP COMPUTER




MAIN Menu:

Business and Finance      Member Directory
Computing Groups          News, Weather, and Sports
Conference                Reference and Education
Custom Forums             Shopping
ELECTROPOLIS (Games)      Travel and Leisure
Entertainment             Using DELPHI
Groups and Clubs          Workspace
Internet Services         HELP
Mail                      EXIT

MAIN>What do you want to do?
Alt-A menu, Alt-H help  BSU     Capture Off        Prn Off   0:09:38
```

A.
THE MAIN MENU.

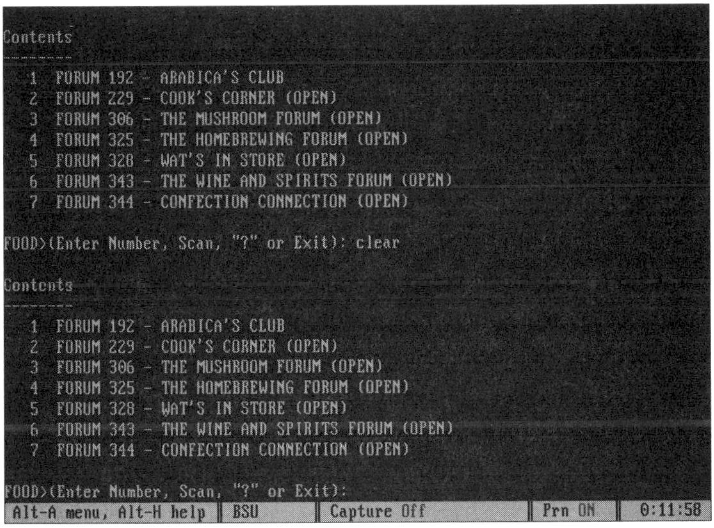

```
Contents
--------
   1  FORUM 192 - ARABICA'S CLUB
   2  FORUM 229 - COOK'S CORNER (OPEN)
   3  FORUM 306 - THE MUSHROOM FORUM (OPEN)
   4  FORUM 325 - THE HOMEBREWING FORUM (OPEN)
   5  FORUM 328 - WAT'S IN STORE (OPEN)
   6  FORUM 343 - THE WINE AND SPIRITS FORUM (OPEN)
   7  FORUM 344 - CONFECTION CONNECTION (OPEN)

FOOD>(Enter Number, Scan, "?" or Exit): clear

Contents
--------
   1  FORUM 192 - ARABICA'S CLUB
   2  FORUM 229 - COOK'S CORNER (OPEN)
   3  FORUM 306 - THE MUSHROOM FORUM (OPEN)
   4  FORUM 325 - THE HOMEBREWING FORUM (OPEN)
   5  FORUM 328 - WAT'S IN STORE (OPEN)
   6  FORUM 343 - THE WINE AND SPIRITS FORUM (OPEN)
   7  FORUM 344 - CONFECTION CONNECTION (OPEN)

FOOD>(Enter Number, Scan, "?" or Exit):
Alt-A menu, Alt-H help  BSU     Capture Off        Prn ON    0:11:58
```

B.
FOOD AND BEVERAGE FORUMS.

73

FIGURE 4.5 CONTINUED
SAMPLE DELPHI SCREENS

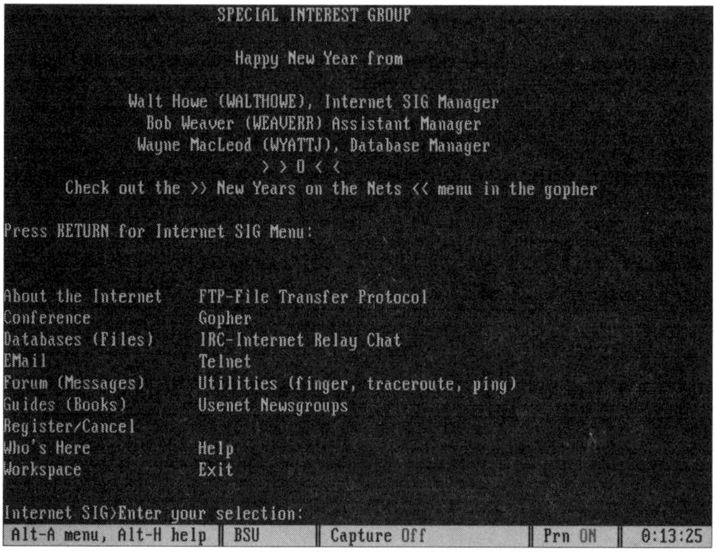

```
                   SPECIAL INTEREST GROUP

                      Happy New Year from

           Walt Howe (WALTHOWE), Internet SIG Manager
             Bob Weaver (WEAVERR) Assistant Manager
            Wayne MacLeod (WYATTJ), Database Manager
                        > > 0 < <
           Check out the >> New Years on the Nets << menu in the gopher

Press RETURN for Internet SIG Menu:


About the Internet    FTP-File Transfer Protocol
Conference            Gopher
Databases (Files)     IRC-Internet Relay Chat
EMail                 Telnet
Forum (Messages)      Utilities (finger, traceroute, ping)
Guides (Books)        Usenet Newsgroups
Register/Cancel
Who's Here            Help
Workspace             Exit

Internet SIG>Enter your selection:
 Alt-A menu, Alt-H help ┃ BSU ┃ Capture Off      ┃ Prn ON ┃ 0:13:25
```

C.
INTERNET SPECIAL INTEREST GROUP MENU.

allowing me to access university archives (Washington University in St. Louis is the largest) with unlimited information on nutrition," says Bushell.

Searching archives of nutritional information on the Internet is just one of the many tools available from DELPHI.

Primary Departments of DELPHI

Business and Finance

You will find numerous business tools online; UPI Business News, Business Wire, Dow Jones Averages and Commodity Quotes, and more. You can check the most recent IPO of a restaurant competitor or stay current on technology with the Product News Press Releases.

Computing

DELPHI offers users of Amiga, Atari, Tandy, and Commodore computers a SIG to compare notes and exchange information. This is important for restaurants running these machines in their kitchens and offices. IBM and Macintosh are featured here also, of course.

Custom Forums

DELPHI allows members to create and host their own special interest groups. Hospitality professionals with initiative can create a custom forum just for sommeliers or food and beverage directors. Custom forums offer great opportunities for diversification and meeting the needs of niche or narrow emphasis groups. Some that exist today include the following:

- People

- Business & Commerce

- Computing

- Professional/Occupational

- Food & Beverage

- Health & Fitness

Entertainment

DELPHI members can stay current on everything from Broadway to Hollywood in the Entertainment section. Operators with coffee houses or wine bars in theater districts can use this area to become more familiar with what their clientele is watching.

Conference

This interactive conversation system is similar to chat on other services. Any hospitality industry company can hold a multiline conference with employees across the country just by setting up a conference. It has a rather complex set of commands that allow you to customize your conference.

If you are in a conference and need command information, type /HELP to get a list of commands. For more information on a command type /HELP <command>.

Groups and Clubs
Some SIGs available in this section include Business Forum, for discussion of a broad range of business issues, and Callahan's Saloon, a virtual pub.

Reference
DELPHI is the only online service that places culinary resources in a Reference area. Online Gourmet contains a large database of recipes. Restaurant operators concerned with AIDS-related issues due to hiring or servicing high-risk individuals will find the AIDS Info Network of value. NRPA Network Dictionary of Cultural Literacy will be of interest to restaurateurs who have multicultural staffs.

Shopping
DELPHI offers a limited shopping section that includes AutoVantage OnLine, Parsons Technology, Books & Guides. Coffee Anyone features a tasting chart that might be of interest to coffee house owners. Restaurateurs interested in learning more about the Internet can purchase several guides online with DELPHI.

Travel and Leisure
EAASY Sabre, Car Rentals, Tours, and Cruises are options to explore in the Travel and Leisure section. If you are inclined to travel to do research for new menus, you can set up your complete trip on DELPHI.

Workspace
A personal workspace is given to members for file storage. This means you can upload files to a private area online for transfer or storage. If you are transferring data files from your restaurant to a sister restaurant, you need this work space to transfer the files on the Internet.

Of Interest to Hospitality Professionals

Online Gourmet
This is an extensive database of recipes, many of which are suitable for upscale, white-tablecloth restaurants.

Food & Beverage Custom Forums

There are several forums available that are formed and hosted by DELPHI members. The Cafe Gourmet, Cooks Corner, Mushroom Forum, Wine & Spirits, and even a Confection Forum are fun to browse.

ELECTRONIC FOOD FOR THOUGHT

Jonathan Lewis is a graduate of the Culinary Institute of America, former food and beverage director for Universal Studios, and owner of a restaurant and Nu West Concepts, a culinary consulting company, in Denton, Texas. Lewis is very enthusiastic about the importance of the Internet to the future of the food industry.

"In the hospitality industry it is a given that the only thing that we can truly count on is that tomorrow everything will be different than today—competitors, products, services, attitudes, cuisine, etc. Hospitality professionals are driven to innovate. The Internet and interactive online services are yet another vehicle that will provide growth for the industry. Our children will use the Internet as we use the telephone today."

Lewis aggressively uses the Internet in his consulting business. He recently did some consulting with an operator concerning the Americans with Disabilities Act (ADA) and found just what he needed on the Internet.

"I downloaded the current ADA guidelines, litigation records, an employer's guide to the ADA, and the hire/fire consequences of the ADA." Lewis accessed the Texas Employment Commission on the Internet to find the documents he needed.

Creative searching of the Internet, leveraging government resources, and tenacity solved his restaurant consulting problem.

The Internet

The Internet connection here offers culinarians and beverage professionals an opportunity to benefit from many of the resources listed in this book. One Internet resource not

FTP, Gopher, and Telnet are navigation tools that assist you in navigating and transferring files on the Internet.

offered by any other commercial online service is Internet Relay Chat (IRC). In addition to the IRC, you will find Internet **FTP, Gopher,** and **Telnet** options.

Navigation

The DELPHI interface is restricted to text. Although the screens are not exciting aesthetically, they are straightforward and easy to use.

You navigate through DELPHI by answering the following question:

```
MAIN>What do you want to do?
```

The first word in each menu selection is enough to move from one menu to the next. For example, if you enter the word INTERNET, DELPHI will display the Internet menu.

The Costs of DELPHI

Becoming a member is easy. While other online services require you to install special software before setting up an account, such as CompuServe's CIM, DELPHI offers a character-based interface. You simply sign up by dialing 1-800-695-4002 with your modem. When connected, press the return key a few times until a prompt appears on your screen. Type Guide and press ENTER.

DELPHI has a 4/10 (4 hrs/$10) and a 20/20 (20 hrs/$20) plan for membership. Full Internet access is available for an additional $3.00 per month. Rates are good from 7:00 p.m. to 6:00 a.m., local time. Additional surcharges will be added to access at other times of the day.

Strengths of DELPHI

Access to the entire Internet is the primary strength of having a DELPHI account. There are many resources on DELPHI that will help you learn about the Internet, including discussion forums where you can learn from other members.

DELPHI also lets you set up your own public message areas, which is unusual. Other online services have predefined forums or bulletin boards, and users must find one that is of interest to them. On DELPHI, members have the opportunity to create their own public message areas. This flexibility is a definite plus. Hospitality professionals can create public message areas to meet their unique needs. Bar owners could create a discussion group about liquor liability, or pastry chefs could congregate in an area that they set up just to discuss pastry techniques. The flexibility extends into personal workspace. DELPHI permits members to store files online.

Weaknesses of DELPHI

For the graphically inclined, DELPHI is a difficult place to spend much time as it is devoid of pictures or color. DELPHI has announced that a more graphical front-end is in development, however.

The sections that are unique to DELPHI are not as extensive as those of some other online services. Outside of using the Internet, DELPHI resources are limited. If you are not interested in spending time exploring and using the Internet, DELPHI might not be for you.

PRODIGY SERVICE

PRODIGY is a family entertainment network with many news, business, and information services. Each day there are over 700,000 logins to PRODIGY. More than 850 bulletin boards contain over 1.7 million public bulletin board messages on a broad range of subjects. In addition to its entertainment features, PRODIGY is expanding its "marriage to the Internet," according to Scott Kurnit, executive vice president. As a result, members can expect increased access to the Internet in the future.

Primary Services

PRODIGY services are divided into three categories: Core areas, Plus areas, and Custom Choices. An example of a Core area is the Weather; a Plus area example would be the Food Bulletin Board. Custom Choices include TimesLink, an online newspaper. See sample screens in Figure 4.6. Here are the major informational and interactive features:

Food and Wine Online

FIGURE 4.6
SAMPLE PRODIGY SCREENS

A.
THE MAIN MENU.

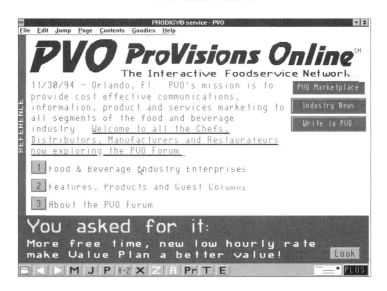

B.
THE MAIN PROVISIONS ONLINE SCREEN.

FIGURE 4.6 CONTINUED
SAMPLE PRODIGY SCREENS

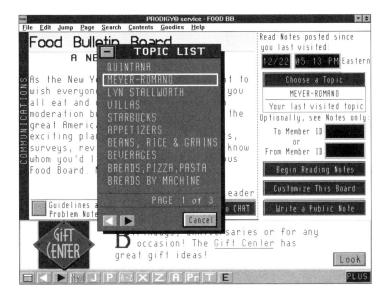

C.
THE FOOD BB MENU.

News/Weather
Members can read the latest news reports from the major news wires; national, regional, and major city weather reports are updated throughout the day. Multi-unit operators can track weather conditions in multiple markets if necessary. Windows users have an added advantage of being able to see photos and hear sound clips along with the news stories.

Business/Finance
Dow Jones Company News offers 21 days' worth of past and present articles on publicly traded companies if you are interested in other hotel companies or competing restaurants. Or, if you are interested in your own company's stock performance you can receive up-to-the-minute quotes.

Sports
ESPN delivers comprehensive sports online with hourly updates on professional sports. Plus, there are polls, contests, and

college sports news. Sports bar owners will find this to be another opportunity to tantalize patrons with more information.

Communications
PRODIGY offers recently enhanced communications services that include free Internet e-mail, personal ads, classifieds, and an address book to include up to 50 Internet mailing addresses in addition to 50 PRODIGY addresses. This is of great value to chefs who need services to receive the Chefs on the Internet e-mail.

Entertainment
Entertainment news from the Associated Press and *Newsweek* help to anchor this section. There is lots of news from the television, movie, and music industry. Restaurateurs in the area surrounding Southern California will find this is an easy way to stay current on their clients in the music and movie business.

Reference
Consumer Reports and *The Mobil Travel Guide*, a movie guide, and an extensive political profile database are just some of the reference material online. Hoteliers looking for coffee makers for their rooms can check out the *Consumer Reports* documentation on the subject.

Shopping
There are dozens of specialty shops on PRODIGY. You can shop until you disconnect at JC Penney and Spiegel. You could even shop for trendy "uniforms" for your bar employees at Lands' End. There are color graphics, and Microsoft Windows users see photos of many catalog items.

Computers
Members find downloads, product support, and *PC NEWS* online. There are many bulletin boards for various computer formats and for interactive communication. Computerized operators will want to plug into this network of knowledgeable members and purveyors.

Travel

City Guides is a helpful travel planning utility where members tell you what's hot and what's not. Find out if your bar or restaurant is on the list! Flyer's Edge compares frequent flier programs for travel-weary executives of national restaurant and hotel organizations to get the most for their travel dollar. EAASY Sabre can book flights, and members can also arrange hotel and car rentals online.

To return to the Highlights page that contains the main menu on PRODIGY, just click on the icon in the lower-left corner of the tool bar on every page.

Home/Family/Kids

This is the section of PRODIGY where the majority of the food- and beverage-related material is provided. Health-conscious members will find fitness and nutrition information and interaction.

Of Interest to Hospitality Professionals

ProVisions Online

ProVisions Online (PVO) is an interactive food and beverage network for industry professionals. This new and ambitious service offers industry news, a message board, and product information. The PVO Forum is an online meeting place for many segments of the industry including chefs, students, distributors, and manufacturers. It functions as an electronic marketplace for the foodservice industry.

The Food and Wine Section

The Food BB is located in the Food and Wine section. Over two dozen topics for public discussion highlight this board, including nutrition, software, and even international cooking. Most participants are weekend gourmets and home cooks, but some of the discussions can be fruitful. An interesting component includes the Wine, Beer, and Spirits area, where there are discussions on beverages of all kinds.

This board is hosted by John Mariani, world-renowned restaurant critic and food writer. He is not the only celebrity in the section, however. Each month the PRODIGY Food section features a prominent professional chef who answers members' questions on all facets of their work.

ELECTRONIC FOOD FOR THOUGHT

Mark Michaud is a DSR in Bangor, Maine, with Northcenter Foodservice, a food distributor. Michaud uses PRODIGY Services and likes the International Cookbook he can access there.

"If I have an account where food costs are escalating I can choose one of the ethnic recipes on PRODIGY with low food cost, download the recipe, and tie it in with products we sell. If they are dragging their feet on menu changes I use Desktop Publisher for MS Works to print new menus for them. I think restaurants should change menus seasonally so I'll bring in newly printed menu samples every six months."

Michaud's online resource, PRODIGY, takes him one step closer to being the consummate professional he strives to be. He depends on his new telecommunications abilities to help him hit ever increasing sales goals.

"Yesterday, one million dollars in sales was good enough to be a sales leader. Today, it's three million. Tomorrow it will be five million."

The Internet resource that features over 7,000 special interest bulletin boards is called the **Usenet**. The individual boards within the Usenet are called **newsgroups**.

The Usenet

The Internet offering on PRODIGY is limited to only a few Internet services, but the Internet bulletin boards known as **Usenet newsgroups** offer many resources. They range from a group that discusses food history or food and wine to one exclusively for food professionals.

ELECTRONIC FOOD FOR THOUGHT

Ed Baker is the sales manager of Earthy Delights, a specialty produce purveyor to upscale restaurants, hotels, and private clubs. Baker went online with PRODIGY initially because he was encouraged by the easy Internet access and was offered a free trial month.

"I am seeking to position my company to be present in what I think will be one of the great marketplaces of the future," says Baker. "I realized that one of the best ways to get my message out in the years to come would be to have my product list available online and learn as much as I can to prepare for the future," Baker continues. "It feels as though this is an almost organic process taking place, and that the best plan would be to follow it where it leads, without too much regard to pre-anticipated outcomes or results." Visionaries from the foodservice industry are growing in number. Many see the great potential of services like PRODIGY to bring the electronic marketplace of the future to the culinarian of today.

Navigation

You navigate through PRODIGY by using one of two methods. You may enter **Jump words,** or keywords that direct you to a particular service. Otherwise you must choose icons on the screen (see Figure 4.7) to lead you through a series of screens to get to your destination.

On PRODIGY, the keywords that are entered manually by members to move to other screens are called **Jump words**.

The Jump word can be entered before going online from the main PRODIGY offline screen. You can also enter it once you have logged in by choosing the JUMP selection on the top menu bar.

The menu bar at the bottom of the screen is a particularly critical navigational tool.

The Costs of PRODIGY

Different membership plans charge for time in the Core, Plus, and Custom Choice areas differently. Users can choose from two different PRODIGY membership plans. In the $9.95 per month plan, you get five hours in either the Core or Plus areas. Extra hours are $2.95 each. The $14.95 plan gives you unlimited time in the Core areas and five hours in the Plus areas. Custom Choices can be added to either plan, but they require enrollment and added fees.

FIGURE 4.7
EXAMPLES OF PRODIGY ICONS

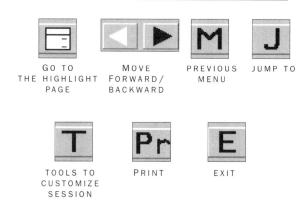

GO TO THE HIGHLIGHT PAGE   MOVE FORWARD/ BACKWARD   PREVIOUS MENU   JUMP TO

TOOLS TO CUSTOMIZE SESSION   PRINT   EXIT

Strengths of PRODIGY

PVO is a strength for PRODIGY. It is one of the most comprehensive in scope of all the services for food and beverage professionals among the Big Boards. The Food and Wine section is also strong and offers the members access to professional chefs and culinary educators. John Mariani is a strength in the Food and Wine area because he has a unique view of the industry as a prominent writer.

Unlimited access to Internet e-mail during your online hours is particularly valuable. There are an increasing number of Internet resources available to hospitality professionals with Internet e-mail.

Weaknesses of PRODIGY

PRODIGY is somewhat difficult to navigate initially. The icons are not intuitively designed, and the screens are confusing due to their cluttered appearance (advertising). The bright colors on each screen are distracting and do nothing to create a focus area on the screen.

PRODIGY's computer related material is not as comprehensive as that of some other services, such as CompuServe. If online support and assistance from computer hardware and software manufacturers are important to you, another service might be a better choice.

CONCLUSION

The Big Boards are much like the smaller, niche-oriented BBSs that pepper cyberspace. They offer public messages, file transfers, real-time conversations, and e-mail. But they differ in two fundamental ways. The first difference between the commercial services and the BBSs is that they have huge memberships. They cover the country, offer local access, and market themselves with multimillion dollar budgets. The second difference is that commercial online services have much more comprehensive information resources. The databases are provided by specialized expert organizations, and the message boards are run by smaller, niche-oriented companies.

While the commercial online services offer a broad range of similar content and features, each is unique. They all have strengths and weaknesses, varying cost structures, and even project different online personalities.

For the hospitality professional, each service has something different to offer. It is important for you, as a food or beverage professional, to think through your information and professional networking needs and compare them to the features and benefits of each service. The result will be a much better online experience and a greater value wherever you decide to spend your money online.

Internet Messaging Across Cyberspace

The Internet is a network of 20,000 computer networks. An estimated 25 million people use the resources on the Internet, and the current growth rate is staggering. In the hospitality industry, every segment is present on the Internet. Restaurants such as Red Sage and Pizza Hut advertise on the World Wide Web. Chefs like Ann Cooper, Putney Inn, Vermont, network with culinary peers. Purveyors of fine foods to restaurants, such as Indian Harvest of Bemidji, Minnesota, explore the Internet for sales and marketing opportunities. For the first time in the history of the industry, professionals have the opportunity to interact with one another, regardless of geographic location, on a daily basis. This chapter provides an overview of the Internet and discusses its basic tools for communicating with written messages.

Many Internet providers have menu-driven e-mail systems in which you make a menu choice instead of typing on a blank command line. Some services even utilize a graphics-based e-mail system so that menus are eliminated and all the user has to do is click the mouse. Actual steps for e-mail may differ slightly depending upon your system.

A service that connects individuals or corporations to the Internet is an **Internet provider.**

A **gateway** is basically a connection between two dissimilar computer systems or applications.

USING THE INTERNET

There are many ways to connect to the Internet. One way is to subscribe directly with an **Internet provider.** Many food and beverage professionals use one of the growing number of commercial online services that provide a **gateway** to the Internet. Another way to gain access to the Internet is through class enrollment at a local university. Finally, your employer might even provide access to the Internet.

Hospitality professionals will find pre-existing communities and an unfathomable amount of information to harvest on the Internet. Chefs gather via e-mail discussion groups. Hotel and restaurant educators discuss the latest developments in related technology and curriculum. More importantly, as more and more hospitality professionals connect, the relevant content on the Internet grows. Communities expand. Greater value on the Internet is created for all professionals as the community grows.

Table 5.1 lists the basic Internet tools and the benefits of each. Scan the features and benefits. We'll explore the tools themselves in detail as we proceed.

TABLE 5.1
INTERNET TOOLS

Internet Tools	Feature	Benefits
Electronic Mail	Private communication	With e-mail, you have instantaneous global message coverage. It provides inexpensive and efficient communication with other food and beverage professionals.
Usenet	Public communication	The Usenet provides discussion groups organized by topic and fast replies from new Internet contacts. Dozens of groups focus on food, wine, or the hospitality industry itself.

TABLE 5.1 CONTINUED

Internet Tools	Feature	Benefits
Mailing lists	E-mail discussion groups	Mailing lists provide focused discussion based on prearranged subjects. Messages are public but are sent to your e-mail box. Several lists exist for chefs, hoteliers, gourmets, and wine experts.
Telnet	Remote login	Telnet provides easy navigation from computer to computer as well as access to libraries containing culinary information.
File Archives	Information storage	Archives provide free access to files, software, and other information including free recipe, bar, and business software.
FTP	File transfers	FTP is a convenient method for file acquisition. It provides efficient information and software transfers.
Archie	File search	Archie finds public files for transfer. You can search for files of interest to food or beverage professionals.
Gopher	Information access	Gopher is a menu-driven, uniform navigation tool to various Internet sites for information such as recipes.
World Wide Web (WWW, The Web)	Hypertext documents	The WWW provides graphic display, multimedia presentations, and linked information. Explore food and beverage supplier files and even competitor Web sites.

ELECTRONIC FOOD FOR THOUGHT

Executive Chef George Sideras of the Dayton Country Club, Dayton, Ohio, is aggressive in expanding his repertoire of online skills.

"I feel that every day is a new event. As I get deeper into the cyberworld and build on the previous day's successes the thrill gets greater and greater," says Chef Sideras.

"The only problem is finding the time to get a real handle on the new technology. I have made the joke that if I do get completely wired at work, no food will ever get cooked. I just find piecing the puzzle together to be so compelling. I have a friend who provides me with a vast amount of tools and a great deal of technical support, which allows me to expand my skills at a rate greater than my comprehension!"

The Internet is incredibly diverse. To try to grasp it in its entirety is impossible. We can, however, take a few bite-size pieces and begin to explore the Internet. A few of its basic components resemble the world of bulletin boards. Other components are on the leading edge of cyberspace, such as the World Wide Web, and are without comparison. The Internet topics covered in this chapter have one thing in common: They are all messaging services. In this chapter you will find discussions and examples of:

• Electronic mail

• Public e-mail discussion groups, called Mailing Lists

• Public discussion groups, called Usenet

Many computers, online services, and BBSs are connected to the Internet but they are *not* the Internet itself. Technically, the Internet is the "stuff" between the networks and services. It is literally the connecting services that lie between the networks. For example, ChefNet BBS is connected to the Internet, but it is not the Internet. America Online is connected to the Internet and provides limited access to the Internet, but it is not, in itself, the Internet. Even DELPHI, which permits total access to the Internet, is not the Internet.

ELECTRONIC MAIL

There are different levels of connectivity to the Internet. E-mail service across the Net is the most limited, but the most common, level of Internet connectivity. On the other hand, connectivity called **Serial Line Internet Protocol (SLIP)** offers a much more complete connection.

E-MAIL ON THE NET

It is estimated that more than 25 million people send e-mail over the Internet. This volume includes members of the commercial online services, corporations, BBSs connected to the Internet, and the more traditional academic and research communications. **E-mail addresses** have even become a status symbol on the old-fashioned business card.

Each e-mail address includes the following:

• A user ID (not necessarily the user's actual name)

• The at symbol (@)

• The name or abbreviation for an organization

• Three letters that indicate the type of organization (company, educational institution, government)

For example, my e-mail address is `holleman@chefnet.com`. Holleman is my user ID, ChefNet is my Internet provider, and .com indicates ChefNet is a commercial Internet user. Another example, and a more famous Internet address, is president@whitehouse.gov.

E-mail on the Internet has the same features as e-mail or public messages on a BBS or online service. You can review Chapter 2 for more details.

The mode of connection to the Internet that allows complete access to all the tools and resources of the Internet with a telephone line, computer, modem, and appropriate software is called **SLIP**.

Each user on the Internet has an **e-mail address** that specifies a unique place of delivery for all electronic communications.

E-mail can accumulate very rapidly in your e-mail box. One technique for managing large volumes of e-mail is to handle each message only once. Make a decision concerning what to do with a message when you read it for the first time. Reply to the sender, delete the message, forward it to another person, or file it away. Don't handle it twice!

Many different e-mail systems and programs to process e-mail on the Internet are available. The following general procedures will help you understand how to send, read, forward, and file e-mail messages. Mise en Place will help you get the necessary information and preparation in place. The procedure will take you step by step through the process and will provide an actual example of the procedure as it progresses.

MISE EN PLACE
Sending Internet E-mail

✓ Find the e-mail address of the person to whom you want to send a message. You may send one to me, if you like, at holleman@chefnet.com.

✓ Log in to your Internet provider.

✓ Start the e-mail program.

PROCEDURE

1. CHOOSE THE SEND OPTION OR GIVE THE SEND COMMAND.

```
% Mail>send
```

2. ENTER INFORMATION IN THE MAIL FIELDS (TO AND SUBJECT).

```
To: SMTP%"holleman@chefnet.com"
Subject: Hello to the author
```

3. TYPE THE BODY OF THE MESSAGE.

```
Enter your message below. Press CTRL+Z when complete, or
CTRL+C to quit:
Gary, what's new on the Internet for chefs?
```

4. SEND THE MESSAGE WHEN COMPLETE.

```
CTRL+Z
```

5. EXIT THE MAIL SYSTEM.

```
exit
```

6. DISCONNECT FROM THE INTERNET PROVIDER.

```
% bye
```

Internet Messaging Across Cyberspace

You will find that the very best way to receive e-mail is to send e-mail. Beverage professionals can send private messages to wineries on the Internet and establish personal relationships with the winery staff. Culinary professionals will find many other chefs in the discussion groups with whom they can discuss business and artistic issues. E-mail is where professional networking begins on the Internet.

MISE EN PLACE
Reading Internet E-mail

✓ Log in to your Internet provider.

✓ Start your log file from your modem software.

✓ Start the e-mail program.

PROCEDURE

1. LIST THE UNREAD MAIL BY USING THE DIR COMMAND.

```
Mail>dir
MAIL
# From                  Date          Subject
1 SMTP%"HOTEL-L@MIZZOU 31-OCT-1994  Re: non-smoking
ordinances in restaurant
2 SMTP%"chefs@halcyon.  31-OCT-1994  LowFat/Fat Free debate
3 SMTP%"chefs@halcyon.  31-OCT-1994  RE: Legume
Standardization
```

2. SELECT A MESSAGE TO READ.

```
MAIL> read 1
#1      30-OCT-1994    16:36:52.08
        MAIL
From:   SMTP%"HOTEL-L@MIZZOU1.missouri.edu" To: GHOL CC:
Subj:   Re: non-smoking ordinances in restaurants
```

3. CONTINUE READING UNTIL DONE. EXIT.

```
Non-smoking ordinances are very different in the state where
I manage a restaurant......
Mail> exit
```

Because it is so easy to duplicate and distribute e-mail on the Internet, take great care concerning what you say to whom.

You may also want to forward a message you receive to another interested individual. Using the message from the previous procedure, the next section will explain how to do this.

FORWARDING INTERNET E-MAIL

Forwarding e-mail is just like sending a letter you receive through the mail to someone else. You return it to the postal service for delivery to a specific person or destination. The difference on the Internet is that you can open the message and read it before sending it back to the Internet postmaster.

MISE EN PLACE
Forwarding Internet E-mail

✓ Log in to your Internet provider.

✓ Start the e-mail program.

✓ Read your e-mail.

✓ When you find an e-mail message you want to forward, locate the e-mail address to which you wish to forward.

PROCEDURE

1. AFTER READING THE MESSAGE YOU WISH TO FORWARD, ISSUE THE FORWARD COMMAND.

```
#1              30-OCT-1994 16:36:52.08
MAIL
From:SMTP%"HOTEL-L@MIZZOU1.missouri.edu" To: GHOL CC:
Subj:Re: non-smoking ordinances in restaurants
Mail> forward
To: wildrice@chefnet.com
Subject: FYI: Smoking ordinances
```

2. CONTINUE READING YOUR MAIL OR EXIT THE MAIL PROGRAM.

```
*exit
```

Internet Messaging Across Cyberspace

Internet e-mail has an immediacy that is fundamental to its value. Answering e-mail demonstrates that you are "taking care of business." For instance, if you receive a message from someone inquiring about your resume as a sommelier that they found online, answering in a timely manner is important. A quick response also builds credibility. However, if you send a message to a winery but neglect to check for a response, you miss creating a prompt reply, and so damage the effectiveness of future communication.

MISE EN PLACE
Saving Internet E-mail
✓ Log in to your Internet provider.

✓ Start the e-mail program.

✓ Read your mail until you find a message you wish to save.

PROCEDURE

1. AFTER READING THE MESSAGE YOU WISH TO SAVE, ENTER THE COMMAND TO EXTRACT OR SAVE THE MESSAGE.

```
MAIL> extract
```

2. GIVE THE SAVED MESSAGE A FILENAME, WHEN PROMPTED.

```
File: smoke.txt
```

MISE EN PLACE
Deleting Internet E-mail
✓ Log in to your Internet provider.

✓ Start the e-mail program.

✓ Read your mail until you find a message you wish to delete.

PROCEDURE

1. AFTER READING THE MESSAGE YOU WISH TO DELETE, ISSUE THE COMMAND TO DELETE OR ERASE THE MESSAGE.

```
MAIL> delete
```

2. RESUME READING YOUR E-MAIL OR EXIT THE MAIL PROGRAM.

```
exit
```

USENET

The **Usenet** is a collection of 7,000 electronic bulletin boards called **newsgroups.** Many new groups are added every day. Each newsgroup is dedicated to a specific topic. Like a forum on a BBS or a public messaging area on a commercial online service, newsgroup messages are **posted** for all interested parties to read and respond. Dozens of newsgroups focus on topics of interest to food and beverage professionals. For instance, subjects range from food history, low-fat cooking, sustainable agriculture, and recipes to brewing beer and enjoying wine.

The Usenet is carried by thousands of Internet providers as well as many BBSs. It is also accessible through DELPHI and America Online.

The names of individual groups reflect an organizational hierarchy by type of newsgroup. There are only a few top-level types of newsgroups that, in turn, branch out to other lower-level types. Figure 5.1 illustrates how the hierarchies work using some newsgroups of interest to food and beverage professionals.

Consider the group called rec.food.historic. The name seems odd at first glance, but it is actually very informative:

- rec indicates its classification in the *rec*reational newsgroups that concentrate on recreational topics.

- food is the category.

- historic is a subcategory.

Sidebar (left column):

Even though disk space becomes less expensive as technology advances, saving e-mail that is of no value is counterproductive. It obscures e-mail that is saved for legitimate reasons. Casual e-mail that is nothing more than chitchat only clutters your e-mail box and files. Delete unimportant e-mail immediately.

A large network of special interest groups, each with its own public message board, is called the **Usenet.**

An individual public message board on the Usenet is a **newsgroup.**

FIGURE 5.1
USENET NEWSGROUPS HIERARCHY

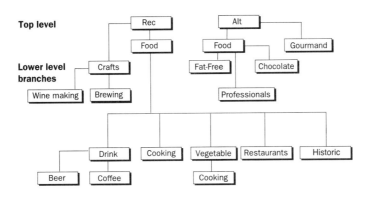

In addition to rec.food.historic, there are the following rec.food newsgroups: rec.food.cooking, rec.food.restaurants, rec.food.recipes, rec.food.drink, and more.

Alt newsgroups are *alt*ernative groups with a narrower focus. They are often more obscure and easier to create on the Internet so they proliferate at a greater rate.

Posting to a newsgroup is similar to sending e-mail, but the communication is public (to a group) instead of private (to an individual).

Let's follow the procedure to send a message to the Usenet group alt.food.professionals. This message is sent from an Internet provider that carries the Usenet at the University of North Carolina, Chapel Hill to the alt.food.professionals newsgroup.

When you place a public message on a Usenet group or BBS, it is called posting. The message itself is a **post.**

MISE EN PLACE
Posting a Message to Usenet

✓ Determine the Usenet group to which you want to post your message.

✓ Log in to your Internet provider.

✓ Access the Usenet area.

99

Food and Wine Online

PROCEDURE

1. SELECT THE OPTION TO POST NEWS.

```
Network News
1.trn - threaded rn
2.trn - won't prompt for new groups
3.rn - line-oriented news reader
4.rn - won't prompt for new groups
5.pnews - post news
6.Download news articles
7.Manipulate .newsrc file
(b)ackup to previous menu, (? or h)elp, (q)uit.
==> 5
```

2. ENTER THE NAME OF THE USENET GROUP TO WHICH YOU WANT TO POST A MESSAGE.

```
Newsgroup(s): alt.food.professionals
Your local distribution prefixes are:
Local organization: launchpad
Organization:                          unc
City:                                  ch
State:                                 nc
Country:                               usa
Continent:                             na
Everywhere:                            world
```

3. DEFINE THE LIMITS OF DISTRIBUTION FOR THE MESSAGE.

```
Distribution (world): world
```

4. CREATE A TITLE OR SUBJECT FOR THE MESSAGE.

```
Title/Subject: New Forum on ChefNet
```

5. CONFIRM THE DISTRIBUTION FOR THE POST.

```
This program posts news to thousands of machines
throughout the entire civilized world. Your message will
cost the net hundreds if not thousands of dollars to
send everywhere. Please be sure you know what you are
doing.
Are you absolutely sure that you want to do this? [ny] y
```

6. TYPE THE MESSAGE.

```
I am looking for organic avocados. Can any professionals
on the Net point me to a foodservice supplier who car-
ries them?
Thanks.
Gary Holleman
```

7. SEND THE MESSAGE.

Send, abort, edit, or list? s

Remember, sending a message to a newsgroup has the potential to reach hundreds, even thousands, of Internet users. Carefully evaluate what it is that you want to say before you post to a newsgroup.

Newsreaders are necessary to read Usenet news postings. There are several different newsreader programs on the Internet; some sites even let you select the newsreader you prefer.

Newsreaders are not easy to learn to use. Once you discover which newsreader your Internet provider supplies, you should find a user guide for the program to learn how to use it most efficiently or ask a friend for help.

With so many newsgroups to browse and so many postings in each group, a good way to see only topics of interest is to use an Internet service that acts as a news filter. The service will send you only the Usenet posts with the keywords that you specify. If you wish to receive a complete introduction to the **NetNews Filter,** just send an e-mail message to netnews@db.stanford.edu and place the word info in the body of the message.

MAILING LISTS:
E-mail Discussion Groups

A **mailing list** is a service unique to the Internet. Imagine a group of hundreds of people with a similar interest, all with e-mail systems, each sending messages to everyone else in the group. Each message you send goes to everyone in the group. Each response to your message goes to everyone in the group. Everything goes to everyone. If you can picture this, you have a good idea of what a mailing list is all about; see Figure 5.2.

A computer program that lets you navigate through the Usenet newsgroups and messages is called a **newsreader.**

The service that returns abstracts of Usenet postings based on keywords supplied by you is called the **NetNews Filter.**

If you want to practice posting to a Usenet group there are special newsgroups just for that purpose:

alt.test
misc.test
biz.test

A system for sending e-mail to a group of people who have chosen to partici-pate in a public discussion is called a **mailing list.** Each message is sent to the entire mailing list.

A **subscriber** is a person who chooses to belong to a mail-ing list by e-mailing a request to join. Unlike other sub-scriptions in your life, you do not pay to subscribe to a mailing list.

A **listserver** is like an electronic traffic cop, automatically handling member-ships to the list, distributing mes-sages, and sending information on the list when requested.

FIGURE 5.2
HOW A MAILING LIST IS STRUCTURED

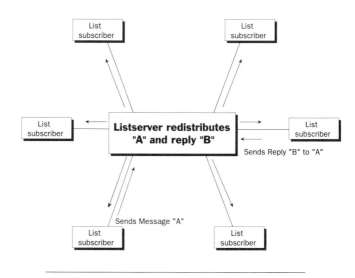

More than a dozen mailing lists have food or beverage topics, including a few that are specifically for culinary pro-fessionals. For example, the list called Chefs on the Internet has more than 100 subscribers from the foodservice indus-try. Another list is for culinary professionals in Canada and those interested in Canadian foodservice from a chef's per-spective.

As with the Usenet newsgroups, there are thousands of topics for mailing lists. Like the Usenet groups, mailing lists let you conduct a public discussion. However, they are much easier to use than the Usenet. If you can send e-mail, you can participate in a mailing list.

A mailing list has two parts: the **subscribers** and the **listserver.** Subscribers send messages to the listserver, which, in turn, sends messages to the list. For example, Hotel-L is a list for the hospitality industry. Participants are lodging and foodservice professionals, educators, and stu-dents. Each hospitality professional on the list is free to send a message to the list. Each post to the list is open to reply by anyone else on the list. It is up to each participant to make sure that the message is appropriate for all list members.

ELECTRONIC FOOD FOR THOUGHT

Chef John Cooney, banquet chef at the Fairmont Hotel, Chicago, Illinois, made these online comments recently concerning his delight with the Chefs on the Internet list.

"Chefs on the Internet has already surprised me in the short time I have been a subscriber. There have been discussions of things ordinary as well as scientific explanations as baffling to me as the first time I pushed my PC's ON button. It is only too true that the techniques of good cooking do not change. This is timeless information, to be learned in schools or in apprenticeships. What does change are the variables: the ingredients, availability, and the consumption trends of the public. In vying for market share, profit margin, creativity, and customer satisfaction one must stay on the edge of both proven techniques and new trends . . . Nothing disseminates information as timely as electronic media," says Chef Cooney.

"As I live in a major metropolitan area, I have been able to not only read about, but see, smell, and taste my way through the shifting cuisine. Here in Cyberspace, the more isolated chef can ask for help in any area from people who have 'hands on' experience to answer with. I have seen postings on the Chef's List not only from the U.S.A.; Canada and England have been heard from . . . I don't feel embarrassed to ask for help here . . . The PC is quickly becoming as indispensable a kitchen tool as the venerable French knife . . ."

John Cooney, banquet chef, Fairmont Hotel, Chicago

A mailing list provides you with a very powerful form of communication. Each member can quickly place any message in front of a large number of individuals. However, with that ability comes responsibility. Members join a list because they want to discuss a particular subject. Messages

103

that are not pertinent to a list's subject are likely to be greeted by disdain and admonishment from other list members. If you post a message to a mailing list, be sure it is relevant!

Benefits of belonging to a mailing list include instant e-mail access to individuals with interests similar to yours. Another benefit is the discussion notes that will be placed in your e-mail box instead of being publicly posted on a bulletin board. In other words, the information comes to you automatically, instead of your going out to collect it.

Subscribing to a list requires only a few steps using your e-mail skills. All you need is the address of the listserver and the name of the list. Generally, the subscription process goes like this.

MISE EN PLACE
Subscribing to a Mailing List
✓ Identify the mailing list you want to join and obtain the address of the listserver.
✓ Determine from the subscription information the specific format for subscribing to the list.
✓ Log in to your Internet e-mail provider.
✓ Start the mail program.

PROCEDURE

Here is the procedure for subscribing to the Chefs on the Internet mailing list:

1. ADDRESS AN E-MAIL MESSAGE TO THE LISTSERVER.

```
%Mail> send
To: majordomo@halcyon.com
Subject: <Return>
```

2. TELL THE LISTSERVER, IN THE BODY OF THE E-MAIL MESSAGE, THAT YOU WANT TO SUBSCRIBE TO THE LIST.

```
subscribe chefs
```

3. SEND THE MESSAGE AND EXIT.

```
Ctrl+Z
exit
%
```

Confirmation from the listserver that you have success-fully subscribed should arrive soon after you send the message. The listserver, **Majordomo,** is automated so the response will be a matter of minutes. Other lists may not be automated and may take several days to return an e-mail confirmation. The confirmation notice will contain more information about the list and its rules.

Majordomo is a specific type of list-server requiring its own unique set of commands.

Even though the process is short and direct, the language used in the message to the listserver must be very specific. In most cases, the listserver is a machine, not a human, so it expects specific words. Usually, a subscription request must contain *only* the following information on the first line of the message:

1. The word subscribe

2. The list name, spelled correctly

Some listservers other than Majordomo, such as Listserv, require a third piece of information, which is your first and last name. Here is an example of my subscription to the list-server of the Hotel-L mailing list, a mailing list for lodging and foodservice professionals, students, and educators.

PROCEDURE

To:
listserv@mizzou1.missouri.edu

FROM:
holleman@chefnet.com

SUBJECT:
<Return>

MESSAGE:
subscribe hotel-l Gary Holleman

When the listserver receives this message it will send a notice, within a few minutes, telling me that I am now a subscriber to Hotel-L.

The address for subscribing is *not* the same as the address you use to post a message to the list. If you are posting to the list, the listserver name is replaced by the name of the list in the electronic address. So, while the address for subscribing to the Chefs on the Internet list is majordomo@halcyon.com, the address for posting to the list is chefs@halcyon.com. The procedure for posting a message to the Chefs on the Internet mailing list follows.

MISE EN PLACE
Posting a Message to a mailing list
✓ Join the Chefs on the Internet mailing list.
✓ Log in to your Internet e-mail provider and start the mail program.

PROCEDURE

1. ADDRESS THE MESSAGE TO THE LIST, NOT THE LISTSERVER.

```
%Mail>
send
To:
chefs@halcyon.com
```

2. CREATE A MESSAGE IN THE BODY OF THE E-MAIL MESSAGE.

```
To all the chefs on the list:
I just learned of a mailing list for Canadian Chefs. If
you are interested....
```

3. SEND THE MESSAGE AND EXIT.

```
Ctrl+Z
exit
```

There is a mailing list that exists for the express purpose of notifying members of new mailing lists on the Internet. To subscribe send an e-mail message to:listserv@vm1.nodak.edu. In the body of the message place the following words, (where *first-name last-name* is your first and last name:) subscribe new-list first-name last-name.

CONCLUSION

The Internet is huge beyond imagination. It is chaotic, heavily traveled, and very useful. Food and beverage professionals find many resources created expressly for them and others that have relevant content.

The most common tools used on the Internet are those that allow you to send written communication to others. These tools include e-mail, the Usenet, and mailing lists.

E-mail allows you to send private messages to individuals anywhere that e-mail is delivered on the planet. For instance, it lets chefs in the United States economically communicate quickly with peers in the United Kingdom on a daily basis. E-mail can be sent, read, saved to a file, forwarded, or deleted.

The Usenet is a message system that allows individuals to congregate around a specific subject and carry on a discussion in a public forum. With more than 7,000 newsgroups, the Usenet carries many newsgroups of interest to food and beverage professionals. Alt.food.professionals is one that is specifically designed for the foodservice industry.

Mailing lists are public discussions that are communicated using e-mail. To receive mailing list messages, you must subscribe to a group and have an Internet e-mail address. Several mailing lists are specifically for hospitality professionals. Chefs on the Internet and Chefs-Canada are for culinary professionals. Hotel-L is for lodging industry professionals.

Obtaining Files at a Distance

Several tools will let you reach out across the Internet to retrieve files, log in to remote computers, or just browse files in random fashion. Professionals in the hospitality industry will find many resources filed away in the deep recesses of the Internet. There are archives for recipes that you can download and use. Libraries around the world can be accessed from your local Internet provider. There are more than 50 different lists of restaurants on the Internet. Many have reviews posted from patrons; others contain overviews of the cuisine, price ranges, and entertainment. Is your restaurant listed? Is the listing correct? The tools that you learn to use in this chapter will help you find the answers to these questions.

This chapter provides you with a working knowledge of the following Internet tools:

- Telnet—a tool that lets you log in to a remote computer

- Anonymous FTP—the tool that allows unrestricted access to many files and software on the Internet

- Archie—a program that searches for files based on a subject you specify

- Gopher—a menu driven program used to access many resources on the Internet

109

Telnet has multiple meanings:

(1) software that allows you to connect to a remote computer over the Internet;

(2) a command used to start the Telnet software;

(3) a verb to describe executing the telnet command.

TELNET

Telnet is a special service available on the Internet that allows you to log in to a remote computer while connected to your Internet provider. A remote computer can be within sight of your terminal or one that is on the other side of the planet.

For food and beverage professionals, Telnet can be a valuable tool. Remember Jonathon Lewis, the chef consultant who uses the Internet to access information used in consulting? He used Telnet to log in to the Texas State Government's Internet site and acquire information on the Americans with Disabilities Act.

There are many government Telnet sites that are of interest to restaurant operators. For example, the address for the federal government, fedworld.gov, is a gateway to many of the government sites on the Internet, including the Food and Drug Administration.

Here is an example of a Telnet session to the LAUNCHpad BBS, which is a Telnet site on the Internet. You get to this site by entering the command telnet, followed by the Internet address of the host computer in Chapel Hill, North Carolina.

MISE EN PLACE
Telnet

✓ Obtain the Internet address of a public Telnet site and the password for entry from an Internet guide such as this text.

✓ Log in to your Internet provider.

PROCEDURE

1. ENTER THE TELNET COMMAND WITH THE INTERNET ADDRESS OF THE HOST COMPUTER.

```
%> telnet launchpad.unc.edu

Trying... Connected to LAMBADA.OIT.UNC.EDU.
```

Obtaining Files at a Distance

```
ULTRIX V4.3 (Rev. 44) (lambada)


  *** ATTENTION laUNChpad USERS ***
Type 'launch' at the login prompt.


login: launch

Last login: Sat Aug 27 20:56:21 from seq.OIT.OSSHE.ED
ULTRIX V4.3 (Rev. 44) System #4: Mon Jul 12 16:55:12 EDT
1993 UWS V4.3 (Rev. 10)
     And now for something completely different....
               ULTRIX V4.3 UWS V4.3
===========================================================
Welcome to UNC's
          L    a    U    N    C    h    p    a    d

                              Administrated by
GIGO, UNC's student high-tech interest group. Your SysOps:
```

Information deleted to conserve space...

2. FOLLOW THE PROMPTS FOR COMPLETING THE TELNET. A NUMBER OF VARIOUS QUESTIONS WILL BE ASKED IN ADDITION TO A REQUEST FOR YOUR NAME. BE PATIENT AND ANSWER THEM AS THEY APPEAR.

```
Your name? gary holleman
Password?  <deleted>


No new system news

Main Menu
    1. Network News
    2. Electronic mail
    3. On-line Information Systems (LIBTEL)
    4. Topical document search (WAIS)
    5. Download files
    6. Find user
    7. User Options
    8. Pherrit - gopher client
    9. Lynx - WWW client
    10. Triangle Free-Net experimental gopher

(? or h)elp, (q)uit.
```

3. AT THIS POINT, THE TELNET IS COMPLETE. YOU CAN NOW SELECT A MENU ITEM OR QUIT. MANY OF THE MOST VALUABLE RESOURCES FOR FOOD AND BEVERAGE PROFESSIONALS ON THE INTERNET ARE AVAILABLE FROM THIS SIMPLE MENU. ITEM #1 GIVES YOU ACCESS TO THE USENET NEWSGROUPS, FOR INSTANCE.

```
==> q

Are you sure you want to quit? [N/y] y
Connection closed by Foreign Host
```

There are no rules for logging in to a remote system. Each system is unique. In some cases, it is easy to "knock at the electronic door" of a remote system yet impossible to get in without prior approval. In other cases, you may be presented with a prompt that will allow public access by using a special command like 'launch' at UNC. In still another instance, no login may be necessary and telnetting to a site may simply generate a menu for navigation of the host system. You will find several Telnet sites that will interest foodservice professionals in Chapter 11.

Many of the computers that act as hosts on the Internet run on a version of the **UNIX** operating system. While it is not necessary to understand UNIX commands to work on the Internet, the serious Net explorer may find it helpful. A classic text on UNIX is Harley Hahn's *A Student's Guide to UNIX*.

FILE ARCHIVES

Files archived on the Internet form a valuable resource for exploration. These archives are one of the foundations on which the Internet is built. Thousands of computers around the globe each have hundreds of files that are archived for the purpose of sharing information. There are files containing research data, spreadsheets, electronic journals and newsletters, video and graphical images, and sounds. The archives also include huge amounts of shareware and freeware, programs for Macintosh, software for MS-DOS and Microsoft Windows, and programs for **UNIX** computers.

For chefs, this means that recipes, food-related software, and nutritional information are readily available. Beverage professionals will find drink recipes, winery information, and consumers' discussions of beer, micro-breweries, and brew pubs. Managers will find small-business-related files that will assist in accounting, marketing, word processing, and communications.

A large percentage of these files are accessible by anonymous or guest users. In other words, you don't have to have a special account on a given computer to download a file contained in the archives. Such unrestricted files are often located in public directories identified by the name pub or /pub/. So, when you review directories of archives on the Internet, the /pub/ directory is often an excellent place to start.

ANONYMOUS FILE TRANSFER

Without the ability to download a file on the Internet, file archives would be of little value. File transfers allow you to move a file from a host on the Internet to your computer.

On the Internet, **File Transfer Protocol (FTP)** is a program that moves files from one computer to another.

File transfers on the Internet are made possible by a program called **File Transfer Protocol (FTP).** FTP is not a program that you can go out and buy, nor is it identical to FTP on a BBS, in that you do not need to specify a protocol. On the Internet, the FTP program defines its own protocol. FTP resides on most full-service Internet providers.

ELECTRONIC FOOD FOR THOUGHT

There are a number of ways to locate Internet sites. One of the easiest methods is just to ask around. Chef Paul Freeman, executive chef, L'Opera Bistro, Santa Barbara, California, is a member of the Chefs on the Internet mailing list, which he receives in his AOL e-mail box. He used the mailing list to find new FTP sites by posting a query online. Chef Freeman saw a reference to a list of FTP sites in a post to the list and pursued the origins in this message:

"I don't know if I missed it, or if it was a private post, but I'd love to have some food-related FTP sites to check into (FTP is one of the few AOL Net access features). Any suggestions?

Thanks in advance,

Paul chefpaul99@aol.com"

Chef Freeman uses commercial online service e-mail to access Internet mailing lists for the purpose of locating FTP sites on the Internet. This chef definitely leverages the technology to expand his culinary horizons!

When a public Internet site lets you log in with no special clearance and transfer a file to yourself, it is called **anonymous FTP**.

Let's look at a session where we FTP (note the use of FTP as a verb!) to The World, an online service for dial-up access to the Internet. The World allows **Anonymous FTP,** so let's take a look at the directory using the FTP program from a public Internet provider. We are searching for a yam recipe that is in the Usenet Cookbook, which is a collection of recipes compiled by a Usenet newsgroup. It is located in the archives of the Online Book Initiative (OBI), a project that seeks to bring texts of many kinds online.

MISE EN PLACE
FTP

✓ Log in to your Internet provider.

✓ Start the FTP program, usually by entering FTP or clicking on the FTP button if your provider has a graphical screen for navigating the Internet.

PROCEDURE

1. ENTER THE FTP ADDRESS OF THE SITE FROM WHICH YOU WANT TO TRANSFER FILES. IN THIS CASE, IT IS THE ADDRESS FOR THE WORLD.

```
FTP>ftp.std.com
Connection opened (Assuming 8-bit connections)
<ftp FTP server (Version wu-2.4(3) Thu Apr 14 16:20:44 EDT 1994) ready.

< <Hello! < <This is the anonymous FTP area for
world.std.com, a public access UNIX <system. Accounts
directly on the system are available via telnet or
<direct-dial (617-739-9753, 8N1, V.32bis (14.4K), V.32
(9600), 2400, etc.), <login as new (no password) to
```

Obtaining Files at a Distance

create an account. Accounts are charged <at $5/mo+$2/hr
or $20/20hrs/month, your choice. Grab the details in
<the world-info directory here if interested.

2. LOG IN AS "ANONYMOUS."

FTP.STD.COM>login anonymous

3. ENTER YOUR E-MAIL ADDRESS
AS THE PASSWORD.

<Guest login ok, send your complete e-mail address as password.

Password: *****

4. SEARCH THE DIRECTORIES
FOR THE DIRECTORY THAT YOU WANT.

FTP.STD.COM>dir
<Opening ASCII mode data connection for /bin/ls. total 394
        Some directory listings deleted to save space...

```
rw-rw-r--     1   0   src    2511   Apr 6   02:43  README
drwxrwxr-x  215 0   src    5120   Jul 4   16:07  obi
drwxrwx--x    3   0   10     512    Jun 29  22:17  private
drwxrwxrwt  148 0   0      5632   Jul 25  20:11  pub
drwxrwxr-x   71  0   10     1536   Jun 28  05:46  src
drwxr-xr-x    2   0   src    512    Mar 22  16:50  world-info
```

<Transfer complete.

After logging in you need to search directories for the file
you want. You must determine the contents of the directory.
Typing **dir** displays a list of files and directories. The directory is quite large; the above listing is only a partial listing.
Continuing, you find the "obi" directory, which is the one
we are looking for.

5. CHANGE TO THE OBI DIRECTORY.

FTP.STD.COM>cd obi

6. SEARCH THE DIRECTORY
FOR THE DIRECTORY YOU WANT.

<CWD command successful.
FTP.STD.COM>dir

<Opening ASCII mode data connection for /bin/ls. total 6662

        Some directory listings deleted to save space...

```
drwxrwxr-x  3 990   src    512 Mar 7   1992  USENET
drwxrwxr-x  3 990   src    512 Jun 16  02:13 USENIX
drwxr-xr-x  4 990   src    512 Oct 13  1992  USElection
```

```
drwxr-xr-x    7 990    src        512 Sep 24    1993 USG
drwxrwxr-x    2 990    src        512 Sep 19    1991 USPatents
drwxr-xr-x    2 990    src        512 Jun 11    1993 United.Nations
drwxrwxr-x    2 990    src        512 Sep 19    1991 Unix
drwxrwxr-x    2 990    src      11776 Sep 19    1991 Usenet.Cookbook
```

To stop the scrolling produced by the dir command, you can do one of two things. Strike the <Pause/Break> key or enter the dir command in the following way:

`ftp>dir . |more`

This will cause the FTP program to move through the directories one page at a time.

The directory entries that begin the line with "drwxr..." are directories. The number to the right of the drwxr... is the number of files contained in the directory. The name of the directory is the text to the far right of the line. For instance obi has 215 files and pub contains 148 files.

7. TO FIND THE CONTENTS OF THE USENET.COOKBOOK, YOU NEED TO MOVE INSIDE THE USENET.COOKBOOK DIRECTORY.

```
FTP.STD.COM>cd Usenet.Cookbook
<CWD command successful.
```

8. TO VIEW THE CONTENTS OF THE USENET.COOKBOOK DIRECTORY, TYPE DIR.

```
FTP.STD.COM>dir

<Opening ASCII mode data connection for /bin/ls. total 4136
```

Moving down through the directory...

```
rw-rw-r—    1 990    src       2436 Oct 31    1989 xmas-icecream
rw-rw-r—    1 990    src       4898 Oct 31    1989 xmas-pudding
rw-rw-r—    1 990    src       2575 Oct 31    1989 xmas-stars
rw-rw-r—    1 990    src       3083 Oct 31    1989 yam-curry
rw-rw-r—    1 990    src       3292 Oct 31    1989 yeast-rolls
rw-rw-r—    1 990    src       3538 Oct 31    1989 yogurt-cakes
rw-rw-r—    1 990    src       2402 Oct 31    1989 yogurt-froz-1
rw-rw-r—    1 990    src       2405 Oct 31    1989 zucchini-ging
rw-rw-r—    1 990    src       3569 Oct 31    1989 zuccotto
rw-rw-r—    1 990    src       3647 Oct 31    1989 zwetschgend
```

9. TRANSFER THE FILE YOU WANT.

```
FTP.STD.COM>get yam-curry
To local file: yam-cury.txt

<Opening ASCII mode data connection for yam-curry (3083 bytes).
<Transfer complete.
```

By entering the get command, a copy of the yam-curry recipe is in your file directory on the Internet provider on which you started the file transfer session.

10. EXIT THE FTP SITE.

```
FTP.STD.COM>bye <Goodbye.
```

11. EXIT FTP.

```
FTP>exit
```

12. TO DOWNLOAD THE FILE FROM YOUR INTERNET PROVIDER TO YOUR HARD DRIVE USING ZMODEM, ENTER THE UNIX COMMAND, SZ FILE-NAME.%SZ YAM-CURRY.TXT

ARCHIE—FINDING FILES ON THE INTERNET

Finding a useful file using FTP can be time consuming and difficult. The time involved in searching for the file could nearly negate the value of the files! This process could require searching thousands of files, in hundreds of directories, on tens of thousands of computers; this is more than any one person can handle. That's a job for **Archie.**

Archie is a powerful searching program that locates specific software programs, databases, or text files. Its name, Archie, is derived from "archive," which is where the search is conducted—in the Internet file archives. Archie can search thousands of computers and millions of files to find files that match your search criteria. Often, it can do all this in just a minute or two. To find Archie, you first need to find an Archie **server.** (See Appendix A.) The best policy is to use the server geographically closest to your Internet provider.

Archie is a computer system that searches indexes of files that are available on public Internet servers.

A **server** is a computer that provides a specific tool or resource.

MISE EN PLACE
Conducting an Archie Search

✓ Locate the electronic address of the nearest Archie server.

✓ Determine what you will use for a keyword in the search. Log in to your Internet provider.

✓ Using your modem software, open a session log file to record the Archie results.

Food and Wine Online

PROCEDURE

1. TELNET TO ARCHIE.

```
%> telnet archie.unl.edu
```

2. LOG IN AS ARCHIE AND USE YOUR COMPLETE E-MAIL ADDRESS FOR THE PASSWORD.

```
Trying... Connected to CRCNIS2.UNL.EDU.

SunOS UNIX (crcnis2)

unl-archie

login: archie
Password: *****
# Bunyip Information Systems, 1993
# Terminal type set to `vt100 24 80'.
# `erase' character is `^?'.
# `search' (type string) has the value `sub'.
```

3. TELL ARCHIE TO FIND FILES BASED ON THE CHOSEN KEYWORD.

```
unl-archie> find recipe
```

4. WAIT FOR ARCHIE TO RETURN THE RESULTS OF THE SEARCH.

```
# Search type: sub.
# Your queue position: 8 # Estimated time for completion: 01:24
working... |

Host ftp.wustl.edu    (128.252.135.4) Last updated 10:08 25 Dec 1993

Location:/graphics/graphics/mirrors/ftp.teleos.com/SHAREWARE/SharewareINFO
FILE
-r--r--r--   2030 bytes  10:33 13 Jul 1993  Numerical-Recipes.TEXT

Location: /systems/amiga/aminet/biz/dbase      FILE
-rw-rw-r--  63564 bytes 06:12 12 Sep 1993  RecipeBox11.lha      FILE
-rw-rw-r--   587 bytes 06:12 12 Sep 1993 RecipeBox11.readme

Location: /usenet/rec.food.recipes/recipes/misc      FILE
-r--r--r--  1822 bytes  23:00  14  Jul  1991  potato-recipes    FILE
-rw-rw-r--  1168 bytes  23:00  14  Jul  1991  potato-recipes.Z
```

```
Host mthvax.cs.miami.edu  (129.171.32.5) Last updated 10:46  5 Aug 1994
Location: /recipes/misc      FILE
-rw-r--r--    7710 bytes  01:00  4 Dec 1991   vietnamese-recipes

Host ftp.wustl.edu    (128.252.135.4) Last updated 10:08 25 Dec 1993
Location: /usenet/rec.food.recipes/recipes/misc      FILE
-r--r--r--  7710 bytes 00:00  3 Dec  1991 vietnamese-recipes    FILE
-rw-rw-r--  4180 bytes 00:00  4 Dec 1991 vietnamese-recipes.Z

Host mthvax.cs.miami.edu   (129.171.32.5) Last updated 10:46  5 Aug 1994
Location: /recipes/misc      FILE
-rw-r--r--   17728 bytes  01:00  3 Jan 1992   weird-recipes

Host ftp.wustl.edu    (128.252.135.4) Last updated 10:08 25 Dec 1993
Location: /usenet/rec.food.recipes/recipes/misc      FILE
-r--r--r-- 17728 bytes  00:00  2 Jan  1992  weird-recipes    FILE
-rw-rw-r--10090 bytes 00:00  3 Jan 1992  weird-recipes.Z

Host mthvax.cs.miami.edu   (129.171.32.5) Last updated 10:46  5 Aug 1994
Location: /recipes/ovo-lacto      FILE
-rw-r--r--    3248 bytes  01:00 18 Nov 1991   persimmon-recipes

Host ftp.wustl.edu    (128.252.135.4) Last updated 10:08 25 Dec 1993
Location: /usenet/rec.food.recipes/recipes/ovo-lacto
FILE    -r--r--r-- 3248 bytes  00:00 17 Nov 1991  persimmon-recipes
FILE -rw-rw-r--    1994 bytes  00:00 18 Nov 1991  persimmon-recipes.Z

Host mthvax.cs.miami.edu   (129.171.32.5) Last updated 10:46  5 Aug 1994
Location: /recipes/turkey      FILE
-rw-r--r--    7783 bytes  00:00 16 Jul 1991   turkey-recipes

unl-archie>
```

When we first began to look at file archives, we found some recipes at the World site and transferred a file for curried yams. Now, using Archie, a search for files using the keyword **recipe** generates many file archive sites to which we can FTP. The value of Archie is clear. Instead of randomly searching FTP sites for files of interest, in the same amount of time you can obtain an entire list of sites with exactly what you are seeking.

TABLE 6.1
DECODING DIRECTORY LISTINGS

Item	Example from Archie	How Item Helps
Host name	mthvax.cs.miami.edu	Tells you where to FTP to get file
Directory	/recipes/misc	Guides you to file
Filename	vietnamese-recipes	Name of file (required for FTP)

Reading the Archie Search Results

For example, here is a file reference returned by Archie:

```
Host mthvax.cs.miami.edu    (129.171.32.5)

Last updated 10:46  5 Aug 1994

Location: /recipes/misc
FILE -rw-r--r-- 7710 bytes  01:00  4 Dec 1991  vietnamese-recipes
```

The file descriptions returned by Archie have three basic items you need to find the file. They are summarized in Table 6.1.

To FTP the file based on Archie's information, just follow the steps for standard file transfers on the Internet:

- Find the location of the host by reading the log of the Archie search.

- FTP to the host.

- Change to the specified directory.

- Get the file.

Customizing Your Archie Search

As you become more familiar with Archie, you may choose to have Archie change the way it gives you results.

There are a number of default settings for an Archie search. To find the default settings, enter the **show** command:

```
unl-archie> show
#  `autologout' (type numeric) has the value `60'.
#  `collections' (type string) is not set.
#  `compress' (type string) has the value `none'.
#  `encode' (type string) has the value `none'.
#  `language' (type string) has the value `english'.
#  `mailto' (type string) is not set.
#  `match_domain' (type string) is not set.
#  `match_path' (type string) is not set.
#  `max_split_size' (type numeric) has the value `51200'.
#  `maxhits' (type numeric) has the value `100'.
#  `maxhitspm' (type numeric) has the value `100'.
#  `maxmatch' (type numeric) has the value `100'.
#  `output_format' (type string) has the value `verbose'.
#  `pager' (type boolean) is not set.
#  `search' (type string) has the value `sub'.
#  `server' (type string) has the value `archie.unl.edu'.
#  `sortby' (type string) has the value `none'.
#  `status' (type boolean) is set.
#  `term' (type string) has the value `vt100 24 80'.
unl-archie>
```

Using the mailto setting to e-mail Archie search results to yourself is helpful if you do not want to wait for the return of the search results. It will also create a text file of the results for future reference.

You can change each of the above default settings by using the **set** command. It has an impact on the search or the display of the results of a search. The **help** command lists more information about each of these settings. For example, to get help on the set command, enter:

```
unl-archie> help set
```

Be sure to enter "done" to exit when you are finished using help. We will set the **mailto** so that we can have the results of the Archie search e-mailed to us if we choose.

```
unl-archie> set mailto holleman@chefnet.com
```

TRAVELING THROUGH GOPHERSPACE

Gopher. Gopherspace. Those uninitiated to cyberspace scratch their heads in wonder at the mere mention of the words. Internet travelers smile with the knowledge that it is an extensive information resource on the Internet—and one of the easiest to use. It is extensive because it accesses a large array of different types of information: databases, libraries, text files, directories, and more. It is easy because it is menu-driven and has a similar appearance across the Internet.

The menu-driven, search tool created for use on the Internet is called **Gopher.**

Gopherspace is the region of the Internet that is encompassed by Gopher.

A **client** is a computer or application that makes use of the resources provided by a server.

For foodservice professionals, **Gopher** provides a unique way to access information about a variety of subjects. Gopherspace is geographically organized so you can quickly move to a Gopher server in Australia, for instance, if you are searching for information on Australian cuisine. If you are searching for information on wine making, you might search Gopherspace in California or a Gopher server at a university that teaches the subject, such as the University of California at Davis.

With a single keystroke, a **Gopherspace** traveler can move from a remote computer in Asia to one in South Africa or simply move from the University of Minnesota campus computer to the university's site at Lake Itasca, Minnesota. For the hospitality professional with little Internet experience this is good news! Instead of constantly changing environments and scenery on the Internet, the culinarian or wine expert is able to use screens that look familiar and require little expertise to navigate.

Originally developed at the University of Minnesota in 1991 (hence the name Gopher, where the Golden Gophers take to the football field each fall), Gopherspace now includes nearly 2,000 Gopher servers worldwide. Each server maintains its own information; for anyone interested, it provides access through the larger Gopher system. The only tools required to access Gopher are an Internet account and a Gopher **client.**

ELECTRONIC FOOD FOR THOUGHT

Eric Scudder is a culinary student at the California Culinary Academy. Scudder is not complacent about his studies and exhausts all resources in his pursuit of culinary information. "As a culinary student at The California Culinary Academy, we are taught to utilize all sources of information in order to learn and to be creative in our approach to food," says Scudder.

Obtaining Files at a Distance

"The Internet is a fantastic vehicle for learning because it allows me to instantly explore recipes and menus from all over the globe. With Gopher, it becomes an excellent reference source for any information I might need—and I can access it in seconds!"

Escoffier never dreamed that culinary students would someday have such tools at their disposal. He would, no doubt, encourage Scudder in his innovative pursuit of culinary knowledge.

———————————————

Selecting menu items is similar to browsing an FTP site. For food and beverage professionals, searching is a quicker, more effective way to find items of interest in Gopherspace. To use Gopher for an online search requires very few keystrokes.

There are two ways to enter Gopherspace. If your Internet provider has Gopher client software, then you may use Gopher by entering the command: %gopher

By following the Gopher command with a Gopher address you can access a Gopher server in much the same way you would use the telnet command. The full Gopher command for a local Gopher client might look like this:

```
%gopher consultant.micro.umn.edu
```

If you don't have a Gopher client with your local Internet provider, you can telnet to a public Gopher client. Log in using Gopher as the user ID and use the Gopher server through the menus provided. For example, from my local Internet provider I type telnet followed by the e-mail address of the Gopher server at the University of Minnesota:

```
%> telnet consultant.micro.umn.edu
```

MISE EN PLACE
Gopher

✓ Log in to your Internet provider.

✓ Access the Gopher client.

PROCEDURE

1. ACCESS A GOPHER CLIENT.

```
%gopher
```

2. CHOOSE A MENU ITEM OF INTEREST.

Each Gopher menu
item ends with a
special character.
The slash (/)indi-
cates that when you
select that item, it
displays another
menu.

```
Connecting..Retrieving Directory\Internet Gopher Information Client
v2.1.-1
Home Gopher server: gopher.tc.umn.edu
    1.  Information About Gopher/
    2.  Computer Information/
    3.  Discussion Groups/
    4.  Fun & Games/
    5.  Internet file server (ftp) sites/
    6.  Libraries/
    7.  News/
-->8.  Other Gopher and Information Servers/
    9.  Phone Books/
    10. Search Gopher Titles at the University of
Minnesota <?>
    11. Search lots of places at the University of
Minnesota<?>
    12. University of Minnesota Campus Information/

Press? for Help, q to Quit
```

The above menu is from the first and greatest of them all—the Gopher server at the University of Minnesota. The menu you see is similar to those of the thousands of other Gopher servers in Gopherspace. Most Gopher menus have a uniform look to them, which accounts for one of Gopher's primary strengths. Note item #5. We now have a menu-driven interface to access the FTP sites on the Internet!

3. SELECT ITEM #2 TO CONDUCT A SEARCH.

```
    1.  All the Gopher Servers in the World/
    2.  Search All the Gopher Servers in the World <?>
    3.  Search titles in Gopherspace using veronica/
    4.  Africa/
-->5.  Asia/
    6.  Europe/
    7.  International Organizations/
    8.  MiddleEast/
    9.  North America/
    10. Pacific/
    11. Russia/
    12. South America/
    13. Terminal Based Information/
    14. WAIS Based Information/
    15. Gopher Server Registration <??>

Press ? for Help, q to Quit, u to go up a menu
Page:1/1
Internet Gopher Information Client v2.1.-1
```

4. ENTER THE KEYWORD "FOOD" TO FIND THE GOPHER SERVERS OF INTEREST TO FOODSERVICE PROFESSIONALS.

```
Search All the Gopher Servers in the World
Words to search for food
Text...
Connecting...
Searching...
\-Search All the Gopher Servers in the World: food
   Food and Agriculture Organization of the UN (FAO)/
-->Food and Nutrition Information Center, USDA/
```

IF YOU SELECT THE SECOND ITEM, GOPHER PRODUCES THE FOLLOWING MENU:

```
  Page: 1/1  -->
Receiving Directory...
Connecting...
Retrieving Directory...
Food and Nutrition Information Center, USDA
-->1. Food and Nutrition Center, General Reference/
   2. FDA/USDA Food Labeling Education Information Center/
   3. Food Guide Pyramid Users' Database/
   4. Food Service Management/
   5. Food and Nutrition Information Center Publications/
   6. Food and Nutrition Software/
   7. Information about the National Agricultural Library/
   8. Other Food and Nutrition-Related Electronic
      Resources/
   9. USDA/FDA Foodborne Illness Education Information
      Center/
   10. WIC-Developed Materials Database/
```

Certainly, this menu will be of interest to food professionals. By choosing a beverage-related keyword, such as "wine" to search Gopherspace, you can find information of interest to beverage professionals.

CONCLUSION

Tools available on the Internet are invaluable to food and beverage professionals. They provide an opportunity to actively pursue information. Learning to use the Internet tools is the key to maximizing the value of your time online.

Telnet is a tool that lets you log in to remote computers to obtain information. Anonymous FTP is a tool that facilitates the transfer of the files in public directories such as recipes, government information, and software. Archie searches the Internet for files related to a specific subject. Gopher is a menu-driven travel aid for the Internet that accesses many types of resources including file archives, libraries, and databases.

Developing the skills to use these tools is essential for effective and complete management of Internet resources for the food and beverage professional.

Exploring the World Wide Web

The World Wide Web may be the most fascinating of all Internet resources. It is certainly the most dramatic and potentially the most valuable. Contrasted with the arcane commands involved in FTPing a file or the stark menus of Gopher, traveling the Web is enjoyable and virtually effortless.

For foodservice workers such as chefs, apprentices, restaurant managers, and culinary students, the Web is where you go to find the most current information on the Net. Suppliers do marketing on the Web; culinary schools advertise on the Web; restaurants post their menus; and newspapers post restaurant reviews. Also, bartenders will find drink recipes posted on the Web. Professionals who are responsible for wine lists and purchasing will find tasting notes and historical information on the Web.

Most important, for professionals who depend on the most current information available, the Web is the Internet resource of choice for nearly all new information placed online. This is particularly true of commercial information.

Food and Wine Online

A **Web page** is an individual file on the World Wide Web.

Hypertext is a form of text where certain words are connected to more detailed information in other files. The documents create a web-like information structure.

A Web page that serves as an introduction to the rest of the document links is called a **home page.** A home page is one of the appropriate places to enter the Web.

A **hotlink** is a portion of text that, when selected, leads to another Web page.

For the Internet, it is "where the action is."

In this chapter you will find the following:

- An overview of the World Wide Web

- A discussion of the tools used to connect and browse the Web

- Instructions for entering URLs to go directly to a Web home page

- Instructions for creating bookmarks

WHAT IS THE WORLD WIDE WEB?

The World Wide Web is a dynamic, fluid, and rapidly growing (at twice the rate of the Internet itself!) service that has few parallels in our daily lives. As with the BBSs connected to the Internet and the Usenet, the Web is a feature of the Internet; it is not the Internet itself. The Web comprises thousands of specially designed documents that are distributed across the Internet. Each document is called a **Web page** and contains **hypertext.** Many of the pages contain graphics that enhance the page contents with illustrations. See Figure 7.1.

The primary page at each electronic address is called a **home page,** and the location is identified by a URL.

A Web page has **hotlinks** that can be clicked, referenced, or entered, to link to a related subject. Some hotlinks connect you to a document on an entirely different computer. That document will, in turn, also contain hotlinks for many other pages. Selecting the new hotlinks can take you on a fascinating journey across the Net. It might produce a video clip or even an appropriate sound bite to bring a subject alive. Web pages can provide information about research, products, or even biographical information about the page owner.

For example, you might connect to the Web page of Van Nostrand Reinhold (the publisher of this book) and select a link to the home page of a new author. When the author's home page appears you may find that she has linked her

FIGURE 7.1
THE STRUCTURE OF THE WORLD WIDE WEB

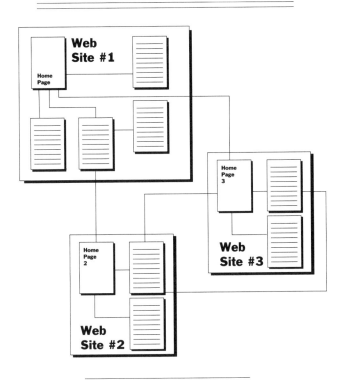

page to some dining-related files on the Web. Selecting a link that looks interesting, you might find yourself at a home page that features dozens of restaurant menus. One more selection and you can find yourself at the menu for the restaurant at Le Cordon Bleu cooking school in Paris, France. With a few quick key strokes, you have taken a culinary tour half way across the planet.

Figure 7.2 shows an example of a foodservice Web page. It was designed and published by Chef Kendall Jackson, Memorial Union Catering and Dining department, Oregon State University.

Chef Jackson's Web page informs others about his foodservice unit at the university. The hotlinks, which are composed of hypertext, can be selected with mouse clicks.

FIGURE 7.2
CHEF KENDALL JACKSON'S WEB PAGE

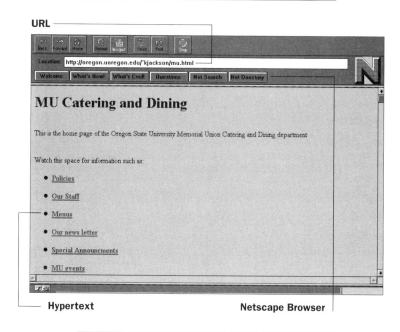

URL

Location: http://oregon.uoregon.edu/~kjackson/mu.html

| Welcome | What's New! | What's Cool! | Questions | Net Search | Net Directory |

MU Catering and Dining

This is the home page of the Oregon State University Memorial Union Catering and Dining department

Watch this space for information such as:

- Policies
- Our Staff
- Menus
- Our news letter
- Special Announcments
- MU events

Hypertext   Netscape Browser

SELECTING A HYPERTEXT LINK

The effect of clicking on the text is like telnetting to another Internet site, except it is much simpler. You do not have to start a Telnet program, find an address, or log in to another computer. All you need to do is click the mouse and you will figuratively travel to the other Web page and view it.

Jackson's page contains no graphics at this time. Other pages, such as the home page for Mark Miller's Red Sage Restaurant, may contain sound clips and graphics. Still others can feature animation or video. Figure 7.3 shows the Gumbo page, produced by UCLA culinary student Chuck Taggart, which contains some graphics as well as hypertext. Notice the hotlinks to various culinary and cultural documents on the Web.

FIGURE 7.3
THE GUMBO PAGES

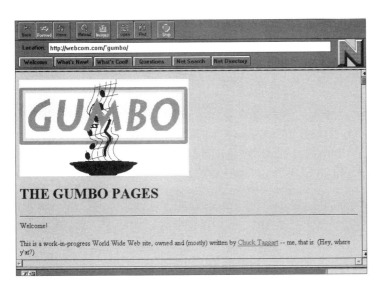

A.

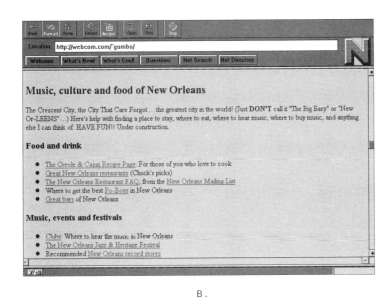

B.

ELECTRONIC FOOD FOR THOUGHT

Culinary student Chuck Taggart created the Gumbo Pages as a result of his great love for the cajun/creole culture and good food. Here is an excerpt from an e-mail message in which he describes his page:

"The page is firmly based in Louisiana cuisine, but it is growing and expanding every day. I'm including more general information on stocks and sauces, and especially my collection of various dishes from around the world that I've come across.

The Gumbo Pages grew out of my two passions—music and food—and particularly as they relate to my home state of Louisiana. I first started the page to disseminate information about my radio show, called 'Gumbo,' and the rest sort of naturally sprang from it. I've been an unpaid music programmer/DJ at KCRW for seven years, and as I mentioned on the (Chefs on the Internet) list, I'm in the midst of career change plans, attending UCLA's Professional Cooking program, offered through UCLA Extension."

Chuck Taggart eamon@netcom.com

"Whatever you is ... BE that!"—Clifton Chenier's barber

NECESSARY INGREDIENTS FOR CONNECTING TO THE WEB

Using the World Wide Web is easy; however, connecting to the Web is not. Even seasoned Internet users struggle to get a working connection that generates the available graphics.

To connect to the Web, either you need an off-the-shelf software package, such as Internet in a Box, or you need to put together a browser with software available from the Internet.

The best graphical connection to the Web with Microsoft Windows requires these items:

FIGURE 7.4
THE NETSCAPE BROWSER

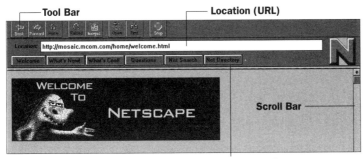

Tool Bar — Location (URL)

Location: http://mosaic.mcom.com/home/welcome.html

Scroll Bar

Directory Buttons

- Trumpet Winsock

- A SLIP Internet connection

- Netscape, Mosaic, or another graphical **Web browser**

- A dedicated phone line

- A fast modem (minimum 9600 bps, 14.4 kbps or faster preferred; the faster the better)

- A fast computer (minimum 486/25 MHz; the faster the better)

- A large hard drive (minimum 210 MB; the bigger the better)

You can obtain **Trumpet Winsock** by using Archie and FTP on the Internet. The SLIP connection allows you to dial up your Internet provider and access the Web. **Netscape** (see Figure 7.4) lets you view the graphics and navigate the Web. The fast hardware and large hard disk are needed to handle the large amounts of digital information (that is, transmitted data) received most of the time during a Web session.

In the following examples, Netscape is installed in Microsoft Windows.

The software that lets you travel across the World Wide Web and access Web documents is a **Web browser**.

Trumpet Winsock is software that allows the Web browser to interface with Microsoft Windows.

The fastest, most advanced browser available for traveling the Web is **Netscape**.

133

MISE EN PLACE
Browsing the World Wide Web

✓ Install a Web browser and related software.

✓ Dial up a SLIP connection with your Internet provider.

✓ Launch your graphical Web browser.

PROCEDURE

This procedure will take you on a tour of the Galaxy page, which has a food and dining focus. The Galaxy home page has links to hundreds of interesting Internet sites; see Figure 7.5. The culinary links are just a small fraction of those selections.

1. FROM YOUR HOME PAGE, CLICK ON A HOTLINK.

FIGURE 7.5
GALAXY HOME PAGE VIEWED THROUGH NETSCAPE

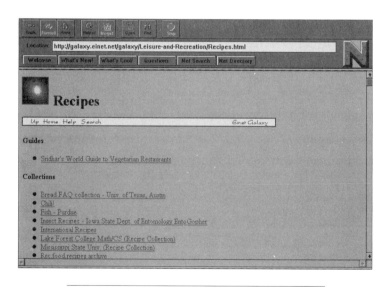

FIGURE 7.6
GALAXY FOOD AND RESTAURANT LINKS

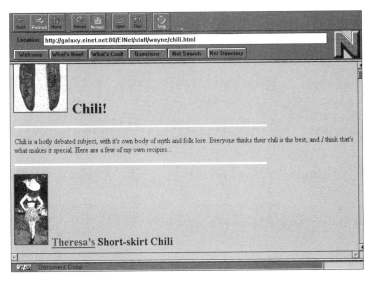

A.

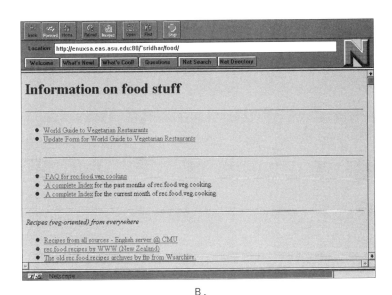

B.

FIGURE 7.6 CONTINUED
GALAXY FOOD AND RESTAURANT LINKS

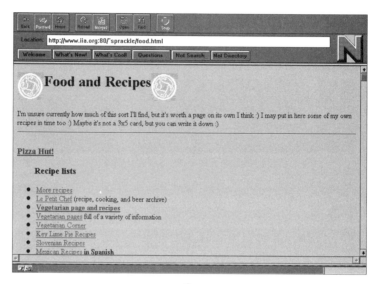

C.

2. USING YOUR MOUSE, CLICK ON A LINK TO MOVE TO OTHER PAGES UNTIL YOU FIND A PAGE OF INTEREST. SEE FIGURE 7.6.

3. DISCONNECT FROM YOUR SLIP CONNECTION.

Lynx is a text-based Web browser, as opposed to a graphical Web browser, that is available free from many Internet providers.

The graphical browser, such as Netscape, is a joy to use. The Web can give you a sense of the power of the Internet, and the colors, graphics, and intuitive feel of Netscape enhance the experience of surfing the Web. Other browsers such as NCSA Mosaic, NetCruiser, WinWeb, and Web Explorer, are also easy to use and just as intuitive.

It is possible to connect to the World Wide Web without a graphical browser. Often, your Internet provider will make a text-based browser, called **Lynx**, available. While this form of Web access may not be as visually exciting, it is a very practical way to access the Web resources.

136

LYNX

Because Lynx is installed on your provider's computer, you do not need to install it. Lynx is also available with limited features from many Gopher sites.

Navigation of the Web using Lynx requires just a few basic keystrokes.

MISE EN PLACE

Browsing the Web with Lynx

✓ Log in to your Internet provider.

✓ Invoke Lynx, usually by typing **lynx** or **www.**

PROCEDURE

1. SELECT A LINK FROM THE HOME PAGE OF YOUR PROVIDER. SEE FIGURE 7.7.

2. CONTINUE TO FOLLOW THE LINKS AS THEY INTEREST YOU. SEE FIGURE 7.8.

3. TYPE Q (FOR QUIT) WHEN YOU FINISH.

NAVIGATING THE WEB USING URLS

You can also access Web pages by entering a URL. Remember, a URL has a very precise syntax and it must be followed exactly. Some URLs are more than one line long, and accuracy is important. Using a URL makes moving to the page you want fast and easy; it is not necessary to browse several pages to get to the one you want. A typical Web URL looks like this:

```
http://host-name/path-name
```
or
```
http://www.tele.fi/~hospitality
```

The URL indicates that the page is hypertext (http), located on a World Wide Web server in Finland (host-name

FIGURE 7.7
LYNX HOME PAGE

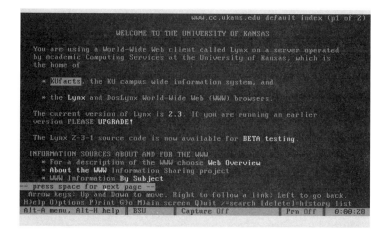

FIGURE 7.8
RESTAURANT-RELATED SITES ON THE WEB

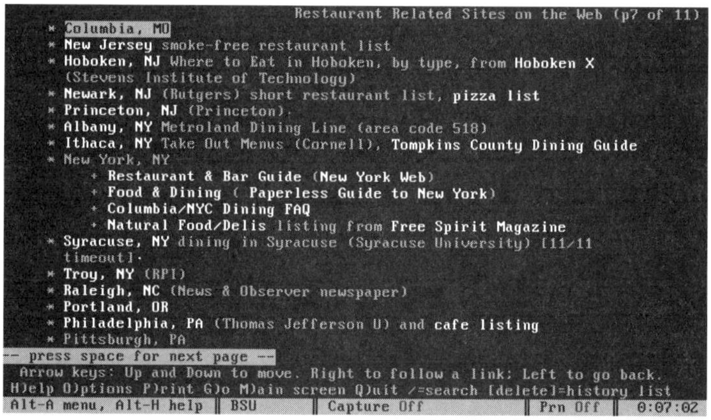

= www.tele.fi), and located in a path called "hospitality," (/~hospitality).

Many different Internet objects can be viewed using a Web browser. If you know the URL for a document, it can be entered and accessed. The URL formats for various resources are listed below.

Exploring the World Wide Web

EXAMPLES OF URLS FOR VARIOUS INTERNET RESOURCES

Type of Resource	URL Format
World Wide Web	http://host-name/path-name
File Archives	ftp://host-name/path-name
Usenet News	news:Usenet newsgroup name
Gopher	gopher://host-name/path-name

MISE EN PLACE
Using URLs with a Graphical Browser
✓ Obtain a URL for a Web home page you want to visit.

✓ Using a graphical Internet access package, connect with your Internet provider.

✓ Launch your browser.

PROCEDURE

1. CLICK ON THE NAVIGATE PULL-DOWN MENU.

2. ENTER THE URL. SEE FIGURE 7.9.

http://itp.thomson.com:9675/vnr/chhome.html

3. FOLLOW THE LINKS AND DISCONNECT WHEN DONE.

FIGURE 7.9
ENTERING A URL

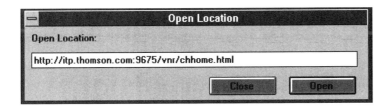

To find out about new Web pages added to the Internet, check out the Usenet newsgroup, comp.infosystems.www.users. Look for messages with subject lines that begin with the word "ANNOUNCE."

To find out more about the World Wide Web, you can look to the World Wide Web FAQ (Frequently Asked Questions). The URL is http://sunsite.unc.edu/boutell/faq/www_faq.html.

MISE EN PLACE
Using URLs with Lynx
✓ Obtain a URL for a page you want to visit.

✓ Connect with your Internet provider.

There is a list of mailing lists on the Web. Using your skills navigating the Web with URLs, check out:

http://www.clark.net/pub/list-serv/lsv11.html

You navigate with Lynx by using the arrow keys. Lynx maintains a record of where you have been on the Web each session. To retrace your steps, press the left arrow key.

PROCEDURE

One interesting Web page deals with coffee and even includes information for "coffee professionals." Using Lynx, you can view the Web's "Over the Coffee" page.

1. START LYNX.

```
%> Lynx

Lynx default home page (p1 of 2)

WELCOME TO Lynx AND THE WORLD OF THE WEB
   You are using a WWW Product called Lynx. For more
information about obtaining and installing Lynx please
choose About Lynx

   INFORMATION SOURCES ABOUT AND FOR WWW*
For a description of WWW choose Web Overview* [This is a hotlink!]
About the WWW Information Sharing project*
WWW Information By Subject*
WWW Information By Type
   OTHER INFO SOURCES*
University of Kansas CWIS*
O'Reilly & Ass. Global Network Navigator


Arrow keys: Up and Down to move. Right to follow a link;
Left to go back. H)elp O)ptions P)rint G)o M)ain screen
Q)uit /=search [delete]=history list-- press space for
next page
```

2. FROM YOUR HOME PAGE, TYPE GO.
```
go
```

3. ENTER THE URL WHEN PROMPTED BY LYNX AND PRESS THE ENTER KEY.
```
--WWW URL to open: http://www.infonet.net./showcase/coffee
Getting http://www.infonet.net/showcase/coffee
                OVER THE COFFEE
   WELCOME! This resource is dedicated to the online
```

```
coffee community.   Select one:
* Read This!
* Retail Vendors
* The Coffee Reference Desk
* Coffee File Archives
* The Usenet Coffee Newsgroups
* CoffeeLink (resources located elsewhere on the
Internet)
* Resources For The Coffee Professional
* Suggestion Box

Commands: Use arrow keys to move, '?' for help, 'q' to
quit, '<-' to


Professional Resources FOR THE COFFEE PROFESSIONAL

The following information is provided for coffee professionals,
shop owners, and others who have a need for profes-
sional/wholesale resources.
This information is not intended for the casual coffee
drinker.
* List Of Wholesale Coffee Resources
* List Of Coffee/Tea Trade Publications
* Specialty Coffee Association of America----(not yet
available)
```

To search for a Web page with a particular subject visit the Web page at:

```
http://web.city.a
c.uk/~cb157/pages
.html
```

4. FOLLOW OTHER HOTLINKS OR ENTER ANOTHER URL.

5. TYPE Q (FOR QUIT) WHEN YOU FINISH.
```
q
Are you sure you want to quit? [y/n] y
```

The same home page looks like Figure 7.10 using a graphical Web browser.

SOME DRAWBACKS TO THE WEB

For all its sophistication and splendor, the Web does have a few negatives associated with it.

1. It is difficult to access its more exciting aspects. Access to video and sound require a solid understanding of both hardware and software. Video and sound also tend to break up over phone lines and take a long time to display (though text is displayed independent of graphics so you

FIGURE 7.10
OVER THE COFFEE WITH NETSCAPE

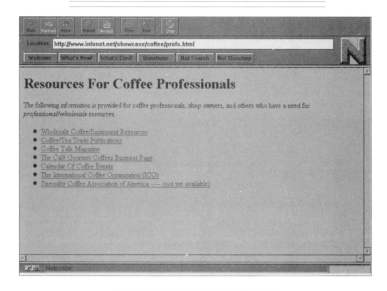

can start to see something before the entire page is drawn).

2. Commercial software packages designed to facilitate Web access are appearing in great numbers on the market, but many tend to be quirky, buggy, and slow.

3. Addresses of Web pages are long, cryptic, and often lead nowhere. Web sites are taken off-line, but the links to the pages remain.

4. You can spend a huge amount of time on the Web waiting and searching.

A link to a Web page that is saved for ready and direct access in the future is called a **bookmark**.

CREATING BOOKMARKS FOR THE WEB

You can create your own list or custom page with your favorite hotlinks and most frequently visited pages. This type of hotlink is called a **bookmark** and allows easy access to pages without having to reenter the URL. So, when you find a Web page that you think you will want to return to in the future, you can save it as a bookmark. Because you will not have to reenter the URL, you can access the page quickly. The bookmarks of a culinarian are likely to be the most interesting food-related sites on the Internet. Beverage professionals will want to have the most active beer, wine, and spirit home pages in their bookmark lists.

MISE EN PLACE
Creating a Bookmark for
the Web with Netscape

✓ Log in to your Internet provider.

✓ Start your Web browser, Netscape.

PROCEDURE

To create and use bookmarks with Netscape:

1. NAVIGATE TO A PAGE YOU WANT TO SAVE WITH A BOOKMARK. SEE FIGURE 7.11.

FIGURE 7.11
PAGE TO SAVE FOR BOOKMARK (VNR)

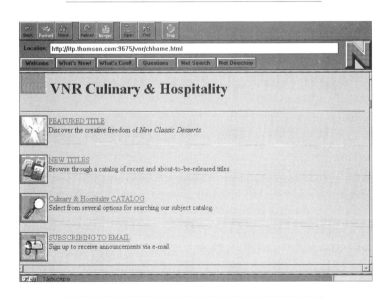

2. TO ADD A BOOKMARK USING NETSCAPE, CHOOSE THE BOOKMARKS MENU AND THEN THE ADD A BOOKMARK COMMAND.

MISE EN PLACE
Creating a Bookmark
for the Web with Lynx

✓ Log in to your Internet provider.

✓ Start your Web browser, Lynx.

PROCEDURE

To create and use bookmarks with Lynx:

1. NAVIGATE TO A PAGE YOU WANT TO SAVE WITH A BOOKMARK.

2. TO CREATE A BOOKMARK USING LYNX, TYPE A (FOR ADD) AFTER YOU LOCATE A HOME PAGE YOU WANT.

3. CONTINUE TO BROWSE THE WEB AND ADD OTHER BOOKMARKS.

4. DISCONNECT FROM YOUR SLIP CONNECTION.

CONCLUSION

The World Wide Web is an exciting Internet tool. Not only is it fun to use, but it is the source for most of the very latest resources placed on the Internet. Food and beverage professionals will find it visually stimulating and intuitive to use.

The Web is a worldwide network of interconnected documents. Each document consists of information with key words that are connected to more detailed information elsewhere in the Net; this is called hypertext. The Web documents, called pages, contain more than just text. Many contain graphics, sound, video, and animation.

Navigating the Web requires browsers that can interpret the hypertext documents. Some browsers let you see only the text on the Web; others reveal the Web graphics and sound capabilities. The most common text browser is called

Lynx, and the most popular graphical browsers are Mosaic and Netscape.

Besides navigating the Web by selecting hypertext words, you can directly enter the URL for a specific Internet resource. This includes not only hyptertext resources, but also Gopher, FTP, and Usenet. Some browsers even support Internet e-mail.

Once you find resources on the Web that are valuable to you as a food or beverage professional, it is important that you save their locations for easy access. You do this by creating bookmarks.

Because of the multimedia potential of the Web, it is the Internet's most important resource to food and beverage professionals. Serious navigators of the Internet will want to explore it, understand it, and profit from it.

The BBS in Culinary Cyberspace

For chefs, information most often takes on one of two forms. Hard information is concrete and descriptive. The price of wild rice, kitchen labor cost, or serving cost per ounce are examples of commonly used hard or factual information. This form of information is often acquired by *computation*. Soft information, on the other hand, is entirely different. It is often vague, laced with opinion, and often needs synthesis and reflection. It is acquired through *communication*.

For the skilled craftsman or technician, hard information and experience are critical. For the artist, soft information and creativity are primary assets. The professional chef is a complex blend of both technician and artist.

The rapidly developing online world presents the chef with many opportunities for both hard information collection and softer information such as professional communication. It is a world where time and space take on a new and exciting meaning. The chef is no longer bound by the 9:00–5:00 switchboards or traditional restaurant closing times to communicate with others in the industry.

147

At the very core of cyberspace is the BBS. The BBS has become a vital part of doing business in many industries. Increasingly, the foodservice industry is looking to the BBS, in many different forms, as an answer to its needs.

The foodservice professional may find many items of interest on any given BBS including the following:

- Accounting software

- Produce market information

- Culinary education information

- Recipes

- Electronic magazines

- Mail-order supplies

- Classified and employment ads

- Time management tips and software

- Marketing advice

- Computer assistance

The number of BBSs available to culinary professionals is growing rapidly. On the following pages are listings of bulletin boards that will be of interest the culinary arts and foodservice professional.

HOTELNET

HotelNet went online in early 1994. It is the first BBS dedicated to the hospitality professional, and it has an emphasis on the lodging segment. However, it includes areas of interest for the food and beverage side of a hotel.

Login is simple and allows you to identify yourself as a Hospitality Industry Professional (HIP). If you identify yourself as HIP, you automatically receive options not accorded those outside the industry.

The board makes use of the increasingly popular RIP (see Chapter 3) graphics, and many screens are designed by the founder of HotelNet, Steve Adams, himself. "We started going outside for some of the development, but RIP looked like something I could do myself," says Adams.

As part of HotelNet, Adams has included a large variety of electronic magazines (called "zines"), which are primarily computer related. These will be of interest to professionals who are deeply involved with computer issues. See Figure 8.1 for sample HotelNet menus.

FIGURE 8.1
HOTELNET MENUS

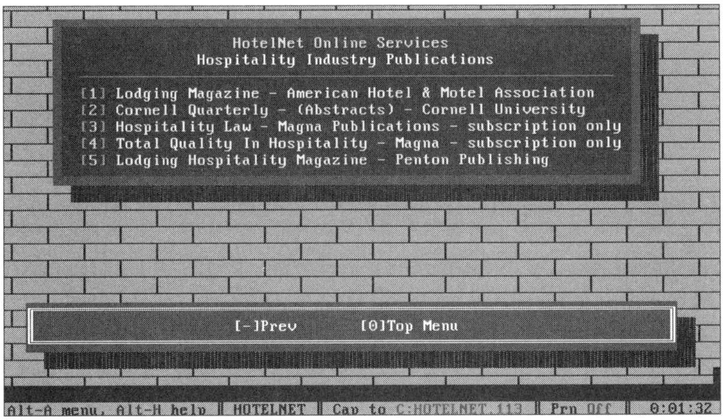

```
              HotelNet Online Services
            Hospitality Industry Publications

    [1] Lodging Magazine - American Hotel & Motel Association
    [2] Cornell Quarterly - (Abstracts) - Cornell University
    [3] Hospitality Law - Magna Publications - subscription only
    [4] Total Quality In Hospitality - Magna - subscription only
    [5] Lodging Hospitality Magazine - Penton Publishing




            [-]Prev        [0]Top Menu

Alt-A menu, Alt-H help ‖ HOTELNET ‖ Cap to C:HOTELNET.113 ‖ Prn Off ‖ 0:01:32
```

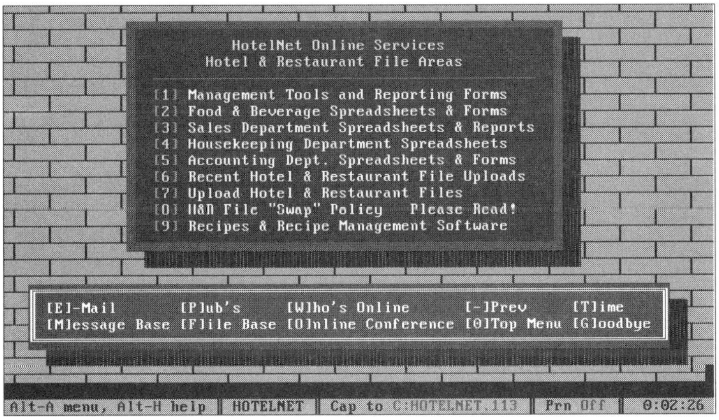

```
                 HotelNet Online Services
               Hotel & Restaurant File Areas

        [1] Management Tools and Reporting Forms
        [2] Food & Beverage Spreadsheets & Forms
        [3] Sales Department Spreadsheets & Reports
        [4] Housekeeping Department Spreadsheets
        [5] Accounting Dept. Spreadsheets & Forms
        [6] Recent Hotel & Restaurant File Uploads
        [7] Upload Hotel & Restaurant Files
        [0] H&R File "Swap" Policy   Please Read!
        [9] Recipes & Recipe Management Software

    [E]-Mail      [P]ub's    [W]ho's Online    [-]Prev      [T]ime
    [M]essage Base [F]ile Base [O]nline Conference [0]Top Menu [G]oodbye

Alt-A menu, Alt-H help ‖ HOTELNET ‖ Cap to C:HOTELNET.113 ‖ Prn Off ‖ 0:02:26
```

TABLE 8.1
HOTELNET INFORMATION

Item	Information
BBS Focus	Provides a platform for discussing hospitality industry issues; provides relevant electronic information of concern to hoteliers
Voice Number	303-296-9200
Modem Number	303-296-1300, ANSI or RIP, 14.4 kbps
Internet Access	Telnet: bbs.ossinc.net Related Internet Sites: http://www.tele.fi/~hospitality http://www.hotelnet.com (early 1995)
Internet e-mail	steve.adams@hotelnet.com
Sysop	Steve Adams
Street Address	1800 Glenarm Place, 7th Floor, Denver, CO 80202
Cost	$30.00 for three months; other plans available; free trial period

FOR THE PROFESSIONAL

Job Search Employee Services is an area used by both employees and employers in the hospitality industry. You may browse the files for candidates to fill an available position, or you can post your own resume.

While the culinary side of HotelNet is currently limited, it promises to grow in the near future. The combination of food and lodging will be attractive to hotel chefs and restaurant managers. HotelNet will become a perfect forum for exploring issues that are common to both the food and beverage and lodging departments in a hotel.

HotelNet has a related Web site (listed in Table 8.1) with up to 15 European hospitality publications online. The BBS features *Lodging* and *Lodging Hospitality* online, which will be of interest to hotel food and beverage directors.

ELECTRONIC FOOD FOR THOUGHT

Founded by Steve Adams, HotelNet is an ambitious full-service bulletin board. Adams capitalizes on his experience as a hotel general manager, owner of a contract management firm, and as a certified executive chef.

"I have spent 25 years in the hotel and restaurant business, 15 of those years in whites. I am an ex-executive chef (or should I say reformed?) <grin> and have managed 82 hotels and full-service restaurants in 35 cities. One of my biggest passions still is cooking and I sneak into the kitchen (ignoring threats from our chefs) whenever I have the opportunity. An area of emphasis that we plan to have on HotelNet is the culinary world.

"We have 20,000 recipes online," says Adams. Such an aggressive recipe file is a testimony to his interest in food and his commitment to hotel foodservice. Section 4 of HotelNet features both a Food, Cooking, & Recipes Forum and a Restaurant Managers forum.

CHEFNET

While many online services focus on the home gourmet cook and the weekend enthusiast, ChefNet meets the online needs of professional chefs; see Table 8.2.

This BBS was developed by Indian Harvest, a specialty rice and grain supplier, as a service for all chefs. ChefNet includes discussion forums just for ChefNet members as well as food and beverage Usenet groups. Also featured are Internet e-mail, teleconferencing, a file library, classified ads, and an Electronic Food Show for suppliers.

Dialing ChefNet with a modem and a computer requires only a standard modem package. New users should log in as "new" to create a new account.

However, if you have an IBM-compatible computer, the easiest method to access ChefNet is to use RIP*term*. As you learned in Chapter 3, RIP*term* provides you with familiar images that help to orient and direct you during the online session. Embedded in images of mailboxes, stoves, and kitchens are "buttons" to click with a mouse to navigate ChefNet; see Figure 8.2. ChefNet provides RIP*term* on diskette upon request. It can also be downloaded from the ChefNet File Library for immediate access.

TABLE 8.2
CHEFNET INFORMATION

Item	Information
BBS Focus	Communication and information source for chefs, culinary arts professionals, and the culinary education community
Voice Number	1-800-346-7032
Modem Number	218-751-5149, ANSI or RIP (disk supplied by ChefNet), 14.4 kbps
Internet Access	E-mail and Usenet only
Internet E-mail	holleman@chefnet.com
Sysop	Gary Holleman
Street Address	PO Box 428, Bemidji, MN 56601
Cost	$8.95 per month; extended free trial period

FIGURE 8.2
CHEFNET SCREENS

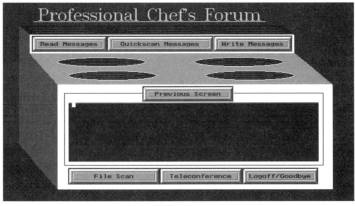

FOR THE PROFESSIONAL

All of the ChefNet discussion forums are specifically for chefs. Subjects discussed include the business of being a chef, pastry chefs, catering, research and development, environmental issues of concern to the industry, and computer uses for chefs. Several organizations, including the Culinary Institute of America, the International Association of Women Chefs and Restaurateurs, and Research Chef Affiliates, also sponsor discussion groups.

Internet resources available include the Chefs on the Internet mailing list and the Usenet groups such as alt.food.professionals, alt.food.historic, and rec.food.cooking. Internet e-mail accounts are given to all members.

The file library includes many recipe management software programs as well as general software of interest to food and beverage professionals. The Electronic Food Show includes exhibits by suppliers, consultants, and employment search firms.

ELECTRONIC FOOD FOR THOUGHT

Steven Frisch is the chef/owner of The Passage restaurant in Lake Tahoe, Nevada. Chef Frisch is a member of ChefNet.

"I log in to ChefNet because it is professionally specific; it is directly useful to my daily work as opposed to having to search through meaningless information online," says Frisch. "ChefNet keeps you up on what's going on in the industry, trends, shows, other chefs, and jobs.

"I have found the discussion of environmental issues especially helpful. I am trying to move our restaurant in that direction—and that is a challenge in this area during the off-season. It has been valuable to read what other chefs have to say about the environment."

TABLE 8.3
ARION COOKING FORUM INFORMATION

Item	Information
BBS Focus	Support for MasterCook II software; recipe database in MasterCook II format
Voice Number	800-444-8104
Modem Number	512-327-9814, ANSI
Internet Access	None
Internet E-mail	info@arion.com
Sysop	Jeff Mayzurk
Street Address	3355 Bee Cave Rd., Ste. 507, Austin, TX 78746
Cost	Free

ARION COOKING FORUM BBS

Arion Cooking Forum doubles as a Technical Support BBS for MasterCook II software as well as a large archive for recipes. There are currently a few chefs online, but the majority of the users are amateur cooking enthusiasts.

Navigation is not as intuitive as in some other BBSs, but a little practice and patience go a long way. New users should log in as "new" to create an account, see Table 8.3.

Arion Software produces a recipe management software package called **MasterCook II**.

For the Professional

The Arion BBS, as a product support vehicle, is successful. If you are using **MasterCook II** in your restaurant, and many chefs do, this BBS is a must. Even if you are not a customer, the BBS should be valuable. There are more than 20,000 recipes online and, if you use MasterCook II, they are already in the format the software requires. There are message forums as well; they include The Recipe Exchange, Macintosh Interests, PC/Windows Interests, Technical Support, and Customer Service. Orders for the software can be placed online.

If you do not use the software, you may be interested in downloading a demonstration version.

TABLE 8.4
CULINARY CONNECTION INFORMATION

Item	Information
BBS Focus	Culinary discussions and information for amateur and professional cooks.
Voice Number	N/A
Modem Number	312-252-FOOD (3663), ANSI or RIP
Internet Access	N/A
Internet E-mail	N/A
Sysop	Andy Biegel
Street Address	3717 Wrightwood, Chicago, IL 60647
Cost	Free; contributions welcome

THE CULINARY CONNECTION

The Culinary Connection BBS is a service for the cooking enthusiast as well as the professional chef. See Table 8.4. The sysop, Andy Biegel, is a graduate of the Kendall College, Evanston, Illinois, culinary arts program and former executive sous chef, Midland Hotel, Chicago, Illinois.

For the Professional

Chef Biegel encourages professionals to participate in the discussion on the BBS. He features an "Ask the Chef" forum and also a "Job Available/Wanted" area that occasionally features foodservice positions. Future upgrades for the BBS include a Chef/Restaurant of the Month feature, which will highlight the recipes and philosophy of a selected chef. There are currently 17,000 recipes online in a database that can be searched. "You can enter the words 'goat cheese' for instance," says Chef Biegel, "and find all recipes that contain goat cheese." Biegel says there are over 1,000,000 recipes to be added to the database as hard disk space permits.

TABLE 8.5
FOODBYTES ON-LINE INFORMATION

Item	Information
BBS Focus	For food technologists and food product development professionals
Voice Number	201-227-1830
Modem Number	201-227-8460, ANSI or TTY emulation
Internet Access	None
Internet E-mail	None
Sysop	Jack Parker
Street Address	1129 Bloomfield Ave., Sparta, NJ 07871
Cost	$225 per year; two-hour free trial

FOODBYTES ON-LINE

FoodBytes On-Line serves the needs of food professionals who work with food ingredients, additives, and flavor profiles. It is dedicated to the work done by product development researchers; see Table 8.5. New users should log in as "new" to create an account. The BBS is not complicated to use.

For the Professional

FoodBytes On-Line provides a network for sharing everything from new product information and sourcing to technical specifications. It also provides headline news, addresses technology issues, and posts an online version of the FDA Enforcement Report. If you need the technical scoop on guar gum or TVP, this is the perfect online resource for you. Seasoned professionals spend time online and post messages in the public forums.

The library has the archives for the FoodBytes newsletter as well as archives of other technical information.

This BBS has been online for more than three years and has over 3,200 users worldwide.

THE JOHNSON & WALES UNIVERSITY BBS

The Johnson & Wales BBS is run by Academic Services and is accessible to the entire school's population of 7,000. See Table 8.6. Only 2,500 of the students are in the culinary

TABLE 8.6
JONHSON & WALES UNIVERSITY BBS

Item	Information
BBS Focus	A local BBS for J&W students, including culinary/pastry students
Voice Number	N/A
Modem Number	401-455-2916
Internet Access	N/A
Internet E-mail	N/A
Sysop	John Lambros
Street Address	N/A
Cost	Free

college, but the BBS is the online home to many talented future chefs. A note to the sysop, John Lambros, will provide you with full access to the board, even if you're not a J & W student. Without permission from the sysop, access is limited.

For the Professional

Johnson & Wales University has an outstanding culinary program. While classified ads for jobs are not a formal part of the BBS, inquiries on the board could bear fruit for employers looking for externs or seasonal help.

At the time this book went to press, the culinary resources were limited to a few shareware files that are cooking related. The library does have a Foodservice Files section and will no doubt grow with time.

NUTRIENT DATA BANK BULLETIN BOARD

The Human Nutrition Information Service (HNIS) of the U.S. Department of Agriculture makes the Nutrient Data Bank Bulletin Board available through a remote login using a telephone line. See Table 8.7.

Online, users will find information on the nutritional content of foods as well as the USDA's Nutrient Data Bank for Standard Reference and the Dietary Analysis Program.

TABLE 8.7
NUTRIENT DATA BANK INFORMATION

Item	Information
BBS Focus	Provides information about the nutritional content of food
Voice Number	301-436-8491
Modem Number	301-436-5078
Internet Access	N/A
Internet E-mail	info-12@info.umd.edu
Sysop	N/A
Street Address	David B. Hayowitz Human Nutrition Information Service 6505 Belcrest Road, Room 315 Hyattsville, MD 20782
Cost	Free

For the Professional

This BBS is most appropriate for foodservice professionals involved with government nutrition programs, such as school foodservice directors. Files available for downloading include information concerning nutritional analysis of foods, conference notes, and government publications for sale.

FOOD-TRAK SUPPORT BBS

FOOD-TRAK is one of the most widely used programs for food inventory management, see Table 8.8. The BBS has an uncluttered and easy-to-use interface. All you need to do is dial in and answer a few questions to be given access.

TABLE 8.8
FOOD-TRAK INFORMATION

Item	Information
BBS Focus	Customer support for FOOD-TRAK restaurant software
Voice Number	602-951-8011
Modem Number	602-951-8071
Internet Access	N/A
Internet E-mail	N/A
Sysop	N/A
Street Address	6560 N. Scottsdale Rd., Ste. H-203, Scottsdale, AZ 85253
Cost	Free

For the Professional

Users have access to upgrades for FOOD-TRAK software and new product news. If you have acquired an affinity for the RIP graphical interface, you can use your RIP*term* here.

The BBS is a valuable resource for FOOD-TRAK users, and customers will find upgrades online in the library. The file library stores demonstration versions of the software for downloading.

THE CHEF BBS

The Chef BBS is cooking related, but it is not just for chefs. In fact, this BBS is directed primarily at home enthusiasts. The Chef BBS has a lot of potential and is very well done. Terry Dawe, the sysop, is actually a police officer who enjoys the kitchen (that's where the BBS is—in the kitchen!); see Table 8.9.

For the Professional

The Chef BBS has two areas devoted to messages about food: Cooking Tips and All About Spices. There is also a Recipe of the Month, which Dawe selects and puts online. The library has more than 8,200 files that include both recipes and shareware. Many of these are business-related software, accounting packages, and even clip art. Chefs and restaurateurs who are looking for inexpensive software for simple business applications will find this valuable.

TABLE 8.9
THE CHEF BBS INFORMATION

Item	Information
BBS Focus	Cooking techniques and recipes
Voice Number	N/A
Modem Number	810-765-2966
Internet Access	N/A
Internet E-mail	N/A
Sysop	Terry Dawe
Street Address	P.O. 293, Marine City, MI 48039
Cost	$12.00 per year

One unique feature of this BBS is what Dawe calls the "Visiting Chef of the Month." Recently, Graham Kerr was the visiting chef; he supplied a biographical and philosophy statement. Kerr also provided a preview of several recipes to be used in his upcoming television special. Messages to Kerr were forwarded by the sysop.

For chefs looking to market themselves online, this BBS will be an ideal venue as it grows and matures. It has been online since March 1994. Chefs who use BBSs frequently check this board out as a place to "give something back" to the online world. It offers an opportunity to contribute and become a recognized "expert" in a new environment.

CONCLUSION

The foodservice professional has many different information and communication needs. Some culinarians require hard facts about products, others need to gather opinions on a prospective employer. Many chefs just want to pass some time with those who understand the pressure of high-volume foodservice. There are a variety of BBSs designed specifically to meet many of those varied needs.

Culinary Usenet Newsgroups

The Usenet is an active and lively place for those who love food. For some professionals, spending time on the Usenet has often been a frustrating experience because so much of the discussion of food occurs from the home cook's perspective. Only recently have professionals found a home in the alt.food.professionals newsgroup.

Yet there is value for the foodservice professional in all of the food-related newsgroups under specific circumstances. A special menu that must be vegetarian might provide the incentive for a chef to spend time in rec.food.cooking.veg. Or a menu reflecting an historical event might prompt a pastry chef to investigate the expertise available on rec.food.historic. As you browse through the listings on the following pages, you will find suggestions for professional application as well as a general description of the newsgroup.

alt.food.professionals

Currently, this is the only newsgroup dedicated to food professionals. It was started in October 1994 and has attracted

Your Web browser can be used to access the Usenet. Select the option on your browser that allows you to open a URL. Enter the following:

`news:usenet-group-name.`

chefs, writers, and restaurateurs from all over the world. Subjects range from industry-specific questions to would-be chefs and restaurateurs looking for advice. Figure 9.1 shows the opening screen using Netscape.

This is an excellent newsgroup for networking with other professionals. Job offers and posts from chefs seeking employment appear in alt.food.professionals. The international exposure of the Usenet gives this group special importance. Very few online venues for chefs and restaurateurs provide such economical access to peers abroad.

rec.food.cooking

rec.food.cooking is the ultimate Internet cooking resource. Hundreds of foodies from around the world gather here to discuss various aspects of cooking. This group discusses everything from saffron to Jello.

One of the great benefits to foodservice professionals is the number of individuals here who have ethnic back-

FIGURE 9.1
USENET ACCESSED WITH NETSCAPE
FROM THE WEB

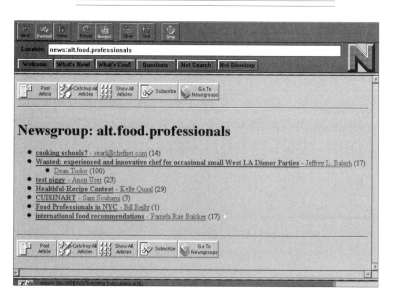

grounds; they provide a wealth of esoteric cooking information. If you are looking for information on authentic Brazilian cooking techniques, ask here! You will probably receive a reply from a home cook in Brazil.

rec.food.recipes

This resource provides an incredible flow of recipes from across the Internet. This newsgroup has as many as a hundred recipes posted on almost any given day. It's almost impossible to keep up with it!

Professionals who request recipes in this group should, in turn, post some of their own. Chefs in major markets can actually develop an audience quickly by contributing recipes of value. Because the participants here love food, it is a perfect forum to market your restaurant or cookbook softly by posting recipes and giving credit to your operation, chef, or publication.

The Internet culture places a great deal of importance to "giving back to the Net." Chefs who use the Internet for research and information gathering should offer to add something to the body of knowledge online—a recipe, cooking tip, or professional insight.

rec.food.veg

This is a vegetarian newsgroup. Usenet participants in this group discuss the specifics of special diets for health, nutritional, and moral reasons. These issues, as well as their dietary implications, are discussed.

With a paradigm shift taking place in the center-of-the-plate, this group will certainly be the center of attention for an increasing number of chefs. The group is populated by possibly the largest number of vegan cybernauts in the world. They are helpful, fanatical, and opinionated! Restaurateurs who offer vegetarian cuisine will benefit from reading the posts from vegetarians.

rec.food.veg.recipes

Vegetarian recipes are the focus of this newsgroup. They range from the very simple to the bizarre and complicated. Many of the vegetarian Web pages contain links to the archives for this group.

The list of Usenet newsgroups is constantly in a state of flux. You can acquire the most current list using Internet FTP. A list is located in the following directory:

ftp://ftp.uu.net/networking/news/config.

In the foodservice industry, the animal protein entrée continues to shrink and the carbohydrate side dish portions continue to grow. Because this trend is relatively new, most restaurants do not have employees skilled in responding to the shift in cuisine. This group can be of great value in educating employees in vegetarian preparations. In this group, you can learn about vegetarian philosophy, explore spice combinations, and acquire recipes for use in your restaurant.

rec.food.restaurants

Where can I find a great Afghan restaurant in Minneapolis? Does anyone know of a cool bistro in the Burgundy region of France? I had a lousy meal at Charlie's in Anytown, Illinois; the bread was stale and the meal was cold! These are the types of questions and statements posted in this newsgroup.

For the restaurateur, this is a great place to lurk and listen as your potential customers discuss what they like, what they don't like, and what they recommend in a restaurant. Many restaurant owners will testify that you will often hear only the good about your restaurant and negative comments about your competitors. Neither of these claims is necessarily accurate. On the Usenet, you never know what you'll read!

This newsgroup can provide an interesting focus group for discussing service, menu design, or even marketing programs, if the subjects are handled gently. The Internet culture frowns on overt attempts at advertising.

rec.food.drink

The pairing of food and beverage is an age-old culinary challenge. On the Internet, rec.food.drink is the newsgroup that focuses on the task of finding the right wine, beer, or other drink to accompany food.

There are many tasting notes that may help chefs, restaurateurs, or even cellar masters find appropriate wines for menus. Jump in anywhere in this group to ask a question or answer a query from a weekend chef. Don't forget to post some of your own opinions and observations. If you have a winemaker's dinner in your restaurant, consider posting some comments from the winemaker in this group. If you have an expertise with a particular area of food and beverage pairing, share it here!

rec.food.historic

This fascinating newsgroup seeks enlightened discussions on the history of food and cooking. From ancient recipes to colonial cooking techniques to lost foods, this is a great forum for culinary professionals.

Because the scope of this group is narrow, this group is not nearly as "busy" as rec.food.cooking or rec.food.recipes. Therefore, it is much easier to manage the information generated and to have a significant impact on the threads of conversation.

Professionals interested in food history will find a great number of reading suggestions in this forum. If you are building a library of food-related books, this newsgroup will provide a great number of text references. The members of this group are generally very well informed. Contrary to what you might experience in some less focused groups, rec.food.historic seldom strays from the subject at hand.

rec.food.preserving

This is the newest of the rec.food.* groups; it deals with all the aspects of canning, drying, and other methods of food preservation.

Chefs who preserve seasonal harvests will find this newsgroup valuable for accumulating the advice of those who have been preserving for decades.

rec.crafts.brewing

The brewing community on the Internet is thriving. The hobby is complex, and the techniques are varied. Discussions are centered not only on ingredients, but also on hardware and tasting notes.

It is commonly thought that advertising is prohibited on the Internet. While this is basically true, there are exceptions. It is acceptable to have a brief comment, two to four lines maximum, at the end of your message with contact information and a phone number. Restaurateurs can list the name, location, and phone number at the end of the message without fear of flaming.

Micro-breweries and brew-pubs are also thriving in the restaurant industry. They are often discussed in this newsgroup, and brew-pub owners can learn from the discussions. Ideas for marketing, promotion, and quality improvement will abound for those operators who are interested.

alt.restaurants

This newsgroup offers a variation on the "Where can I find X type of restaurant when I visit such-and-such city" theme. This is a great place for guerrilla marketing, if you do it without blatant advertising. On the Internet, no one would know you own the restaurant you are recommending! A bonus feature of this newsgroup is that recommendations will often elicit echoes and endorsements or warnings and caution. Either will be valuable to the operator with an eye toward improving business.

When a Usenet message is posted to several newsgroups at once, it is called **cross-posting**.

Public message forums have a certain amount of very targeted, pointed information (signal). They also have posts that are inane and off-subject (noise). The balance between the two is called the **signal-to-noise ratio**. If the ratio is high, the information is easier to find.

alt.creative_cooking
alt.creative-cooking
alt.creative+cooking
alt.creative=cooking
alt.food

All of these Usenet groups are quite similar and are available sporadically across the Internet. They are not necessarily available everywhere because many Internet providers do not have to carry all newsgroups. These newsgroups tend to be clones of one another. In fact, messages posted to one group are often **cross-posted** to the others. They are all recipe discussion groups, but they have a low **signal-to-noise ratio.** While there may be newsgroups that have more to offer professionals, you will occasionally find discussions of interest. Check them out if you have some spare time.

alt.gourmand

This is a desolate and empty newsgroup with great potential—if gourmands would actually gather here. If you have a small group of culinarian friends who need a home online, you might consider gathering here.

alt.good.gourmand (moderated)

Discussions of all things good and gourmet. Because the forum is **moderated,** the signal-to-noise ratio should be high.

A newsgroup that has a person who filters and controls the messages posted to the group is called a **moderated** newsgroup.

alt.food.wine

Group members in this newsgroup discuss food and wine, as the name suggests. Often the discussion may turn to food and wine pairings, although the discussions certainly are not limited to these topics. Generally, the topics dwell on wine, not food.

Professionals will find tasting notes, requests for suggestions (another opportunity for guerrilla marketing), and recipes. For wine lovers, this is a comfortable way to make new friends and enjoy good conversation.

rec.food.sourdough

This is one of the older newsgroups dealing with food, specifically sourdough. The group covers all facets of sourdough production — starter, flour, technique, and more.

Professionals can obtain sources for sourdough ingredients by networking here.

alt.org.food-not-bombs

This group deals with primarily political issues surrounding food, including feeding the homeless and organic food supplies. This group has a very radical side to it.

Alt.org.food-not-bombs is a suitable place for contacts if you are heavily involved in the activism surrounding these foodservice issues. The activist chef will often find like-minded individuals posting messages here.

ba.food

ne.food

misc.triangle.dining

These are regional newsgroups for Bay Area food, New England food, and dining in the golden triangle of North Carolina. The discussion is primarily focused on regional cuisine and restaurants. The concentration of high-tech companies in these areas has given birth to an active regional discussion.

Restaurateurs in these areas of the country benefit from not having to wade through the national scope of the rec.food.restaurants to find comments on operations of local interest. The regional groups are likely to be carried only by Usenet providers in the appropriate areas of the United States.

alt.food.fat-free

A free-ranging discussion of foods without fat takes place here. Recipes, techniques, and nutritional issues are common points of interest.

Chefs find that cooking with less fat is a mandate from the customer in some operations. This group is a good resource to work through options and ideas for your restaurant.

alt.college.food

This newsgroup is dedicated to the foodservices at universities, from the student's perspective. If you want to know what is the most popular wrinkle in college foodservice, check this out. There are active discussions about the quality of new programs, brand marketing, and even the previous night's special.

Culinary Usenet Newsgroups

alt.food.mcdonalds
alt.food.dennys
alt.waffle-house
alt.food.taco-bell

These four newsgroups are the domain of fast food junkies. If you are in the business of fast food management, you can find consumer response to your newest marketing campaign, product offering, or even the way you queue your lines in the restaurant!

Line employees and young managers can meet here and discuss work with others across the country. Bold chain restaurant managers might even stop in to defend a burger or dessert.

alt.food.chocolate

Few ingredients invoke such fanatical followers as chocolate. This newsgroup is the home of chocoholics on the Internet. Discussions are broad and include the culinary side as well as commercial subjects. For instance, recent topics include tempering chocolate, brand names, and online ordering.

CONCLUSION

The Usenet is a very distinctive and diverse environment on the Internet. It features forums for professionals, hangouts for foodies, and depositories of trivial information. Newsgroups are fertile ground for creative food professionals. You can conduct product or marketing research on the Usenet, find a focus group with very specific interests, and network with peers across the globe.

While some Usenet newsgroups may not consistently offer a lot of valuable information to the foodservice professional, they often point to other information resources. Many Usenet posts point readers to Web pages that are new and of interest to the group.

Mailing Lists and E-Mail Discussion Groups

FOR FOOD PROFESSIONALS AND CULINARIANS

Mailing lists, also known as e-mail discussion groups, are a valuable resource for professionals in the busy world of foodservice. Messages are targeted by subject. They are delivered to your e-mail box, and membership often imparts a sense of community.

CHEFS

Chefs on the Internet (see Table 10.1) is the first mailing list created by and for professional chefs. This list is exclusively for professional chefs and was conceived by David Alexander Lee. His vision for an online community of chefs has catalyzed a great deal of chefs' activity on the Internet. Chef Lee, a research chef, is associated with Essential Foods in Seattle, Washington.

"I would suggest your first message to the list be a note of introduction so all on the list will know WHO and WHERE you are," says Lee.

TABLE 10.1
CHEFS ON THE INTERNET LIST

Item	List Information
Focus	Also called Chefs on the Internet; discussion group for professional chefs, culinary students, and educators only
Subscription Address	majordomo@halcyon.com
Subscription Message	subscribe chefs
List Posting Address	chefs@halcyon.com

If you want to know who is currently subscribing to the Chefs on the Internet list, send an e-mail message to

`majordomo@ halcyon.com`

and place the following words in the first line of the message:

`who chefs`

The listserver will send you an e-mail message with the members of the list.

If you have Internet e-mail and your time online is limited, this is the single most important resource you can access. It is focused, informative, and the best online source of information about the professional chef's presence in cyberspace.

Discussions span the entire range of interests of chefs: employment, ingredients, cooking techniques, education, business issues, trends, and technology.

CHEFS-CANADA

Chef Norman Myshok created the Chefs-Canada mailing list to give Canadian chefs an opportunity to discuss issues of a uniquely Canadian nature, including professional organizations, suppliers, ingredients, and cuisine. See Table 10.2.

Chef Myshok invites interested chefs from all over the globe to participate in the list. American chefs can network with chefs north of the border and can locate sources for Canadian produce, fish, and game. European chefs can learn more about Canada's indigenous foods.

Currently, the list is low volume so subscribing to stay current won't flood your e-mail box to an unmanageable level.

TABLE 10.2
CHEFS-CANADA LIST

Item	List Information
Focus	Discussion for Canadian professional chefs
Subscription Address	majordomo@primetime.org
Subscription Message	subscribe chefs-canada
List Posting Address	chefs-canada@primetime.org

HOTEL-L

Hotel-L is dedicated to fostering the exchange of views on hotel and restaurant educational issues among hotel and restaurant educators and students (see Table 10.3). List members are primarily educators and students in hospitality programs. Many are from outside the continental United States.

Discussions are primarily hotel-related but restaurant management issues are presented occasionally. The list is historically skewed to issues concerning technology in the hospitality industry.

Hotel-L is particularly fertile ground for hotel chefs to influence the industry and address issues at the core of many educational programs. List members are influential educators with innovative and progressive viewpoints. There were just over 100 list members when this book went to press.

To receive a list of the Hotel-L list subscribers, send an e-mail message to listserv@mizzou1.missouri.edu and include the following words in the first line of the message:

`review hotel-l`

The listserver will return a list of members in your e-mail box.

TABLE 10.3
HOTEL-L LIST

Item	List Information
Focus	Hospitality education; lodging, food, and beverage
Subscription Address	listserv@mizzou1.missouri.edu
Subscription Message	subscribe hotel-l *first-name last-name*
List Posting Address	Hotel-L@mizzou1.missouri.edu

FOODWINE

The FoodWine mailing list, Table 10.4, is very similar to the many general cooking and recipe newsgroups available with Usenet, but it arrives in your e-mail box. Several dozen messages are distributed each day. Many postings are recipes; others are comments concerning wine tastings or food and beverage pairings.

If you have questions about a particular wine or food and wine pairing for your restaurant, and no time to browse the Usenet groups, this list will serve you well. Although some participants are novices, others are very knowledgeable.

To remove yourself from the FoodWine mailing list, send a message to the list-server address (not the posting address) with the following words in the first line of the message:

`signoff listname`

You will receive an e-mail notice that you are removed from the list.

TABLE 10.4
FOODWINE LIST

Item	List Information
Focus	Topics related to food and wine
Subscription Address	listserv@cmuvm.csv.cmich.edu
Subscription Message	subscribe foodwine *first-name last-name*
List Posting Address	Foodwine@cmuvm.cc.vt.edu

EAT-L

Eat-L is a mailing list that deals with food lore as well as recipe exchange (see Table 10.5). However, it is quite broad in scope. This list is very active, with dozens of messages sent each day. Lack of attention to your e-mail can result in a full e-mail box from this list alone.

TABLE 10.5
EAT-L LIST

Item	List Information
Focus	Food lore, eating, and cooking
Subscription Address	listserv@vtvm1.cc.vt.edu
Subscription Message	subscribe eat-l *first-name last-name*
List Posting Address	eat-l@vtvm1.cc.vt.edu

FATFREE

The Fatfree list is concerned with fat-free cooking and includes recipes for extremely low fat, mostly vegetarian diets (see Table 10.6). With the prevalent concern regarding reducing fat consumption in dining, chefs will find this a helpful resource when rewriting menus. List members have experience with fat-free cooking and can provide helpful hints and guidelines.

To remove yourself from Eat-LF, send an e-mail message to listproc@apollo.it.luc.edu with the following words in the body of the message:

`signoff eat-lf`

TABLE 10.6
FATFREE LIST

Item	List Information
Focus	Fat-free food and cooking
Subscription Address	fatfree-request@hustle.rahul.net
Subscription Message	Place the word ADD in the subject field
List Posting Address	fatfree@hustle.rahul.net

EAT-LF

The Eat-LF mailing list is concerned with eating low-fat foods (see Table 10.7). For restaurateurs and chefs not familiar with a low-fat focus on foods, this list can provide valuable insights into low-fat cuisine. It also presents an opportunity to interact with those who are devoted to this style of eating.

TABLE 10.7
EAT-LF LIST

Item	List Information
Focus	Eating low-fat food
Subscription Address	listproc@apollo.it.luc.edu
Subscription Message	subscribe eat-lf *first-name last-name*
List Posting Address	eat-lf@apollo.it.luc.edu

VEGGIE

The Veggie list involves an active discussion of vegetarianism and the vegetarian lifestyle; see Table 10.8. Restaurateurs with a vested interest in this cuisine and lifestyle can network and learn from the members of this list.

TABLE 10.8
VEGGIE LIST

Item	List Information
Focus	Vegetarianism
Subscription Address	veggie-request@maths.bath.ac.uk
Subscription Message	subscribe veggie *first-name last-name*
List Posting Address	Veggie@maths.bath.ac.uk

VEG-COOK

Vegetarian diners often complain about the lack of variety and imagination involved in vegetarian cooking. See Table 10.9. To avoid alienating this growing customer segment, subscribe to this list and learn directly from the customer!

TABLE 10.9
VEG-COOK LIST

Item	List Information
Focus	Vegetarian food preparation
Subscription Address	listserv@netcom.com
Subscription Message	subscribe veg-cook
List Posting Address	veg-cook@netcom.com

VEGAN-L

The vegan diet is the most specific and restrictive of all vegetarian diets. The Vegan-L list (Table 10.10) is concerned with the diet, the philosophy, and many related issues. The vegan consumer is the most narrow niche of all vegetarian markets and requires the most detail in culinary preparation. If you wish to serve this niche, this group can provide a platform for questions and answers about the vegan diet in a restaurant setting.

**TABLE 10.10
VEGAN-L LIST**

Item	List Information
Focus	Vegan diet and lifestyle
Subscription Address	listserv@vm.temple.edu
Subscription Message	subscribe vegan-l *first-name last-name*
List Posting Address	vegan-l@vm.temple.edu

VEGLIFE

The VegLife list is another e-mail discussion group that will help acquaint the chef and restaurateur with the finer points of vegetarianism. See Table 10.11.

**TABLE 10.11
VEGLIFE LIST**

Item	List Information
Focus	Vegetarian lifestyle
Subscription Address	listserv@vtvm1.cc.vt.edu
Subscription Message	subscribe veglife *first-name last-name*
List Posting Address	veglife@vtvm1.cc.vt.edu

VEGGIES

The Veggies list originates in the United Kingdom and offers still another view of vegetarianism and opportunity to interact with its adherents. See Table 10.12.

**TABLE 10.12
VEGGIES LIST**

Item	List Information
Focus	Vegetarianism
Subscription Address	veggies-request@newcastle.ac.uk
Subscription Message	subscribe veggies *first-name last-name*
List Posting Address	veggies@newcastle.ac.uk

BEEF-L

Beef-L is not a very busy list, but all subscribers have an interest in beef (see Table 10.13). Some members are from the beef industry; others are just admirers of red meat. If your expertise is in serving beef, this is a great forum for you to mentor others and attract attention as an industry expert. With a short reference to your restaurant at the end of the messages you post here, it can become a viable soft-sell opportunity as well as a chance to share your knowledge.

TABLE 10.13
BEEF-L LIST

Item	List Information
Focus	Beef
Subscription Address	listserv@wsuvm1.bitnet
Subscription Message	Leave the subject heading blank; include the following words in the body of the message: subscribe beef-l *first-name last-name*.
List Posting Address	beef-l@wsuvm1.bitnet

J-FOOD-L

The J-Food-L list is dedicated to discussing Japanese food and culture; see Table 10.14. Even though it has many subscribers, it remains focused and, compared to other lists with memberships this size, has a relatively low volume of messages.

The advent and growth of Asian fusion cuisine in the restaurant industry give added importance to a group of this nature. Japanese culture and food are complex. If you serve a market where Japanese influence is great, this list will help you become more knowledgeable and comfortable with the Japanese culture.

TABLE 10.14
J-FOOD-L LIST

Item	List Information
Focus	Japanese food and culture
Subscription Address	listserv@jpknu01.bitnet
Subscription Message	sub J-FOOD-L *first-name last-name*
List Posting Address	j-food-l@jpknu01.bitnet

MASTERCOOK

The MasterCook list (see Table 10.15) is a very active pipeline for recipes and is facilitated by the recipe software creators at MasterCook II and Arion BBS (see Chapter 8). If you are using the MasterCook II software in your restaurant and wish to collect more recipes, this mailing list is an effortless way to do so. Don't forget to post some of your own as a thank-you to the other contributors.

TABLE 10.15
MASTERCOOK LIST

Item	List Information
Focus	Recipes in the MasterCook II format
Subscription Address	mail-server@mind.org
Subscription Message	Leave the subject field blank and include the following text in the message portion: subscribe mastercook quit
List Posting Address	mastercook@mind.org

BSS-L

The BSS-L list has roughly 50 subscribers and actually meets in person at a different sushi bar once a month in the Boston area (see Table 10.16). Restaurants with sushi service in Boston will certainly want to subscribe to this mailing list. Other restaurants across the United States can learn from the reviews and information posted on the sushi mailing list.

TABLE 10.16
BSS-L LIST

Item	List Information
Focus	Also called Boston Sushi Society List; discusses sushi in the Boston area
Subscription Address	listserv@netcom.com
Subscription Message	subscribe bss-l
List Posting Address	bss-l@netcom.com

FOOD-LAW

Food-Law is a low-volume message list that deals with the legal aspects of commercial food production. See Table 10.17.

TABLE 10.17
FOOD-LAW LIST

Item	List Information
Focus	Legal issues in the food business
Subscription Address	listserv@vm1.spcs.umn.edu
Subscription Message	subscribe food-law
List Posting Address	food-law@vm1.spcs.umn.edu

FOODLINK

Foodlink concerns itself with food safety issues (see Table 10.18). Consulting chefs, executive chefs, research chefs, foodservice managers, and caterers can benefit from engaging in food safety discussions. The list is currently not very active, so if you have specific needs, you might want to introduce yourself to the group and share your request with its members.

TABLE 10.18
FOODLINK LIST

Item	List Information
Focus	Food safety issues
Subscription Address	listserv@wsuvm1.csc.wsu.edu
Subscription Message	subscribe foodlink
List Posting Address	foodlink@wsuvm1.csc.wsu.edu

CHILE-HEADS

The Chile-Heads list is an e-mail discussion group for anyone who wants to elevate their understanding of chiles and spicy food; see Table 10.19. You will find posts that promote cooking, growing, handling and enjoying chiles. If you enjoy, serve, or sell chiles, this list will be a valuable resource for you.

TABLE 10.19
CHILE-HEADS LIST

Item	List Information
Focus	All things hot and spicy
Subscription Address	chile-heads-request@chile.ucdmc.ucdavis.edu
Subscription Message	subscribe
List Posting Address	chile-heads@chile.ucdmc.ucdavis.edu

CONCLUSION

Mailing lists are valuable resources. They are easy to access, are focused, and often provide a sense of community. It is important to become familiar with the rules and commands for each list that you join so that you can navigate successfully and interact intelligently. As a professional, you must demonstrate respect and wisdom in your interactions with others.

Food, Cooking, and Restaurant Resources on the Internet

The Internet has long featured foods and recipes for the enjoyment of the educators and researchers who have historically dominated the network. Today, food professionals on the Internet are growing in number. As a result, many new items that are specifically used by the professional chef, culinary student, and educator are available. Even though the resources listed in this chapter are designed exclusively for professionals, they should be of interest to those who desire to learn and grow.

Most of the resources discussed in this chapter have three common features. First, each resource has a title, which is taken directly from the resource itself, when available. Otherwise, a title has been chosen that seems appropriate. Second, each resource has a URL to help you locate the item on the Internet. You may want to review Chapters 5-7 if you need to reacquaint yourself with URLs. Last, most of the resources listed have short descriptions or summaries of the content available.

When an Internet site carries the identical files of another site, it is said to be a **mirror**.

RECIPE RESOURCES

This section will list recipe file archives to provide an overview of what's available on the Net. Because many sites are considered **mirrors** of other servers, many of these files and directories may be found in several different places on the Internet. In some cases, alternative sites for a resource are noted in this chapter because access to some servers is difficult at certain times of the day. Many sites can be accessed using several different tools on the Internet. For instance, the rec.food.recipes archive containing "ovo" recipes at the English Server is available through both the Web and Gopher; these are essentially two routes to the same destination.

The Creole & Cajun Recipe Page

http://www.webcom.com/~gumbo/recipe-page.html

Even if you are not operating a restaurant in New Orleans, this recipe Web page will be of interest.

Ovo-Vegetarian Recipes

http://english-server.hss.cmu.edu/Recipes.html

gopher://nutmeg.ukc.ac.uk/11/.archive/uunet/usenet/rec.food.recipes/ovo

Ovo-vegetarians are individuals whose meatless diet permits the consumption of eggs. Therefore, these recipes may contain eggs, but no meat. Restaurants with vegetarian sections on their menus will find many usable recipes here.

Lacto-Vegetarian Recipes

http://english-server.hss.cmu.edu/Recipes.html

gopher://nutmeg.ukc.ac.uk/11/.archive/uunet/usenet/rec.food.recipes/lacto

Lacto-vegetarians permit dairy products in their diets, so these recipes may contain dairy products. A well-rounded vegetarian menu should include an entree meeting this need.

Low-Fat Vegetarian Recipes

http://english-server.hss.cmu.edu/Recipes.html

ftp://ftp.halcyon.com/pub/recipes/general

Food, Cooking, and Restaurant Resources

Here are recipes from the Fatfree Mailing List archives. If you offer a menu with a low-fat emphasis, having a large file of recipes on hand in your restaurant is a must.

Veggies Unite!

http://www-sc.ucssc.indiana.edu/cgi-bin/recipes/

This is a new and growing Web page for vegetarians. Online are more than 900 recipes that can be searched by keywords. You will find vegan-related files and mail-order sources. There are also hundreds of other links to nutrition, health, and food- and drink-related WWW and Gopher resources.

Other Fat-free Archives

ftp://ftp.geod.emr.ca/pub/Vegetarian/Recipes/FatFree

gopher://gopher.geod.emr.ca/Recipes

http://geod.emr.ca/index.html

ftp://ftp.halcyon.com/pub/recipes

ftp://ftp.informatik.tu-muenchen.de/pub/rec/cooking/fatfree

These archives are more options for obtaining fat-free recipes for your files.

Recipes for Traditional Food in Slovenia

http://www.ijs.si/slo-recipes.html

Unique Slovenian recipes include Young Goat with Wine, Marinated Catfish, and Beef Liver Chasseur. This page is from a European server and has links to other food and wine pages from Slovenia and beyond.

Usenet Recipe Index/Database

http://me-www.jrc.it/cook.html

This is a fascinating attempt (the owner calls it experimental) to create a Web resource with a searchable database of more than 2,500 Usenet recipes.

If you find a site listing on the Internet that is not in service or can't be located, don't give up. Try again at a later date to be sure that the server wasn't down for repairs.

Recipe Index from Amy Gale

http://www.vuw.ac.nz/who/Amy.Gale/recipe-index.html

Amy Gale is a foodie from New Zealand as well as the keeper of the rec.food.cooking FAQs. This is the index of the rec.food.cooking archives.

Sourdough Mailing List Archives

ftp://ils.nwu.edu/pub/sourdough

If you are just getting acquainted with sourdough, you might want to check out the archives for the mailing list to "get up to speed."

Sourdough Bread Recipes

gopher://gopher.utexas.edu:3003/00/pub/sourdough/FAQ.recipes.v1.0

gopher://gopher.utexas.edu:3003/00/pub/sourdough/FAQ.recipes.v2.0

Sourdough lovers, bakers, and pastry chefs can find a variety of ideas in these files.

Recipe Archive at the World

gopher://world.std.com/11/obi/book/HM.recipes/TheRecipes

ftp://ftp.std.com/obi/HM.recipes/TheRecipes

This is a large and diverse recipe file including some Thai pantry items, medieval recipes, and even cabernet sauvignon ice.

Galaxy Nutrition Page

http://galaxy.einet.net/galaxy/Medicine/Nutrition.html

This consists of more than 20 pages of links to other nutrition servers, international papers on nutrition, and even software resources. Nutritionists, country club chefs with healthy menus, and institutional foodservice professionals will find this page valuable.

Food, Cooking, and Restaurant Resources

ELECTRONIC FOOD FOR THOUGHT

Lenard Rubin is a chef in Moscow, Russia. As the former chef of the Phoenician, Scottsdale, Arizona, he does not lack for talent or experience. Yet, even he has found the recipe resources on the Internet to be valuable.

"When moving across the world," says Chef Rubin, "it is difficult and very expensive to take even a small amount of cookbooks and the various other resources that are needed as a chef. Through the Internet I can access volumes of recipes or simply ask for them through the various culinary newsgroups and mailing lists and receive a large variety of responses quickly.

"The ability to communicate online is like being fluent in a foreign language; it opens up a whole new world, a whole new culture and broadens your whole life," says Rubin.

"While living and working in America I enjoyed being able to communicate with other chefs across the country and reading what others had to say to each other. It is the best way to keep up on current trends and attitudes in the foodservice industry, from all sectors of the business and regions of the world. You can reach a broad and wide-ranging group of people who share your interests and needs with a few simple keystrokes."

Chef Rubin also notes, "There are quite a few executive recruiters online, as well, who can be of help when I am ready to come back to the USA."

To expand your Web browser bookmark file, you can find new resources by using only a portion of a URL. The Galaxy Recipe page is just one link of hundreds on the Galaxy Home Page. By removing the path and using only the server address in a URL, you can often find new pages to explore. The Galaxy server address is the first portion of the URL:

`http://galaxy.ein et.net`

Galaxy Recipe Page

`http://galaxy.einet.net/galaxy/Leisure-and-Recreation/Recipes.html`

This is an extensive collection of links to both the classic and obscure recipe resources on the Internet. The entire offering on this server, of which the recipes are just a portion, is well done.

Insect Recipes

gopher://gopher.ent.iastate.edu/00ftp%3aThomomys%3aEntogopher%3
        //aTasty%20Insect%20Recipes

What culinarian can be professionally fulfilled without a recipe for Rootworm Beetle Dip or Chocolate Chirpie Chip Cookies with crickets in their recipe file? You'll find these and other priceless gems on this page.

The Usenet Cookbook

ftp://gatekeeper.dec.com/pub/recipes

This is a huge collection of recipes collected from Usenet groups.

Seafood Recipes

http://www.vuw.ac.nz/who/Amy.Gale/seafood/seafood.html

This contains more recipes from the keeper of the rec.food.cooking FAQS.

Metric Conversions for Chefs

http://www.ijs.si/recipes-conversions.html

If you can't find a culinary textbook with the metric conversions in it, start your modem and point your Web browser here.

Chile-Heads Recipe Collection

http://chile.ucdmc.ucdavis.edu:8000/www/recipe/recipe.html

Chile-heads and restaurants with southwestern-style menus are fired up about this page!

Online Book Initiative Recipes Collection

ftp://obi.std.com/obi/Recipes

This resource is one of the increasing number of books published on the Internet. It is another huge recipe collection.

Online Book Initiative Usenet Cookbook

ftp://obi.std.com/obi/Usenet.Cookbook

The Usenet has spawned many recipe collections, including this one from the Online Book Initiative.

Food, Cooking, and Restaurant Resources

Archives for rec.food.recipes

ftp://mthvax.cs.miami.edu/recipes

ftp://wuarchive.wustl.edu/usenet/rec.food.recipes/recipes

ftp://ftp.wustl.edu/usenet/rec.food.recipes

ftp://ftp.uu.net/usent.rec.food.recipes

The rec.food.recipes newsgroup is one of the most prolific producers of recipes on the Internet. The archives of recipes sent to the newsgroup are mirrored on several sites.

Indian Recipes

ftp://wpi.wpi.edu/recipes

This is an interesting accumulation of authentic recipes from India for the adventurous chef.

The Callahan's Cookbook

ftp://suphys.physics.su.oz.au/mar/cookbook

Callahan's is a virtual bar on the Internet; these recipes are from the kitchen's files.

Vegetarian Recipes

ftp://ftp.geod.emr.ca/pub/Vegetarian/Recipes

Vegetarians have inhabited the Internet in a big way. Recipes abound—this is one more set.

The English-Server Recipe Collection

http://english-server.hss.cmu.edu/Recipes.html

This is the home of not-so-subtle hints about vegetarian diet. Read recipes for "Dead Cows" or "Dead Bunnies" at this Web page. If you modify the recipes for nightly dinner specials, you might want to change the names.

Cuisine of Karnataka

http://www.nmsu.edu/~subbarao/recipes.html

For chefs into ethnic cuisine, this is a set of regional Indian recipes.

Food and Wine Online

National Capital FreeNet of Ottawa

The National Capital FreeNet of Ottawa, Canada has two areas that contain food-related material. To reach the resources, log in to your Internet provider, then:

1. Telnet to the FreeNet.
   ```
   telnet freenet.carlton.ca
   ```

2. Log in.
   ```
   Login: guest
   ```

3. For general cooking information, type the following at the command prompt:
   ```
   Go Food & Cooking
   ```

4. For international health-food recipes type the following at the command prompt:
   ```
   Go culture
   ```

Then select Sunshine Recipes.

Miscellaneous Recipe Sites (Directories)

```
ftp://ugle.unit.no/pub/misc/recipes
ftp://halcyon.com/dec/.0/recipes
ftp://sunsite.unc.edu/pub/docs/books/recipes
ftp://ftp.halcyon.com/pub/recipes
ftp://ftp.cc.mcgill.ca/pub/things_of_interest/recipes
ftp://etext.archive.umich.edu/pub/WELL/outbound/Yanoff/recipes
ftp://calypso-2.oit.unc.edu/pub/docs/recipes
ftp://life.slhs.udel.edu/interp/recipes
ftp://sierra.stanford.edu/pub/mead/recipes
ftp://ftp.ee.rochester.edu/pub/recipes
```

BOOKS, PERIODICALS, AND LIBRARIES

Publishing on the Internet is still in its infancy, but both large publishers and do-it-yourselfers are finding the electronic medium attractive. You can also explore libraries for abstracts of books that might assist you in your pursuit of culinary knowledge. Here are some literary resources of interest to foodservice professionals.

The Electronic Gourmet Guide (eGG)

`http://www.deltanet.com/2way/egg`

The electronic Gourmet Guide is a very popular online magazine for foodies and professionals. The guide is published every two weeks with an entirely new issue that contains interviews, feature articles, classifieds, and recipes.

Kate Heyhoe, the editor, says that an average of 10,000 people each day scan the pages of the eGG. It is lively, colorful, well organized and informative. It is an important link to be included with your bookmarks.

The Culinary Professional's Newsletter

The Culinary Professional's Newsletter is an electronic newsletter that informs food and beverage professionals about new online resources. The newsletter covers BBSs, the Internet, and commercial online resources. The newsletter is intended to supplement *Food and Wine Online*. For more information about the newsletter, see Table 11.1.

TABLE 11.1
FOODWINE LIST

Item	Newsletter Information
Focus	New online resources of interest to food and beverage professionals
Subscription Address	majordomo@list.vnr.com
Subscription Message	subscribe vnr-cul

Virtual Reference Desk

`gopher://gopher-server.cwis.uci.edu`

This contains abstracts from industry publications including *Restaurant Hospitality*.

Food and Wine Online

VNR Culinary and Hospitality

http://www.vnr.com/cul.html

You can view the latest releases by the hospitality industry's premier publisher, check out titles to be released soon, and even find links to the Internet's best hospitality pages.

List of Recommended Cajun and Creole Cookbooks

http://www.webcom.com/~gumbo/food/cookbooks.html

These recommendations are from the Web page of student chef Chuck Taggart. If you are looking for cajun menu items, you might check out these cookbooks.

University of Wisconsin–Stout

Telnet: lib.uwstout.edu

Login: library

The UW Stout library catalog is accessible via the Internet using Telnet. UW Stout has a large and respected Hospitality Education program, and the library is well stocked with related periodicals and books. A simple search of the library's online catalog using the subject keyword "food" generated over 3,500 listings. Each listing is sorted by a subheading and has an abstract describing the book location, publisher, content, and other important information needed to obtain the publication.

Cornell University Library

Telnet: cornellc.cit.cornell.edu

To log in, use the down arrow or tab to move past the first two fields and type the word "library" in the COMMAND field. Press the Enter key.

Cornell has a very prestigious hospitality program, and the library reflects the seriousness of its program. Where else in the world could you find a rare French copy of *Le Memorial de la Patisserie* published in 1903 by Pierre Lacam? Below is the record found online by searching the subject "Chefs."

```
5BOOK - Record 5 of 40 Entries Found
Brief View
TITLE:  Le memorial historique et geographique de la
patisserie :
contenant 3000 recettes de patisserie, glaces et liqueurs,
orne de gravures dans le text
AUTHOR:  Lacam, Pierre, b. 1836
PUBLISHED:  Paris : En vente chez l'auteur, 1903.
---------------------------------------------------------
LOCATION:Hotel Admin Library
CALL NUMBER:TX773 .L27 1903
STATUS:Not checked out Rare (Non-Circulating) Page  1 of 1
```

Vegetarian Journal, Simply Vegan, and Other Articles

ftp://ftp.geod.emr.ca/pub/Vegetarian/Article

These archives store articles of past issues for several vegetarian magazines. If you are just considering adding vegetarian entrees to your menu, these articles can provide some background on the philosophy, cuisine, and lifestyle associated with vegetarianism.

The Electronic Newsstand

gopher://gopher.enews.com

Telnet: enews.com (login: enews)

The Electronic Newsstand was launched in July 1993 with only eight magazines. Today it carries more than 160 titles. The Newsstand is accessed more than 50,000 times each day.

The service offers you the opportunity to scan a table of contents for recent and current issues of each magazine. It also allows users to read entire articles specifically selected for online reading. Other services offered include placing subscription orders for each magazine and even searching all magazine articles online by keyword.

A quick search using the keyword "cuisine" returned a wonderful variety of foodie fiction, dining reviews, and articles on regional and ethnic cuisine.

There are no culinary magazines online as this book goes to press, but *Decanter*, an interesting magazine covering the wine industry, is available through the Electronic Newsstand.

RESTAURANT LISTS

This is a list of lists—dining and restaurant lists. If you have a restaurant in any of the regions covered by a restaurant list, check to see that the information is accurate. Often, the producers of the list are identified in the file; you can contact them to correct any errors.

DC Area Dining

gopher://gopher.american.edu/11/dc/dining

Guide to Vegetarian Restaurants

http://www.cis.ohio-state.edu/hypertext/faq/usenet/vegetarian/guide/top.html

Bay Area Restaurants

http://netmedia.com/ims/rest/ba_rest_guide.html

Guide to the Good Life: Stanford Area Restaurants

http://gsb.stanford.edu/goodlife/home.html

Bay Area Restaurants

gopher://lindy.stanford.edu:2270/1GOPHER%20WYLBUR%20COPY%20FROM%20WYL.GO.CIR.GOPHER.CUISINE.LIST

Byte Bar & Grill Menu

http://matisse.net/files/bytebar.menu

Palo Alto Area Restaurants

http://www.commerce.digital.com/palo-alto/chamber-of-commerce/entertainment

Palo Alto Restaurant–Mini Reviews

href="http://www.service.com/PAW/thisweek/mini_reviews.html

Irvine, CA Restaurant Reviews

gopher://confserv.cwis.uci.edu:7009/00/Restaurant.Guide

San Diego Restaurants

gopher://teetot.acusd.edu/00/toys/Entertainment/San%20Diego%20Restaurants

Food, Cooking, and Restaurant Resources

San Diego Coffeehouses

http://mls.saic.com/mls.coffee.html

Yale University Area Restaurants–New Haven, CT

gopher://yaleinfo.yale.edu/11/Yale/Campus/Publish

Atlanta Restaurants

http://zaphod.cc.ttu.ee/vrainn/aeats.html

Carbondale, IL Restaurants

gopher://cwis.c-fiber.siu.edu/11/geninfo/area/dining

Champaign-Urbana Restaurants

gopher://ns.cso.uiuc.edu:105/2?restaurant

This is Chicago!

http://www.ncsa.uiuc.edu/SDG/IT94/Venue/Restaurants.html

Chicago/Hyde Park Restaurants

gopher://gopher.uchicago.edu/00/chi/food-hp

Chicago Ethnic Restaurants

gopher://gopher.uchicago.edu/00/chi/food-chi

Chicago Restaurants

http://www.psych.nwu.edu/biancaTroll/chicago/restaurants/names.html

Chicago/Rogers Park Restaurants

gopher://gopher.luc.edu/11/Chicago/menus

Evanston, IL Restaurants

gopher://nuinfo.nwu.edu/11/localentertainment/restaurants/evanrest

Chicago Cafe Guide

gopher://nuinfo.nwu.edu/11/localentertainment/cafes

Bloomington, IN Restaurants

http://cs.indiana.edu/docproject/bloomington/restaurant/restaurants.html

Framingham, MA Restaurants

gopher://ftp.std.com/11/periodicals/Middlesex-News/restaurant-reviews

Food and Wine Online

Boston Restaurants

http://www.osf.org:8001/boston-food/boston-food.html

MIT Area Menus

http://web.mit.edu/afs/athena/user/w/c/wchuang/www/menus/menus.html

Boston Dining Guide

gopher://software.bu.edu/11/MetroGuide/Dining%20Out

MIT Restaurants

gopher://gopher.mit.edu:71/0D%20tiserve.mit.edu%209000%2025387%201nf

Ann Arbor, MI Restaurants

gopher://mpcc.org/11/area/aa/restaurant

Hoboken, NJ Restaurants

http://www.stevens-tech.edu/hobokenx/where.html

Princeton Area Restaurants

gopher://gopher.princeton.edu/00/.files/carolynh/restaurants

New York/Rutgers Restaurants

gopher://quartz.rutgers.edu/11/nyc/restaurants

Raleigh, NC Restaurants

http://www.nando.net/epage/nao/links/restaurants.html

Rhode Island Restaurants

gopher://gopher.brown.edu/00/local/restaura

Texas Restaurants for the Health-Conscious

http://gopher.metronet.com:70/1/North-Texas-Free-Net/Directs/Rests

Japanese Restaurants and Food

http://www.ntt.jp/japan/living/lm7.html

Milwaukee Restaurants

gopher://alpha1.csd.uwm.edu/00/Milwaukee%20Information/Restaurant%20Guide

Knoxville, TN Restaurant Reviews

http://www.netlib.org/utk/people/ReedWade/rest_review.html

Food, Cooking, and Restaurant Resources

Austin, TX Restaurants

http://www.quadralay.com/www/Austin/AustinFood/AustinFood.html

Austin, TX Food

gopher://cactus.org/11/Austin/Food

Bryan, TX Restaurants

gopher://gopher.tamu.edu/11/.dir/restaurant.dir

Houston, TX Restaurant Reviews

http://www.cs.utexas.edu/~throop/food/houston/review.html

University of Texas Restaurant Reviews

http://www.cs.utexas.edu/~throop/food/clearlake/review.html

Madison, WI Restaurant Reviews

http://poona.cs.wisc.edu/Restaurant_Reviews/HomePage.html

Milwaukee Restaurants

gopher://csd4.csd.uwm.edu/00/Milwaukee%20Information/Restaurant%20Guide

New Orleans Restaurants

http://www.webcom.com/~gumbo/no-rest.html

Po-Boys

http://www.webcom.com/~gumbo/food/po-boys.html

Creole and Cajun Food

http://www.webcom.com/~gumbo/food/socal-la-rest.html

Cajun Restaurants

http://www.webcom.com/~gumbo/cajun-rest.html

Virginia Tech Area Restaurants, Blacksburg, VA

http://crusher.bev.net/community/restaurants.html

Dining Out on the Web from John Troyer

http://cornelius.ucsf.edu/~troyer/dish/diningout.html

Kosher Restaurants

gopher://jerusalem1.datasrv.co.il/11/comm/comm

Amsterdam Restaurants

http://www.cs.ruu.nl/people/otfried/html/resto.html

Southern Australian Restaurants

gopher://x500.utexas.edu:7777/1Mst%3dSA%2c%20c%3dAU

The Not-Quite-'Compleat' Central Philadelphia Cafe List

http://www.seas.upenn.edu/~cpage/coffee.html

Austrian Restaurants

http://www.lib.uchicago.edu/keith/austria/restaurants.html

Restaurant Lists from Palo Alto

http://www.commerce.digital.com/palo-alto/chamber-of-commerce

Brew-Pubs List

ftp://sierra.stanford.edu/pub/homebrew/docs/publist

RESTAURATEURS ON THE INTERNET

The Digital Deli & Red Sage Web Home Page

Access: http://town.hall.org

The Digital Deli is located at the Web site that is the home of Internet Talk Radio, an audio Internet resource. Visitors to this WWW resource can see an image of the restaurant, a photo of the Red Sage hostess, a copy of the menu, and more.

Owner Mark Miller's venture into Internet marketing is one of the first from the restaurant industry, but surely not the last. Miller is proving to have a vision for more than just southwestern cuisine.

Food, Cooking, and Restaurant Resources

Burk's Cafe Menu

http://www.halcyon.com/burk

Burk's Cafe, a Cajun and Creole restaurant, has a very interesting and creative Web page. You will find the menu, a note from the chef, recipes, and even some photos online.

Country Fare Restaurant Menu

http://www.service.com/cf/home.html

Here is another Web page by an enterprising restaurateur.

Chef Kendall Jackson's OSU Catering and Dining Page

http://www.orst.edu/Dept/mu_catering/mu.html

Quite likely the first Web page designed and converted to hypertext by a chef, Kendall Jackson's page is for customers and culinary peers alike. As the executive chef for Oregon State University Memorial Union, Jackson provides menus for students and faculty as well as recipes of his fare.

For his peers in foodservice, Chef Jackson provides links to other restaurant home pages.

Advertisement for Scott's Seafood Restaurants

http://netmedia.com/ims/rest/ADS/scotts/scott_main_final.html

The Scott's Seafood in Palo Alto has really done a first-rate job of building a solid Web page for marketing the restaurant. In addition to the menu, there is a wine list, weekly specials, a review from the San Jose newspaper, *Mercury News*, photos, and even videos of the entrance, outside patio, and banquet area.

The New Orleans Restaurant FAQ

http://www.webcom.com/~gumbo/food/norstfaq.txt

This page features the frequently asked questions about New Orleans restaurants.

Le Cordon Bleu

http://sunsite.unc.edu/expo/restaurant/restaurant.html

This is a fascinating page with menus from Le Cordon Bleu and information about classes at the world famous cooking school.

MISCELLANEOUS FOOD RESOURCES

There are a lot of food-related resources on the Internet that do not fit into a specific category. They often lead to new and unique Internet sites. Following are a few for browsing.

San Francisco Chronicle and Examiner Food Page

http://sfgate.com/fun/food

The online service of the two San Francisco papers is full of dining information for the Bay area. Find reviews, lists, and menus.

Hospitality Web

http://www.tele.fi/~hospitality

This is primarily a European hospitality Web site, and it is interesting from that viewpoint. Seldom do we hear about the restaurant and lodging industry in countries other than the United States. This page has links to European hospitality trade magazines and is produced in cooperation with Steve Adams, the founder of HotelNet BBS.

Food Stuff Page

http://eunxsa.eas.asu.edu/~sridhar/food/

Food Stuff is mostly vegetarian stuff! You can access FAQs and archives from the rec.food.veg.cooking newsgroup and nearly 15 sites of vegetarian recipes.

Software for the Kitchen (MS-DOS only)

ftp://oak.oakland.edu/msdos/food

If you want to FTP some software, this site in Oakland, California, will provide MS-DOS programs related to food.

Food, Cooking, and Restaurant Resources

The Food Resource

http://www.orst.edu/food-resource/food.html

Oregon State University provides a valuable resource for food professionals with this new Web page. The Web space is occupied by all types of information—archives, lists, images, and text. Even though the page is still under construction there are several items worth checking out.

One of the unique features of the Food Resource is the Images of Food selection. There are dozens of pages of images of all manner of food. A cruise into the images of apples will yield at least three pages of images of both obscure and famous apples. These will provide the professional with an enjoyable and educational visit to a virtual orchard.

The Food Resource also lists information on food-related associations, links to newsgroups, and government resources.

Mother-of-All Bulletin Boards

http://www.cs.colorado.edu/homes/mcbryan/public-html/BB/28/summary.html

Don't be fooled by the title, this *is* a Web server, and more importantly, it is one that has some interesting dining-related hotlinks. They are all accessed by choosing the link to "Best Places to Eat." Once you are linked to this item, it becomes apparent that this is no ordinary list. You are greeted by a page titled "Kebab Vans of the World." This multipaged link is filled with reviews of kebab vans. If you don't know what a kebab van is, don't despair. There is a link called "What is a Kebab Van?" Choosing this link provides the following information:

```
        [IMAGE] KEBAB VANS OF THE WORLD ITEM 25
Title: *** WHAT IS A KEBAB VAN ***
Author: Richard M Date: May 24
Item: A Kebab van is a very specific sort of junk-food
place. It does _NOT_ refer to any old place of culinary
delight, but specifically to literal vans, usually old
and dodgy, which park by a section of pavement/sidewalk
and sell kebabs (pita-bread stuffed with dodgy meat &
```

salad, with some sauce to top it off), hot-dogs, burg-
ers, possibly spuds (potatoes), and even chips (fries).
They are usually run by foreigners, for some reason, and
they operate between about 8pm and 3am.

This truly unique resource demonstrates the value and
power of the Internet for culinary use. Not only does it
point users to other resources, but it provides a glimpse of a
food concept not experienced in the New World: kebab
vans.

Maribor Food and Drinks

http://www.uni-mb.si/mb_food.html

Maribor food is a regional Slovenian cuisine. One of the
most interesting things about this page is that it demonstrates what an inspired group of people can do to popular-
ize a very obscure subject. There are links to this page all
over the Web!

Food and Religious Holidays

http://www.umiacs.umd.edu/research/lpv/YU/HTML/food_religious.html

A Web page with an unusual perspective on food, this is an
interesting historical resource for chefs who want to learn
more about the history of food.

FAQ Links Page

gopher://bongo.cc.texas.utexas.edu:3003/11/pub/sourdough

This resource provides links to the primary FAQs dealing
with bread, sourdough, and other fermentation procedures
such as brine for olives.

Basic Bread

gopher://gopher.utexas.edu:3003/00/pub/sourdough/FAQ.basic_bread

Bread bakers will find 48 pages of information on bread,
tools, and troubleshooting.

Sourdough Cultures

gopher://gopher.utexas.edu:3003/00/pub/sourdough/FAQ.culture.bank

If you are just beginning to explore sourdough, this FAQ
will lead you to sources for sourdough cultures.

Food, Cooking, and Restaurant Resources

Vegetarian Page

http://catless.ncl.ac.uk/vegetarian/

This page offers a glossary of a few terms such as "vegan," a list of vegetarian mailing lists, and vegetarian Usenet groups.

Sourdough

gopher://gopher.utexas.edu:3003/00/pub/sourdough/FAQ.sourdough

This is the premier document on the Internet about sourdough. It features everything you ever wanted to know about sourdough. Pass a copy of this FAQ on to your bakery.

Sourdough Starter

gopher://gopher.utexas.edu:3003/00/pub/sourdough/FAQ.starter.doctor

Having trouble with your sourdough? This Gopher server may have the answer. For troubleshooting your sourdough starter, point your Gopher client here.

Russian Black Bread

gopher://gopher.utexas.edu:3003/00/pub/sourdough/FAQ.black.bread

This is an interesting resource for information on the Eastern European specialty, Russian black bread.

Sourdough Mailing List Archives

gopher://gopher.utexas.edu:3003/00/pub/sourdough/FAQ.mail-archive

This archive holds an historical record of the Sourdough mailing list. For the baker or chef inspired by sourdough, this is a great resource.

Brine for Olives

gopher://gopher.utexas.edu:3003/00/pub/sourdough/FAQ.brine.cure

More and more restaurants make their own condiments. This guide to brine for olives is a good start to creating a pantry of unique items.

Sauerkraut FAQ

gopher://gopher.utexas.edu:3003/00/pub/sourdough/FAQ.sauerkraut

Making sauerkraut is nearly a lost art. You can learn here from individuals who have taken it to a new level.

Department of Food Science and Nutrition U of MN

http://galaxy.einet.net/galaxy/Medicine/Nutrition.html

Nutritionists and dieticians will want to place this Web page in their bookmark list. This is a comprehensive food and nutrition server with 21 pages of related links.

Cooking Page

http://akebono.stanford.edu/yahoo/Entertainment/Cooking/

This page has a variety of recipes and links to other Web culinary pages including the alt.callahans cookbook.

Food and Nutrition Information Center (FNIC)

gopher://cyfer.esusda.gov/11/fnic

gopher://ra.esusda.gov:70/11/fnic

The FNIC is a valuable online resource. It has been instrumental in documenting the electronic resources for those interested in food and nutrition. That commitment is evident in the offerings at this Gopher server.

Food and Cooking Site List

http://www.vuw.ac.nz/who/Amy.Gale/other-sites.html

Amy Gale has put together a broad cross-section of Internet food and cooking sites—recipes, drinks, commercial sites, and much more.

Professional Cutlery Direct

http://www.dash.com/netro/sho/ema/procutdt/pcutlery.html

Offering more than 1,000 knives from around the world, this is a commercial Web page that markets the "Chef's essential tools, knives, and a whole lot more."

Food and Nutrition Software

gopher://cyfer.esusda.gov/00/CYFER-net/program-m/fnic/fnic7

This Gopher resource identifies software that is commercially available, reviews each one, and provides ordering information.

Pgh.food Archives

http://www.cs.cmu.edu:8001/afs/ece/usr/hread/info/Food

Food, Cooking, and Restaurant Resources

These files are the archives of the pgh.food newsgroup for Pittsburgh food.

Agriculture and Food Page

http://www.einet.net/galaxy/Business-and-Commerce/Industry-Sectors/Agriculture-and Food.html

There is a growing interest, among many restaurateurs and chefs, in farming as a part of the food supply chain. This Web page is a mix of links from the subjects of farming and foodservice.

Chile Today-Hot Tamale

http://emall.com/Chile/Chile1.html

Chile Today is a commercial Web site that contains "chile factoids" and offers a Chile of the Month and a Hot Sauce of the Month.

Gumbo Home Page

http://www.webcom.com/~gumbo/

A wonderful resource that is informative and entertaining, chefs look to this page as the authority on the Internet for Cajun- and Creole-related links.

Chile-Heads Page

http://chile.ucdmc.ucdavis.edu:8000/www/chile.html

The Chile-Heads Page has a number of chile resources and features the archives of the Chile-Heads mailing list.

Urban Agriculture Notes

http://unixg.ubc.ca:780/~cityfarm/urbangnotes1.html

If you are attempting to grow food in a city to serve in your restaurant, this page may be of help.

Bed and Breakfasts on the Internet

http://www.webcom.com/~gumbo/bnb.html

gopher://ftp.std.com/11/vendors/NE-bed%2bbreakfast

gopher://UNLV.UNL.EDU:71/00/nebtrav/travel1.bandb.guide

gopher://gopher//gopher.brown.edu/11/local/hotels

If you own a bed and breakfast, you'll want to check out these guides for various regions of the country. You can learn what others are doing and check to see if your B&B is included in the appropriate list.

CONCLUSION

The culinary and food resources on the Internet are quite varied. This chapter explores the recipes, books and libraries, restaurateurs, and other food-related items on the Internet. You can use these resources to lead you to information, marketing opportunities, and even customers.

Government Resources Online

The U.S. Government has funded the Internet for many years and has used online services to reach out to consumers of government services. There are government resources online that will be of interest to food and beverage professionals. Although they may not become part of your daily online routine, there are BBSs, Telnet sites, and Web pages funded by the government, with your tax dollars, for you to use when the need arises.

TECHNOLOGY TRANSFER AUTOMATED RETRIEVAL SYSTEM (TEKTRAN)

The Agricultural Research Service (ARS) of the U.S. Department of Agriculture makes research available through TEKTRAN, see Table 12.1. Users will find research information on food, human nutrition, and agriculture. Interpretive summaries are available online, provided by the Food and Nutrition Service, Food Safety and Inspection Service, the Food and Drug Administration, and the Human Nutrition Information Service.

TABLE 12.1
TEKTRAN INFORMATION

Item	Information
BBS Focus	Provides information on nutrition and agriculture
Voice Number	301-504-5345 Technical Support: 301-504-5198
Modem Number	Must be obtained from the Agricultural Research Service
Internet Access	None
Street Address	Agricultural Research Service, USDA Room 404, Bldg. 005, BARC-West Beltsville, MD 20705
Cost	Free

For the Professional

The latest studies in nutrition, agriculture, and food will be of interest to food and nutrition educators, as well as researchers and consultants. Activist food professionals who are investigating nutritional and agricultural issues as they relate to the foodservice industry will find this a rich resource.

FOOD AND DRUG ADMINISTRATION BBS

The FDA BBS (Table 12.2) is primarily for information dissemination; it is the voice of the Office of Public Affairs for the FDA. As such, it holds all the press releases distributed by the FDA. The BBS is not dedicated exclusively to food; it also contains information related to FDA drug issues.

You can type HELP from any prompt for assistance and QUIT to leave. The FDA BBS permits scanning of topics for easy browsing. However, unlike most other BBSs discussed throughout this book, it is not interactive. That is, you cannot leave messages for the FDA. The government tells you what they want you to know; this is *not* a reciprocal relationship.

TABLE 12.2
FDA BBS INFORMATION

Item	Information
BBS Focus	Online resource concerning announcements relating to FDA regulatory issues
Voice Number	1-301-443-3285
Modem Number	1-800-222-0185, 7-Even-1
Internet Access	Telnet: FDABBS.FDA.GOV Login: BBS
Street Address	FDA Press Office, HFI-20, Rockville, MD 20857
Cost	Free

For the Professional

Online are topics such as AIDS as it relates to food preparation issues, import alerts concerning food products in the marketplace, and testimony by the FDA in the U.S. Congress. Recently, users found press releases entitled New Food Labeling and Advice on Consumption of Raw Shellfish, and the press release announcing the introduction of the Flavr Savr Tomato, the first genetically engineered vegetable to reach the market. For chefs concerned about environmental issues, this BBS serves as a valuable resource for up-to-date information on FDA rulings concerning labeling and genetic engineering.

AGRICULTURAL LIBRARY FORUM (ALF)

The National Agricultural Library and the U.S. Department of Agriculture have produced this BBS to distribute nutrition-related information; see Table 12.3. There is information on food labeling, human nutrition, and agricultural topics. The Food and Nutrition Information Center's publication list is available online, as is the Microcomputer Software List.

TABLE 12.3
ALF INFORMATION

Item	Information
BBS Focus	Nutrition and labeling
Voice Number	301-504-5113
Modem Number	301-504-6510, 301-504-5111
	301-504-5496, 301-504-5497
	ASCII or TTY terminal emulation
Street Address	National Agricultural Library
	Food and Nutrition Information Center
	Room 304, 10301 Baltimore Blvd.
	Beltsville, MD 20705
Cost	Free

For the Professional

If you have a restaurant with a retail food profit center, this BBS will be useful to you as labeling laws evolve and change. Also, research chefs and product development professionals may find this BBS valuable when producing labels and nutritional information for products.

FDA Prime Connection

The FDA Prime Connection is made available by the FDA's Center for Food Safety and Applied Nutrition; see Table 12.4. Users will find information on sanitation, toxins, and FDA enforcement.

TABLE 12.4
FDA PRIME CONNECTION INFORMATION

Item	Information
BBS Focus	Sanitation and FDA enforcement
Voice Number	202-205-8140, Preregistration required
Modem Number	Provided with preregistration
Street Address	FDA Prime Connection, 200 C Street, SW - HFS-625
	Washington, DC 20204-0001
Cost	Free

For the Professional

Many restaurants are launching retail product lines. If you are involved in a retail product roll-out, and if regulatory issues and policies are important to your project, this BBS is for you. Dairy and seafood products receive a special emphasis on this government service.

CONCLUSION

In recent years, the goverment has taken an active role in regulating the activities of the restaurant industry. You may find that online resources will help keep you abreast of federal interest in your business. Government online services deal with nutrition, labeling, and food safety. They are free, many have Telnet access, and all are supported by your taxes.

Networks and Commercial Resources

FOR FOODSERVICE PROFESSIONALS

THE RESTAURANT ASSOCIATION NETWORK

The Restaurant Association Network (RAN) is a service that is offered to National Restaurant Association (NRA) members. This is the most comprehensive resource for restaurant professionals to obtain information online. However, it is also the most expensive. The cost is $48 per month and 75 cents per minute. But for many restaurateurs, particularly high-volume, multi-unit organizations, it is worth every penny. The reason? RAN offers unparalleled industry news, information, and statistics, with updates daily.

The service is offered by the NRA, but the operation, including the technical support, is the responsibility of Information Inc., a company that specializes in bringing entire industries online. Their technical support is excellent. They offer assistance in getting online, adapting scripts and automating access programs to the network as well as periodically polling users for their opinions and suggestions.

Food and Wine Online

Below is the Main Menu for the Restaurant Association Network. The interface is strictly text and can be accessed via a local phone call from many areas on any one of several telephone networks such as SprintNet. Information Inc. will even supply you with shareware communication software if needed.

```
                          Welcome to
        The Restaurant Association Network
        (A service of the National Restaurant Association)

1    Foodservice Industry News
2    Government Affairs
3    Foodservice Information and Numbers
4    Association Member Services
5    Foodservice Industry Suppliers
6    Travel Services
7    Communications Services
Enter item number, <I>ndex, <BAN>ner, <H>elp or <Q>uit:
```

Food Industry News

Food Industry News is clipped and entered daily from more than 750 publications to provide up-to-the-minute information for restaurant operators. When the source is a regional newspaper, online publication often precedes industry periodicals by two weeks to 60 days! For large chains that must react quickly to a marketplace in flux, this is an invaluable resource.

Government Affairs

Government affairs, a major focus for the National Restaurant Association, is appropriately included on RAN. Here members can read about the most up-to-date legislative concerns and even send messages to Congress.

Foodservice Information and Numbers

The Foodservice Information and Numbers is another important area. It includes database access, market statistics, commodity pricing information, and P & L trends. Here is the menu from Foodservice Information and Numbers:

```
            Foodservice Information and Numbers
1   Dineline Database
2   "Pro-Motion" Calendar of Events
3   Foodservice Employment at a Glance
4   Monthly Foodservice Market Measure
5   Prices and Commodity Statistics
6   Income Statement Ratios
7   Economic Trends Update
8   CREST Quarterly Summary
9   Special Reports
Enter item number, <P>revious, <M>ain menu, <H>elp or
<Q>uit:
```

Dineline

While culinary items on the RAN are few, Dineline is the one resource that is heavily skewed to food and cuisine. This is an abstract database of all materials archived by the National Restaurant Association. The database is easily searched using menus provided online:

```
Dineline Database
1   About Dineline
2   Search Dineline
Enter item number, <P>revious, <M>ain menu or <Q>uit:
```

```
DINELINE DATABASE
Select by <AB>stract, <TI>tle, <DA>te, <SO>urce, <AU>thor,
<P>revious, <M>ain menu or <H>elp:
Enter TEXT or <H>elp:
```

By selecting the field to search (summary text in the abstract, for instance), users can receive a listing of all material relevant to a keyword, then request the full text from the association library. Searching by types of cuisine, ingredients, or restaurant style will yield volumes of information. There really is no other database in the foodservice industry that comes close to duplicating this service.

With time online quite costly, quick navigation is a must. You may use the following commands online:

Go Commands

Use GO commands at any RESTAURANT ASSOCIATION NETWORK prompt to bypass menus and go directly to a RAN menu option. Simply type GO followed by one of the terms listed below.

```
-----------------------------------------------------------
to access                                       type

DailyNews                                       GO MONDAY,
                                                GO TUESDAY, etc.
Foodservice Wire News                           GO FWIRE
Wire Services (UPI, Reuters, Knight-Ridder, etc.)  GO WIRES
President's Report                              GO PRES
Action Alerts                                   GO ALERT
Washington Weekly                               GO WASHINGTON
Governmental Affairs Daily Roundup              GO GAR
Daily Legislative Report                        GO LEGDAILY
Today's Congressional News                      GO CN
Committee Hearings/Action Database              GO COMM
Daily Federal Register Briefing                 GO FR
Federal Legislation Database                    GO LDB
Special Reports                                 GO REPORTS
State Legislative Affairs                       GO STATE
State Legislative Bulletin                      GO SBUL
Issue Updates                                   GO ISSUES
Business Meal Sponsors                          GO SPONSORS
Dineline Database                               GO DINE
Foodservice Market Measure                      GO FMM
Prices and Commodity Stats                      GO STATS
Income Statement Ratios                         GO INCOME
Economic Trends Update                          GO TRENDS
CREST Quarterly                                 GO CREST
Foodservice Suppliers Database                  GO GUIDE
Software Services Database                       GO SOFT
Ask National Restaurant Association             GO ASK
Association Contacts                            GO CONTACT
Calendar of Events                              GO CALENDAR
Training and Seminars                           GO ED
Consultant Services Database                    GO CONSULT
Official Airline Guides                         GO OAG
Electronic Mail                                 GO MAIL
Subscriber Directory                            GO DIR
Bulletin Board                                  GO BBS
```

If the most current industry information available is important to the success of your operation, this service will be a good resource for you.

For more information contact:

Information Inc.

7700 Old Georgetown Rd.

Bethesda, MD 20814-6100

301-215-4688

FOODNET INFORMATION SERVICE

FoodNet Information Service is scheduled for full-service operation in the spring of 1995. FoodNet seeks to "link manufacturers, reps, brokers, dealers, and restaurateurs." It facilitates processing quotes and product-related sales and promotion tasks. Users can find new product release information, e-mail, and a communication tool for contacting participating purveyors.

The only way to gain access to this service is to call the number listed below for a special software package that will connect you. The service is projected to cost less than $10 per month, but there is an $8 per hour charge to use the 1-800 number for access. While not actually toll-free, the 1-800 number does provide long distance service that costs the same all the time and is billed separately from your telephone service.

For more information contact:
FoodNet
460 S. Arrowhead
San Bernadino, CA 92408-1309
1-800-366-3875
Fax: 909-885-8286

CHRIE'S HOSTEUR NETWORK

CHRIE, the Council on Hotel, Restaurant, and Institutional Education, created the HOSTEUR Network, an electronic recruiting service, to link employers with potential job candidates. The key to the network is that the skills of each candidate and the skills desired in a candidate by each employer are carefully cataloged in a sophisticated database.

Charter subscribers to the HOSTEUR Network are Brinker International, Hyatt Hotels Corporation, Marriott International, McDonalds Corporation, and Renaissance Hotels & Resorts. Each of these subscribers uses the network to access potential job candidates.

The service is currently offered via dial-up with a modem or by fax. CHRIE expects to offer Internet access via the World Wide Web in the near future.

Employer Services

Employers pay a fee to access resumes and search for candidates whose skills match their needs. "Assisted Search Service" is done on a "contingent on hire" basis. The "Direct Access Service" is a self-help service for frequent users.

Candidate Services

The Feedback Service is for job candidates who subscribe to the network. This service provides candidates with a quarterly report listing the employers who have retrieved their resumes. There is no charge to submit your resume to the HOSTEUR Network.

For more information contact:
CHRIE's HOSTEUR Network
PO Box 8440
Gaithersburg, MD 20898-8440
202-331-5990

AMERICA ONLINE

The growth in AOL features for food and beverage professionals has been extensive recently. You will find chat opportunities, message boards just for pros, and an increasing number of professionals online.

"Back of the House" Chat

It has been said that chat is one of AOL's greatest strengths. Chefs have taken that to heart and formed a chat group that convenes each Monday evening. From all across the country, chefs enter the room to visit in an electronic culinary meeting. Participants come from all segments of the industry including contract foodservice, education, food companies, and upscale restaurants. Students and chef-wannabes are encouraged to attend.

To attend a chat session at 10:00 p.m.(EST) every Monday night, do the following:

Click **The People Connection.**

Click on **The Lobby.**

Click on the **Rooms** icon.

Scroll through the Event Rooms to "Back of the House."

Enter the Room and introduce yourself!

Wine & Dine

Wine & Dine is a group of message boards, databases and files that are food- and beverage-related. To get to Wine & Dine, select **Go To** from the tool bar above the screen, then select **Keyword** and enter either the word **Wine**, **Dine**, or **Restaurants** (they will all take you to the same place!).

Chef/Instructor Abby Nash is a professional who acts as a recipe resource online for AOL members. Nash teaches Matching Food and Wine at Cornell University's hotel and restaurant management school. By clicking on the Newsstand, members will find recipes provided by Chef Nash. These are not the typical home-spun recipes found online over and over again. These are sophisticated and contemporary preparations that speak of quality and a love for great food. They are worth browsing.

Also online in Wine & Dine is a reference library. Members can access the Wine Connoisseur's Cookbook for culinary inspiration when cooking with wine.

One of the most complete and thorough online databases for restaurants exists in the Wine & Dine Forum. Members can search the DineBase for restaurants by selecting a state and then browsing the listings. Specific entries include type of cuisine, contact information, awards received, and check average.

Anyone can set up this chat room on AOL, so if you arrive at the chat area and there is no room named "Back of the House," just follow the on-screen prompts to create a room with that name. You will enter the room when it is created and then, as others arrive, the room will be ready and you will be waiting to greet them!

There are files for uploading and downloading in the Food & Cooking section of Wine & Dine. There is a file for "Restaurateurs Only" with 380 messages between restaurant professionals. Also included here are software demos.

The Recipe Exchange has an interactive area called Ask a Chef, where amateurs pose questions to be answered by professionals. The professionals include any chefs online who wish to answer a question, so you can jump in anywhere. If you enjoy giving advice and mentoring, this area will appeal to you.

The Recipe Exchange also features several other folders and message areas of interest to professionals. There is a Cooking With Beer folder, and a recipe folder arranged by food item (e.g., turkey, pork, rice, and grains). If you want to see what AOL members are saying about your restaurant or one of your competitors, check out the US Restaurant Reviews section, which is arranged by state.

Restaurant Hospitality

One of the most widely read restaurant trade magazines is now online in Wine & Dine. To access this area, go to Wine & Dine, select **Restaurants,** and scroll down the listings until you get to *Restaurant Hospitality*.

The magazine articles have yet to be placed online for reading, but restaurateurs have plenty of opportunity to interact with the publisher and other operators. *Restaurant Hospitality* magazine strives to provide hands-on information to operators; the topics covered in the various folders reflect that commitment.

Topics that restaurant professionals can participate in include the following:

• Introduce Yourself

• Stress Busters

• Question of the Month

• Job Opportunities

- Cooking Equipment

- Ads & Offers

- Management Etc.

- Messages *TO* Your Hosts

- Subscribe to RH

- This Month's Issue

- Computers and Communication

- Cooking Tipsheet

- Kiosk: Upcoming Shows/Events

The advantages of participating in the *Restaurant Hospitality* section are many. It is one of the most visible and accessible areas in cyberspace for interacting with other restaurant operators. AOL is now the largest online service and, therefore, offers a greater opportunity to reach out to more professionals. This section gives you an opportunity to communicate with the editors of *Restaurant Hospitality* magazine in a much more informal manner. If you have always longed to see your restaurant mentioned in a trade magazine, answering the editors' questions with a thorough and intelligent response is a good start. This area of AOL is positioned to become a premier online resource for the industry.

The Cooking Club
The Cooking Club is another public message area, unrelated to Wine & Dine, that features cooking, recipes, and software resources, some of which are specifically geared for professionals. This section of AOL can be accessed by entering the keyword "cooking" after selecting **Go To**... from the tool bar. Once in the Cooking Club, you will find several cooking-related sections.

One of these sections, the Celebrity Cookbook, may not hold a lot of interest for professionals. However, it is a searchable database of recipes and could be helpful if you are running out of recipe resources when looking for a particular item.

The Cupboard section of the Cooking Club includes a message board for Tips & Techniques, Health & Nutrition, and Cookbooks and Software Reviews.

Most importantly, you will find the Culinary BBS located in the Cookbook and Software Reviews Folder of the Cupboard Section of the Cooking Club! This is a bulletin board set up for food professionals to interact on a variety of subjects. It is, currently, not very heavily used, most likely due to its obscure location. You would never find it if you went looking for it without knowing its location on AOL!

There is also a Cooking Library in the Cooking Club. It contains DOS, Mac, and Windows software demos and information that can be downloaded for testing and reading.

Last, there is a Kitchen Conference Room in the Cooking Club. Many times during the day you can find members chatting about food, restaurants, and even professional cooking issues.

COMPUSERVE

CompuServe has the oldest online culinary sections of the larger commercial online services. As such, it provides a real sense of community to active participants. Recent changes in CompuServe's forum design permitted the creation of a section just for professionals within the context of Cook's Online.

Cook's Online Forum

Cook's Online Forum is the primary CompuServe offering for culinary enrichment. To access Cook's, select **Go To**... from the **Services** menu and enter **Cooks** to go to the forum. Cook's offers 22 public message sections:

1. General/System Help

2. New Uploads

3. First Course

4. Herbs & Spices

5. Desserts & Sweets

6. Meats, Poultry, and Fish

7. Ethnic Recipes

8. Outdoor Cooking

9. Breads

10. Microwave Cooking

11. Fruits & Vegetables

12. Salads & Dressings

13. Dining Out

14. Nutrition & Fat Fighters Club

15. Tools & Books

16. Vegetarian

17. Potpourri

18. Soups & Sauces

19. Eggs/Cheese/Casserole

20. Culinary Pro & School

21. Pizza & Pastas

22. Visual Recipes

Of these 22 sections, the most specific to the professional is the Culinary Pro/School section. Cyberchef Gary Jcnanyan is the Section Leader and provides a solid, professional foundation for the service. Members find discussions as varied as the industry itself. Topics include starting a restaurant, attending culinary school, obtaining new ingredicnts, and many more.

Section 4, Herbs & Spices, features the expertise of Michail Aichlmayr. In addition to the normal herb banter he submits "Herb Bites" twice a week to Cook's Online. This posting contains information on the use and history of herbs.

Food and Wine Online

Some of the most valuable assets to Cook's Online are the libraries that exist for each of the public message sections. The Culinary Pro/School library is just beginning to flourish; it includes lists of culinary programs and schools, diaries of a culinary student, and transcripts of online conferences such as Starting a Restaurant. Also included in files of the Cook's Online library are listings of mail-order sources for hard-to-find ingredients.

Also of interest in other libraries on Cook's Online are vast collections of recipes and shareware for culinarians. The forum elects a Cook of the Month (COM), and the winner uploads a recipe file that is indicative of his or her interests. These COM recipe collections are a wonderful resource for anyone searching for new recipes.

All in all, this is one of the most friendly kitchens in cyberspace!

ELECTRONIC FOOD FOR THOUGHT

There are few chefs in the United States who have cooked with more of the world's great chefs than CompuServe's section leader, Gary Jenanyan. As the executive chef at Mondavi's Great Chefs School, Jenanyan has worked alongside such greats as Julia Child, Joel Robuchon, the Troisgrois brothers, and many more. Even after spending kitchen time with some of this century's greatest chefs, he still finds his time on CompuServe to be of great value.

"I find Cook's Online to represent a broad cross-section of the public with expertise in many areas, but who share this common denominator of an interest in cooking," says Jenanyan. Of his first time online he says, "I finally got the nerve up to leave an introductory message with a note that I would welcome the possibility of answering questions since I was actually a cook for living."

That small step has paid off in a big way for Jenanyan. "Over the years I have developed relationships and met people online all over the world—France, England, Mexico, Italy, Spain, and the United States—with whom I communicate on a regular basis.

"One thing is certain, I have learned much more on Cook's Online than I have contributed. The range of expertise on subjects other than COOKING is astonishing. I think it is important to be both a teacher and a student of our craft. Cook's Online, as well as other bulletin boards such as ChefNet, give me that opportunity.

"We must understand that it is our responsibility as professionals to invest in those who are interested in our craft and profession and set an example of conduct and camaraderie. There is so much misinformation transmitted, especially on TV cooking shows that are commercially driven, that a solid, steady voice from professionals is vital."

KNOWLEDGE INDEX

CompuServe's Knowledge Index is a compilation of more than 100 full-text and bibliographic databases. It is an excellent resource for food and beverage professionals because it contains, in its records, many foodservice and beverage publications.

Many, but not all, of the databases provide the full text of articles online. If articles selected during a search are not available online, CompuServe will mail a hard copy of the articles for $7.50 each. If an article is available, capturing the text as it scrolls by online costs $0.40 per minute.

Almost any subject can be used to initiate a search; any search can be done in a number of different ways. Here are the steps:

1. Select **Go**... from the **Services** menu and enter **KI**.

2. Then choose #3) **Business Information**.

3. From the next menu select #3) **General Business**.

4. Select #1) **ABI/INFORM**.

5. Choose #1) **Subject Search**.

6. Enter the keywords for which you wish to search.

For example, suppose you are looking for information on southwestern cuisine. Below are the results of the search using "southwestern cuisine" as search keywords. Notice that not all of the articles look appropriate. However, many of the articles look promising as sources of valuable information. Several articles are even from foodservice industry trade publications such as *Restaurant Hospitality, Restaurants & Institutions*, and *Nation's Restaurant News.*

```
Option                  TITLE  No.
1    New restaurants heat up San Francisco dining duel
2    Ham hocks: The soul of flavor
3    Tequila today
4    Kimco recruits Gilmore, Sedlar for 2 ventures
5    The country's hottest restaurant market
6    Let's do lunch^ A diner's delight:
     The top 100 restaurants
7    Site selection: Phoenix & Scottsdale
8    RealMart '93 - It's your deal!
9    America the Beautiful
10   Careers: Lost in Gotham
11   Home on the mid-range
12   Pasta, Potatoes and Rice:
     Signature Sides & Scrumptious Entrees
13   The Very Private World of Ross Perot
14   R&I Ivy Winners: Coyote Cafe
15   R&I Ivy Winners: Cafe Annie
16   Market Segment Report: Mexican
17   Southwestern Cooking Heats Up
18   Regional Wines
19   Menu: Breakfast and Brunch
20   Diversification Key in Iffy Economy
21   West Coast Restaurant Ventures: Eclectic Enterprise
22   Breakfast Bonanza
23   Ultimate Fusion
24   Mexican
25   Global Warming
```

I chose to download 10 of these articles. The entire search took less than 11 minutes and cost less than $4.50—a bargain at twice the price. This service is available on evenings and weekends only.

ELECTRONIC FOOD FOR THOUGHT

When Dick Carr, executive chef for Marriott Foodservice, Phoenix, Arizona, wanted to research Total Quality Management in foodservice he turned to the Knowledge Index.

"I had never really done anything like it before and I found it very easy to use," says Carr. "I used the keywords 'TQM,' 'Demming' (the name of the father of modern quality control), and 'food.' It generated over 100 articles! After reviewing the descriptions of the articles I made my choices and began to download," said Carr. After downloading he printed out the articles and began his study of Total Quality Management. Chef Carr views the information harvest a bargain, even at the $10 to $15 it cost to obtain the articles.

DELPHI

DELPHI allows members to create and manage forums in which other members can participate. Several have been created for those interested in food. These are not specifically designed for professionals, but there are some pros who frequent them.

Food and Beverage Custom Forums

Several food-related forums are available that are formed and hosted by DELPHI members. The Cook's Corner and the Confection Forum are the most likely Custom Forums to be of any interest to foodservice professionals.

Cook's Corner Forum is accessed by typing **go custom 229** from any DELPHI menu prompt. Cooking enthusiasts post recipes and messages. A menu selection here will give you access to the cooking related Usenet newsgroups.

The topics for discussion in this group are as follows:

- General Discussion

- Appetizers & Soups

- Salads & Veggies

- Meat/Poultry/Fish

- Breadmaking

- Ethnic Cooking

- Desserts & Sweets

- Food Discussions

- Diet Support

- Announcements

- Recipes for Special Diets

- Miscellaneous Recipes

- Support for Diabetics

- Ask It

- Basket

- Gifts

- Crafts & Entertaining

The Confection Forum is accessed by typing **go custom 344** from any DELPHI menu prompt. This forum covers both candy making and cake decorating. While this is not a pointedly professional resource, this forum may be of interest to you if you enjoy giving advice.

The topics for discussion in this forum are as follows:

- General Discussion

- Candy Corner

- Decorating Den

- Recipe Rack

- Classifieds

ONLINE GOURMET

According to DELPHI, "The Online Gourmet is a collection of classic and modern recipes. It is written for those who possess knowledge, sophistication, and appreciation of fine food."

Here is how you access The Online Gourmet. Choose **Reference and Education** from the Main Menu by typing **reference**. Then choose **Online Gourmet** by typing **online.** Do this and you will be presented with the following menu:

Online Gourmet Menu:

- About the Recipes

- Salads

- New Recipes

- Side Dishes & Appetizers

- Meat & Chicken

- Desserts

- Diet Recipes

- Vegetarian

- Fruits & Vegetables

- Seasonal Selections

- Soups

- Fish & Seafood

Each section contains recipes for home preparation. These recipes will provide a resource for those professionals brainstorming comfort food, seeking to add to a recipe database, or just exploring new ideas. The recipes are, however, primarily of interest to home cooks.

PRODIGY

PRODIGY offers two areas of interest to culinarians and restaurateurs. The first is the Entertainment/Dining section, which contains bulletin boards and databases primarily designed for hobbyists, but of use to professionals also. Second, ProVisions Online is an electronic marketplace designed especially for foodservice operators.

Entertainment/Dining

You can access the Dining section on PRODIGY by selecting **Entertainment** from the main menu and then **Dining.** It consists of six different areas:

- The Zagat Restaurant Guide
- The Mobile Travel Guide
- Cooking Class
- Food BB
- Wine, Beer & Spirits BB
- Premier Dining Club Ad

Many professionals consider John Mariani, board leader, Dining section, to be an asset to the food-related message areas. Articulate, opinionated, and well-known, Mariani is an interesting centerpiece for the board. He is not the only professional in the limelight here, though. Recent visitors to the Dining section found Chef Michael Lomonaco, "21" Club, fielding questions from PRODIGY members.

The Food BB subject list includes the following:
- Appetizers
- Beans, Rice & Grains
- Beverages
- Breads, Pizza, Pasta
- Breads by Machine
- Cookbooks

- Desserts & Sweets

- Eating Out

- Ethnic

- Fish & Seafood

- Food Exchange

- Food Forum

- Food Software

- Garden

The messages posted in PVO Marketplace will be visible to members only once (old messages are not visible once read) so if you are posting product or service announcements, you should repost every 10 days or so to maintain visibility on the board.

ProVisions Online

ProVisions Online, a PRODIGY offering, is also specifically geared for professionals in the foodservice industry. Designed to function as an online marketplace to connect buyers with purveyors, PVO also provides online news from the industry. Frank Winzig, Jr., a former senior buyer for Walt Disney World and the founder of PVO, launched the interactive foodservice network with a vision for bringing quality communication to all segments of the industry.

PVO is divided into five primary areas, and with each area, it offers multiple choices for interactive participation. These areas are PVO Marketplace; Industry News; Food and Beverage Industry Segments; Features, Products, and Guest Columns; and About PVO.

The PVO Marketplace is an area for posting advertisements and needs. There are subdivisions for items such as breads, aqua-farming, beverages, and new products. Services such as brokerages, consulting, employment search firms, and marketing are given their own sections online. These areas are open for posting by interested industry professionals.

Industry News is clipped from a wire service. It often includes government actions such as FDA enforcement, food safety issues, and commodity pricing news.

The F&B Industry Segments offers current information on trade and marketing associations. You can also receive timely reports on the 1996 Culinary Olympics Team.

Features, Products, and Guest Columns is a compilation of miscellaneous editorial content. Guest Columns give industry insiders an opportunity to express views and opinions.

About PVO contains background information on the interactive service. This includes a missions statement and a discussion of the plans for expansion for PRODIGY'S first service offered exclusively for foodservice professionals.

CONCLUSION

The nature of professional resources on various networks and commercial services is a mixed bag; some contain strictly professional information, such as the RAN, while others are directed at the consumer. In DELPHI Custom Forums, for example, mentoring and advice-giving are the best use of the service for professionals.

It is important to recognize what resources are located on which services so that, when the need arises, you will know where to look. Since many services offer free one-month trials, sampling all of the services is a useful exercise.

Beverage BBSs

Beverage BBSs most frequently focus on beer and brewing. There are, however, a couple of notable exceptions that feature wine as the primary interest. The beer BBSs are usually technically oriented for the home brewer; their secondary purpose is to provide a forum for general beer appreciation. Nearly all of them list suppliers of brewing equipment, which are either mail-order or regional suppliers. It is not unusual to be required to name your favorite beer when creating your account on a brewers' BBS.

As stated throughout this book, finding a home on a BBS is not always easy. You need to find one that matches both your personality and your interests.

MURRAY HILL BBS— THE VIRTUAL TASTING ROOM

The Virtual Tasting Room is a forum on a new BBS that takes its mission very seriously—the down-to-earth discussion of wine; see Table 14.1. High-minded, pretentious exchanges are not permitted! The participants are as friendly as they are knowledgeable, so don't hesitate to ask questions. This BBS will be of interest to culinarians who enjoy wine, as well as those who solely pursue their love of the grape.

TABLE 14.1
THE VIRTUAL TASTING ROOM INFORMATION

Item	Information
BBS Focus	Discussions of interest to wine lovers and freedom of speech issues
Voice Number	N/A
Modem Number	212-683-1448
Internet Access	N/A
Internet E-mail	N/A
Sysop	David St. Marie and Amy Louise Pommier
Street Address	N/A
Cost	Free

The public message area for wine enthusiasts is accessible from the main menu by selecting **V,** for Virtual Tasting Room. David St. Marie is the technical energy behind the board; he also heads up another forum on the Murray Hill BBS that concerns itself with freedom of speech issues.

For the Professional

The Virtual Tasting Room is hosted by Amy Louise Pommier, also known as the Wine Goddess. She is a wine professional, a retail wine shop owner, and a freelance writer. Her professional ties to the wine community and organizations help provide this BBS with event notices that benefit both enthusiasts and the wine industry. Although the emphasis is on East Coast events, some events with a national scope are listed. For culinarians, The Virtual Tasting Room welcomes discussion concerning wine and food pairings and cooking with wine.

"We will be adding a special 'private' area soon for beverage professionals such as wine stewards and cellar masters," says St. Marie.

Beverage BBSs

The board also has a file library with wine-related shareware for downloading, tasting notes, and general wine discussions.

THE WINE CONNECTION BBS

The Wine Connection BBS (see Table 14.2) went online in November 1993 so that "lovers of fine wine can have an easily accessible medium to communicate to each other about wines they would like to buy, sell, or trade," according to sysop Paul Sennett. He also wanted to provide a forum for discussing other subjects associated with wines.

The BBS is easy to navigate. Screens are simple and direct with plenty of "help" options to consult.

TABLE 14.2
WINE CONNECTION INFORMATION

Item	Information
BBS Focus	Wine-related discussions and collector trading
Voice Number	818-718-8470
Modem Number	818-718-5994
Internet Access	N/A
Internet E-mail	N/A
Sysop	Paul Sennett
Street Address	PO Box 2389, Winnetka, CA 91396-2389
Cost	Free limited access 30 minutes each day; for $15 per year, full access for two hours each day

For the Professional

This BBS offers two primary sections of interest to professionals. One section contains information about wine and includes wine terms, varietal information, winery information, and

When a BBS exchanges messages with other BBSs on a regular basis, the network is called an **echo** network.

It is common for a BBS to add short advertisements to outgoing messages on an echo or Usenet message. The short advertisement is called a **tagline** and usually contains a quote and the BBS's modem number.

Los Angeles area wine events. The second section is for public messaging between collectors, buyers, sellers, and tasters. One of the most interesting offerings in this section is a marketplace that allows collections to be listed along with prices for trading or selling. Users are charged a fee to list wines.

Activity on the BBS is not extensive, and advertisers, which the sysop encourages to participate, are few. There are messages posted by professionals in the serving and retailing side of the business, including a beverage manager from a private club working on Sommelier Certification. Sysop Sennett is beginning to advertise in *Wine Spectator,* so traffic among professionals should soon be on the increase.

IN HEAVEN THERE IS NO BEER BBS

The discussion on this BBS (see Table 14.3) is typical of many that focus on beer and home brewing. It is technical in nature and dedicated to problem solving. The BBS has an **echo** message base. Therefore, you will notice **taglines** at the end of many messages from other BBSs. While the BBS may be typical of home brew BBSs, it is exceptional in the amount of beer-related conferences or forums. It also features many beverage-related Usenet groups.

TABLE 14.3
IN HEAVEN THERE IS NO BEER
BBS INFORMATION

Item	Information
BBS Focus	Home brewing and beer appreciation
Voice Number	N/A
Modem Number	619-667-0159
Internet Access	N/A
Internet E-mail	N/A
Sysop	Tony Quinn
Street Address	N/A
Cost	Free

Beverage BBSs

For the Professional

This BBS offers the professional beverage director or brew-pub owner one-stop access to most of the more popular beer-related resources. You can read the latest mailing list posts, follow the FIDO echo conferences (a worldwide network of BBS message areas), and download software and information from the library. Here is a screen log of the beer- and wine-related resources on the In Heaven There is No Beer BBS.

```
Message Areas
*10...Usenet Mailing List: Homebrew Digest
*11...Usenet Mailing List: Cider Digest
*12...Usenet Mailing List: Mead Digest
*13...Usenet Mailing List: Lambic Digest
*14...Usenet Mailing List: Beer Judge Digest
*15...Usenet Mailing List: New England Beer Club
*16...Usenet Mailing List: Libertarian Beer Digest
*20...FidoNet Echo: Zymurgy
*21...FidoNet Echo: Vin Maison
*22...Usenet Conference: Rec.crafts.brewing
*23...Usenet Conference: Rec.crafts.winemaking
*24...Usenet Conference: Alt.beer
*25...Usenet Conference: Rec.food.drink.beer
*26...Usenet Conference: Alt.Hangover
*27...Usenet Conference: Alt.beer-like-molson-eh
*28...Usenet Conference: Alt.zima
*29...Usenet Conference: Francom.biere_vins
```

This is a substantial BBS for home brew information as well as micro-brewery discussions. Beverage directors and micro-brewery owners and managers should add it to their calling directories.

HOME BREW UNIVERSITY

This trio of BBSs is not actually associated with a university; the name is symbolic of their dedication to studying and learning about home brew; see Table 14.4. These BBSs are interesting for both their scope and their regional emphasis. If you own a brew-pub in the Midwest or Southwest United States, you should check to see what beer aficionados are saying about your pub.

Billing itself as "all things beer and wine," the Milwaukee BBS features discussion forums on brewing and wine making.

TABLE 14.4
HOME BREW UNIVERSITY INFORMATION

Item	Information
BBS Focus	Brew pubs, wine making, and home brew
Voice Number	N/A
Modem Number	Milwaukee Campus Modem: 414-238-9074
	Chicago Campus Modem: 708-705-7263
	Southwest Campus Modem: 713-923-6418
Internet Access	N/A
Internet E-mail	N/A
Sysop	Jeff Kane (Milwaukee), Andrew Patrick (Chicago), Steven Moore (Southwest)
Street Address	N/A
Cost	Free

If you are looking for a BBS to call that is closer to your home, in order to reduce long distance charges, start reading the taglines of messages on the BBSs you call. Sooner or later you will likely find one nearer to your home that has a similar message base.

The Milwaukee "campus" is the newest of the BBSs. Online are FAQS, supplier lists, and lists of brew-pubs and beer bars. The file library is full of graphical images of beer labels of all kinds, coasters, posters, and much more.

For the Professional

Besides the technical information on brewing and wine making, you will find an extensive list of beer tasting and brewing events in the regions covered by the BBS. This is a great trio of BBSs for informal focus groups and for staying current on beer trends and news.

NO TARMAC BREWING BBS

This BBS features a D.C. area beer echo and a cooking echo; see Table 14.5. If you are looking for a local BBS in the D.C. area dealing with these subjects, this BBS may fit the bill.

TABLE 14.5
NO TARMAC BREWING INFORMATION

Item	Information
BBS Focus	Beer and home brew
Voice Number	N/A
Modem Number	703-525-3715
Internet Access	N/A
Internet E-mail	N/A
Sysop	John DeCarlo
Street Address	N/A
Cost	Free

For the Professional

There are many interesting software selections and information files on this BBS. In addition, the cooking echo provides a foundation for some culinary software, recipe archives, and other information in the cooking library. If you are involved in a brew-pub or restaurant in the Baltimore/Washington area, this BBS will provide a nice hometown feel, with subjects that interest you.

CONCLUSION

There are beverage BBSs for both wine and beer interests. The wine BBSs tend to focus more on wine appreciation, discussing specific wineries, vintages, and tasting notes. The beer BBSs primarily concentrate on home brewing, which involves recipes, supplies, and techniques. As a professional, just interacting with individuals who have such a deep appreciation of the beverages can be valuable. But more importantly, if you are concerned with staying ahead of the competition, you can often learn what the opinion leaders in your market are saying about various beverages, pubs, and brands.

Beverage-Related Mailing Lists and E-Mail Discussion Groups

As the professional beverage community increases, online there will, no doubt, be mailing lists that are directly relevant to the industry. However, currently the only lists are those committed to serious wine appreciation and hobbyist home brewers. Food and beverage directors, cellar masters, and sommeliers will find valuable information and camaraderie on these mailing lists, which are actually e-mail discussion groups. Even if you subscribe just to keep tabs on certain varietals and how they are aging, these lists can be valuable. Brew-pubs will find many of their most ardent admirers on the various beer and ale lists.

241

THE WINE LIST

Wine enthusiasts from all over the world subscribe to this list. Tasting notes, updates on the harvest and weather in the wine-growing regions, and even mentoring of those with an undeveloped appreciation of wine are common themes of posts to this list.

TABLE 15.1
WINE LIST INFORMATION

Item	List Information
Focus	General wine appreciation
Subscription Address	majordomo@ee.pdx.edu
Subscription Message	subscribe wine
List Posting Address	wine@ee.pdx.edu

For the Professional

One of the most broad-based of several wine discussion lists, this list will serve as a general wine reference for professionals interested in tasting notes and comments. You can use this list for leads to other Internet resources as they are created on the Internet.

AUSTRALIAN WINE LIST

Australian wine has gained a growing following in recent years. This list originates in Australia and fosters the love of wine from down under.

TABLE 15.2
OZWINE LIST INFORMATION

Item	List Information
Focus	Australian wine
Subscription Address	maiser@koala.cs.cowan.edu.au
Subscription Message	subscribe ozwine
List Posting Address	ozwine@koala.cs.cowan.edu.au

For the Professional

If you carry Australian wine on your wine list, this is an excellent source for expert information. Use it to track newcomers to the market and check the tasting notes on obscure varietals.

FOODWINE

FoodWine is a very active Usenet group that discusses food, wine, and sometimes the relationship between the two. It is very busy with posts from first-time wine drinkers to very experienced tasters.

This list, FoodWine, has a large number of posts each day. If you are overwhelmed and do not want to continue receiving it, send the following message to `list serv@cmuvm.csv.cm ich.edu`: `signoff foodwine`

TABLE 15.3
FOODWINE LIST INFORMATION

Item	List Information
Focus	Primarily wine, with occasional food-related posts
Subscription Address	Listserv@cmuvm.csv.cmich.edu
Subscription Message	subscribe foodwine *first-name* *last-name*
List Posting Address	Foodwine@cmuvm.cc.vt.edu

For the Professional

This is a good resource for staying abreast of what is happening in the world of wine on the Internet.

Many postings are recipes, while others are comments concerning wine tastings or food and beverage pairings. If you want to know about a particular vintage, varietal, or wine maker, this is a great place to ask.

BEER-L

This list offers the latest information on trends and techniques in home brew. Also common are posts dealing with equipment and suppliers for hobbyists and professionals.

Archived messages from the Mead-Lovers list are available at ftp://sierra.stanford.edu/pub/mead. Send an e-mail message to `listserv@sierra.stanford.edu` with the following word in the body for complete instructions on obtaining the archives by e-mail: `help`

TABLE 15.4
BEER-L LIST

Item	List Information
Focus	home brew and beer appreciation
Subscription Address	Listserv@ua1vm.ua.edu
Subscription Message	subscribe beer-l *first-name last-name*
List Posting Address	beer-l@ua1vm.ua.edu

For the Professional

If you own a brew-pub, interacting with "experts" in the market may be the biggest advantage to participating in this list. You will also find frequent posts about new Internet resources related to beer and beer making.

MEAD-LOVERS LIST

Mead makers (mead is an alcoholic beverage made with honey and water, among other things) will find this a very useful resource. This list is quite active, and the discussions are very targeted. Subscribers discuss technique, equipment, ingredients, recipes, and problem solving.

TABLE 15.5
MEAD-LOVERS LIST

Item	List Information
Focus	Making mead, a beverage made from honey and water
Subscription Address	mead-lovers-request@eklektix.com
Subscription Message	Send a written request including your name and e-mail address
List Posting Address	Mead-lovers@eklektix.com

For the Professional

Mead lovers are a special breed of consumer. This is a great way to get to know them, and their craft, a little better.

LAMBIC BEER LIST

Subscribers discuss all aspects of lambic, or Belgian, beer brewing and tasting.

TABLE 15.6
LAMBIC LIST

Item	List Information
Focus	Belgian-style beer, drinking, and brewing
Subscription Address	lambic-request@lance.colostate.edu
Subscription Message	Send a written request that includes your name and e-mail address
List Posting Address	lambic@longs.lance.colostate.edu

For the Professional

If imported Belgian beer or lambic brewing is an important part of your beverage business, this list will be valuable to you. The discussion is heavily geared toward brewing techniques.

NEW ENGLAND BEER CLUB

Subscribers discuss pub tours, brewery reviews, and general New England beer news.

TABLE 15.7
BEER LIST

Item	List Information
Focus	New England beer industry from a consumer's point of view
Subscription Address	beer-request@rsi.com
Subscription Message	Send a written request with your name and e-mail address
List Posting Address	beer@rsi.com

For the Professional

If you own a pub or a micro-brewery in New England, you should definitely subscribe to this list. It will keep you in close contact with potential customers and opinion leaders in the market. You will also be able to monitor competitors' activities.

CONCLUSION

The beverage-related e-mail discussion groups offer targeted discussion and e-mail convenience for professionals in the beverage industry. You can use them on a limited basis, subscribing when you are working on specific projects, or you can become a member of the community and build your network. Either way, these e-mail discussion groups offer creative operators a unique way to interact and stay informed.

Internet Resources for Beverage Professionals

The Internet is populated with a large number of people who like to drink, and drink well-informed about their beverages. This chapter explores the resources they have placed on the Net. Included are a varied group of resources that focus on beer, brewing, coffee, wine, and spirits.

BEVERAGE USENET NEWSGROUPS

The beverage-related Usenet groups are similar in many ways to the cooking-related Usenet groups. The primary contributor of message posts is the hobbyist and enthusiast. Professionals are online here in small numbers, and they are destined to grow in number as the Net becomes more accessible. For operators looking for information on obscure wine varietals, new beers, and the trends for the next decade, this is a great place to begin.

alt.callahans

Alt.callahans is a unique presentation of "virtual beverage service" and it is included here as a professional curiosity.

Food and Wine Online

Callahans is a virtual reality bar based on the books by Spider Robinson. This Usenet group is very different from most others on the Net. Here participants post messages while speaking of themselves in the third person. Characters from the books show up occasionally as authors of the posts. Many messages are posted in the form of a "toast." So when something happy or sad happens in a member's life, it is often transmitted as a toast.

There is even virtual furniture, such as the Virtual Pizza Machine, and members can spend time in a virtual hot tub. The Callahans FAQ says "bathing suits are optional but keep your hands to yourself."

rec.food.drink.coffee

For the beverage professional or restaurateur interested in being on the leading edge of the coffee crowd, this newsgroup will be useful. It can be used to cull information on competitors or new coffee resources. It also becomes an interesting focus group for those who consider themselves gourmet coffee experts. Consumer views, while not scientifically obtained, can also be extracted for commercial analysis.

alt.coffee

This group is not as widely distributed as rec.food.drink.coffee, but the focus is similar and cross-posting is common. The postings are from suppliers as well as aficionados, and discussions include the topics of equipment, bean varietals, and preparations.

alt.hangover

Although there are not a lot of posts to this newsgroup, you might find a remedy to pass on to your customers.

alt.zima

The charter says the group is for those who like Zima and want to discuss the beverage. However, the postings are from detractors as well as admirers. Currently the group serves as a barometer for Zima's advertising campaign.

alt.beer-like-molson-eh

If you serve a lot of the Canadian brew, Molson, you may take an interest is what the masses are saying about it.

alt.food.cococola

This is where you will find discussions of cola in general: Royal Crown, Pepsi, etc.

alt.drugs.caffeine

Coffee is the obvious topic here, but subscribers also debate the merits of Mountain Dew, Jolt, tea, chocolate, and even Vivarin.

alt.beer

Beer. Beer as a micro-brew. Brew-pubs. Ice beer. Beer, beer, beer. Drink it. Cook with it. Drink it. Make it. Drink it. Buy it. Drink it. alt.beer . . .

alt.food.wine

This newsgroup is a mixed bag of food messages, wine messages, and combination food and wine posts. Tasting notes are common, as are discussions of the pairing of food and wine. Also posted here are items of news that would be of interest to Net wine enthusiasts, such as new Web pages.

rec.crafts.brewing

As even the casual observer will notice, the Internet seems to have an unusually high number of home brewers online. They are aggressive in posting questions and answers on their hobby. Brew-pubs find this newsgroup to be a great source for trivia on brewing and related information.

rec.crafts.winemaking

If you are involved in wine making this newsgroup will certainly be of interest to you. If not, you might learn a bit about the process from this group.

rec.food.drink.beer

For beer lovers and professionals who have a large stake in the beer business, few places on the Net are more important than this newsgroup. Resources in the form of both files and knowledgeable individuals abound in this group.

Archives for rec.food.drink.beer are located at ftp://sierra.stanford.edu./pub/homebrew/rfdb.

BEER AND BREWING ON THE INTERNET

This section provides listings of resources on the Internet concerning beer and brewing. The majority of the resources are Web pages and contain current and high-quality information on the craft.

Spencer Thomas's Beer Page

http://guraldi.ith.med.umich.edu:80/Beer/index.html

Thomas says the page is "geared to home brewers, with a little bit of general beer info." Moreover, it is well organized with interesting and unique entries. With the help of a Mosaic browser, visitors can view more than 223 beer labels online. Basic hypertext materials include brewing FAQs and recipes.

Most notably, Thomas has created a useful search capability for the Homebrew Digest, a compilation of messages from the Homebrew mailing list. This allows you to search for keywords in the digest. There is a fascinating listing of previous searches conducted (to reduce repeat searches) that is more than 76 pages long.

Eric Wooten's Beer and Home Brewing

http://pekkel.uthscsa.edu/beer.html

Wooten's page is a window into the world of Texas beer. It includes information on the Texas Brewer's Festival and Texas brew-pubs. In addition to the usual links for other beer pages, Wooten supplies information about brewing competitions and a forum for a brewer's recipe exchange.

What's in the Mashtun?

http://mashtun.jpl.nasa.gov/yeast.html

For the serious brewer this page offers many FAQs including a Mashing FAQ, Brewing FAQ, Maltose Falcon FAQ, and a Belgian Beer FAQ.

Metabisulphite Club

http://www.abdn.ac.uk/~csc133/metabisulphite.html

The Student Society of Aberdeen, Scotland provides information and links pertaining to home brew and wine making. Also online is the *Small Murmurings Newsletter,* the group's oracle.

The Virtual Pub

http://lager.geo.brown.edu:8080/virtual-pub/index.html

The Virtual Pub is the Web page for "network beer aficionados" and concentrates on drinking beer, which means tasting notes galore. Joel Plutachak is the self-named "janitor" for the Virtual Pub and has put together a wonderful resource for beverage professionals and aficionados alike.

Patrons of the Virtual Pub can read about IRC (Internet Relay Chat) Tastings that take place in a real-time teleconference, beer in Belgium, beer around the world, and, of course, beer in the United States. You will also find a depiction of beer glasses and access to the FAQs for all the major beer-related Usenet groups. There are links to other home pages related to the barley brew as well, and if you are really motivated, you can even find out how to set up your own page.

The usage figures, which are available on the server, show that this page is growing at an exponential rate. One week in February 1994 (presumably the page's first week) 105 patrons accessed the page. By May 1994, the patrons numbered 5,176 in one week; by August 1994, the Virtual Pub attracted more than 7,100 visitors in one week.

Dan Brown's Beer Page

http://www.eff.org/dan/beer.html

Dan Brown offers access to the alt.beer newsgroup, numerous FAQs (old and new), and several other beer pages.

Home Brewery Kits and Supplies

gopher://ftp.std.com/11/vendors/home brewery

This is a commercial site for obtaining home brew equipment. It is one of a growing number of commercial brewing Web pages that market supplies to brewers.

Cat's Meow WWW

http:..guraldi.itn.med.umich.edu/Beer/Cats-meow/top-page.html

This is a large collection of brewing recipes for pale ale, lager, stout, and cider, to name just a few.

Peat-Smoked Malt

http://guraldi.hgp.med.umich.edu/dynamic/Beer/peat-smoked-malt.txt

Suppliers of specialty malt, general brewing, and wine-making equipment are provided here.

Brewers Supply 1-800 Telephone Numbers

http://guraldi.hgp.med.umich.edu/dynamic/Beer/800-numbers.html

Three full pages of toll-free numbers for brewing supplies are listed here.

Brew-Pubs List

ftp://sierra.stanford.edu/pub/homebrew/docs/publist

This huge guide is nearly 400 pages long and covers brew-pubs worldwide. The author of this guide says that the list is the result of a project that is five years or more in the making. The references cover multitudes of countries, and most entries have notes on significant features of the pub.

The Dowling Page

http://www.primenet.com/commercial/dowling.html

Dowling, a brew equipment supplier, uses the WWW to offer access to its mail-order brewing supplies. Items in this extensive selection include recipes for beer, equipment, and various malts. Orders cannot be placed from the Dowling Web Page, but ordering instructions are given online.

The Beer Home Brewing Guide CD-ROM

http://micromedia.com/www/catalog/titles/beer.htm

This is an online pitch for a CD-ROM that serves as a guide to creating your own home brew beer.

Charleston Beer Works

http://www.sims.nct/organizations/chasbeerworks/chasbeerworks.html

Charleston Beer Works offers a complete line of beer brewing supplies including kits for micro-breweries, equipment guides, and more.

Zeno's Pub

A tradition for students in State College, Pennsylvania, Zeno's Pub has a loyal clientele that started a Web page to share their passion with others locally and around the globe. Using a graphical browser, you will find a photo of the bartender. Also on Zeno's page is the beer menu and a list of activities at the pub.

Cascade River's Beer-of-the-Month Club

http://venus.mcs.com/~cascade/html/beer.html

A commercial Web page markets a beer-of-the-month offer for two six-packs each month and a newsletter. Orders can be placed online.

COFFEE AND CAFFEINE ON THE INTERNET

Coffee lovers abound on the Internet, and they have the online resources to prove it. On the Internet you will find commercial offers, tasting notes, lists of where to drink coffee, and even information on its harmful effects.

Mr. Coffee Caffeinated Home Page

http://www.paranoia.com/~lizardo/caffeine.html

This page is all about "that most beloved of drugs," caffeine. Find links to files that deal with the effects of caffeine, FAQs about caffeine, and leads to other caffeine resources.

Over the Coffee

http://www.infonet/showcase/coffee

This page is maintained by Tim Nemec, tim@ins.infonet.net, who oversees this comprehensive guide for coffee lovers and beverage professionals. This is a creative, informative, and useful page for beverage professionals who have a large stake in the coffee business.

The page opens with selections of various types. The first is a listing of retail coffee vendors. The second is the Coffee Reference Desk, which is a mix of news, information on equipment, and trivia. It also includes a five-page glossary where you can learn synonyms for "bodum" or that "cafecito" is a Cuban coffee drink made from espresso and sugar. The Reference Desk will soon contain coffee recipes and a traveler's guide to coffee houses.

Other sections include the Coffee Archives, which contains info on the Usenet groups related to coffee. Professionals will certainly want to browse the Resources for Coffee Professionals. Visitors to Nemec's Over the Coffee page can subscribe to *Coffee Magazine* and learn of other coffee-related publications.

The Other Resources section includes a link to Capulin Coffee. This is a fascinating description of a very specific condition of coffee by Seth Appell of Ash Creek Orchards.

Matt Loew's Cafenet

http://www.me.mtu.edu/personal/partners/Loew/public-html/caffeine.html

This home page for Matt Loew consists of both caffeine and coffee links. They include FAQs, caffeine pages, newsgroups, and links to cafe lists.

Mothercity Coffee:
A Guide to Seattle Coffee Houses

http://www.seas.upenn.edu/~cpage/mothercity.html

For an overview of the coffee scene in the city that started it all, point your browser to this page. There are reviews of bean roasters and the "bean juice" they serve as well as reviews of simple coffee houses.

Professionals wishing to order Seattle roasted coffee can browse three pages of mail-order references. There are also links to other fine beverage pages that are wine- or spirit-related.

The Xerox Database of Coffee Folksongs

http://www.xerox.com/digitrand?coffee

The truly creative beverage professional will somehow find value in the words to such songs as "I'd Rather Make Coffee Than Love." Someone at Xerox has compiled six pages of coffee songs with hotlinks to the words.

San Diego Coffee Houses

http://mis.saic.com/mls.coffee.html

This is a list of five pages of addresses, phone numbers, and entertainment at San Diego coffee houses.

WINE AND SPIRITS ON THE INTERNET

The wine and spirits resources on the Internet span the globe. They provide interesting information on little-known wine regions as well as the most famous districts. There are tasting notes, lists of bars, and even drink recipes.

Great Bars in New Orleans

http://www.webcom.com/~gumbo/no-bars.html

You can check out great bars in a city where bars are king!

Great Dive Bars in Louisiana

http://www.webcom.com/~gumbo/food/la-bars.html

If you have an interest in the other end of the upscale market, Chuck Taggart has some things to share with you.

Brad and Dri Brown's Wine Page

http://augustus.csscr.washington.edu/personal/bigstar-mosaic/wine.html

The Brown's wine page is well designed and an important professional resource. The page links to several very interesting resources, and new links are added frequently.

The first selection on this wine page is the Tasting Archive, which the Browns consider an "experimental, interactive tasting-note compendium." It contains wine reviews, tasting notes, and winery/tasting room reviews.

The other selections include a link to other wine pages and resources, such as a huge Wine FAQ. The FAQ is over 160 screens long and is currently "under construction." The Wine FAQ is essentially an encyclopedic style reference to wine in general and includes other notable electronic hard cover reference works.

Visitors to the Brown's Wine Page can also tour select Washington wineries (the Browns live in the Northwest). The Napa Wine Page has a link here as well as the UC Davis Page, from the Department of Viticulture and Enology.

The Wine FAQ is an ambitious effort for even a Web resource, and it makes this page a must on any beverage professional's custom bookmark page.

Wine-list Page

http://www.ee.pdx.edu

Tim Trautmann is the owner of this page, and he seeks primarily to archive the postings to the Wine-list. You will also find information on wine, wine regions, and wine research.

Wine.com Page

http://www.wine.com/wine/

The owners of this page, promote it as "connecting the Worldwide Wine Community together."

Wine.com offers information on wineries in Solano County, Napa County, and Northern Michigan. They also include a number of resources available elsewhere on the Net. Such resources include *Decanter Magazine, Grapevine,* The Wine Society Page from Bath University, and the Slovenian Page.

The Outrageous Wine Lover's List on Wine.com consists of several hundred posts from the Usenet. Legal Issues is concerned with the legal issues regarding wine consumption.

Wine in Hungary

http://www.fsz.bme.hu

This short Web resource details aspects of Hungary's 17 wine-growing regions.

Wine Society Page

http://www.bath.ac.uk

The Bath University Student Union Wine Society produces this page, which appropriately provides local information from the United Kingdom, as well as Vintage Club tasting notes and access to other wine pages, such as the ubiquitous Slovenian page.

South African Wines

http://www.wimsey.com/teletimes.root/wine_9402.html

This is a five-page overview of the South African wine industry.

Wine Research

http://aruba.nycaes.cornell.edu:8000/fst/market/wineres.html

This page provides a brief but detailed description of the Wine Research Program at Cornell University. The program leader is Dr. Thomas Henick-Kling, Associate Professor at Cornell.

Drink Recipes from the Usenet Group, rec.food.recipes

gopher://nutmeg.ukc.ac.uk/11/.archive/uunet/usenet/rec.food.recipe/drinks

A large archive of drink recipes can be accessed from this Gopher server.

Grapevine—The Wine Drinkers Forum

http://www.opal.com/grapevine

The folks at *Grapevine* promote themselves as providing the first Web-accessible magazine dedicated to the wine lover. The magazine includes reviews of Italian, Australian, and U.S. wines as well as access to the rec.food.drink archives. This magazine accepts articles and review contributions. For details, send an e-mail message to grapevine@opal.com.

Food and Wine Online

Visitors can also rent space on the Grapevine Web server. Given the profile of *Grapevine* readers this may be an interesting vehicle for creative merchandising by beverage industry entrepreneurs. See this Web page for details and rates.

Gordon Biersch: Wine List

`http://www.commerce.digital.com/palo-alto/chamber-of-commerce/`

`entertainment/restaurants/pictures/gb-logo.gif`

Check out this famous wine list with a graphical Web browser.

rec.food.drink.beer FAQ

`http://www.cis.ohio-state.edu/hypertext/faq/usenet/beer-faq/faq.html`

Frequently asked questions about beer-related topics are featured in this important document for beverage professionals and micro-breweries. The FAQ is divided into four basic categories and is at least 50 pages long.

The sections are as follows:

1. Beer — Common terms as well as information on how beer is enjoyed

2. Where to get beer and frequently asked questions about making beer

3. Where to find more information on beer

4. General facts about rec.food.drink.beer

Wines of Slovenia

`http://www.ijs.si/wine_uvod.html`

Learn about Slovenian wines in the context of the world history of wine making (it predates Roman production). The Slovenians present facts and figures about annual vintages and details of six extraordinary vintages this century.

Maribor—Food and Drinks Page

`http://www.uni-mb.si/mb_food.html`

The regional Slovenian cuisine of Maribor is undergoing rapid changes. What was once typical Central European or

Viennese in nature is now being influenced by other areas. Read about these changes, find links to Slovenian recipes, and use references to the Slovenian muscatel and Riesling wines.

Slovenia Wine Regions

http://www.ijs.si/wine_regions.html

This is a brief, four-page description of the wine growing regions of Slovenia.

Global History of Wine Making

http://www.ijs.si/wine_history.html

This is a short but comprehensive history of wine making from the wine lovers in Slovenia. It begins in prehistory, moves through Babylonia, and in four pages ends with a brief discussion of phylloxera, the vine disease ravaging the Napa Valley.

Wine Net News

http://augustus.csscr.washington.edu/personal/bigstar-mosaic/newsletter.html

The first issue of this newsletter is a 45-page compendium of well-written, extensive tasting notes by experienced tasters from several continents. The page also features a request for more reviewers.

CONCLUSION

A rapidly growing number of Internet resources feature beer, coffee, wine, and spirits. Professionals will find that new trends show up early on the Internet. Close attention to some of the active and well-attended resources can create unique opportunities for operators. You might find tasting notes on a particularly good but obscure wine. New micro-brews are mentioned often in some of the brewing resources and afford the aggressive marketer an early look at developing brands. Find the pages and servers you like best, place them in your hotlist or bookmark list, and return to them frequently for new updates and information.

Beverage Resources on the Big Boards

The beverage resources available on the Big Boards offer the professional easy access to the opinions, thoughts, and impressions of many articulate connoisseurs of fine beverages. They also offer a new way to communicate with many wineries and other beverage manufacturers that have been attracted to the new online media. If you are a beverage professional, you will find it beneficial to use the free trial offers often extended by the larger online services to explore the wine, beer, and spirits message areas and file libraries.

AMERICA ONLINE

America Online provides a growing volume of beverage resources, many of which will be of interest to professionals who wish to interact with wineries online or obtain new information on varietals.

Wine & Dine

Wine & Dine can be accessed by selecting **Go To** from the main menu and then selecting **Keywords** and entering **wine**. The Wine & Dine selections of interest to beverage professionals include those that are wine- and spirit-related as well as beer and brewing resources.

For wine resources, you can select the Message Boards, Chat, and Library items from the Wine & Dine menu. The Wine Message Center has folders for you to post comments on wine topics, picks and pans of vintages, and comments on wineries. You can connect with traders and collectors, and there are special areas to discuss specific varietals. Of special interest to professionals is a folder for "jobs in wine." Professionals will also enjoy the Winery News message area with announcements and interaction with several fine wineries, including Fetzer, Simi Winery, and Enoteca.

Select the Wine & Spirits & Ratings item to access software for cellar managers that can be downloaded, many files for tasting notebooks, and databases of wineries and varietals. These include the Winery Directory, with more than 1,500 winery addresses and phone numbers; the Winebase, a database of wine ratings; and the Wine Dictionary, which lets you search for encyclopedia style articles on various wine-related subjects.

Last, the wine resources include scheduled conferences. Using AOL's strength in chat services, Wine & Dine features occasional conferences, "live" with experts.

Beer and brewing is a popular subject on Wine & Dine. The message boards feature folders for comments on regional beer and pubs, festivals, and general beer-related information. The brewing message boards include recipes and information on laws and regulations. Professionals will be interested in the Business Opportunities folder with business plans and posts on starting a micro-brewery and opening a brew-pub. Selecting Beer & Brewing will give you an opportunity to download brew-pub guides, notes on brewing famous beers, and software such as an Alcohol Calculator. There are also transcripts from the periodic beer-related conferences held online.

There is also a message board for Pipes & Cigars. With folders on Cigars & Food, as well as tobacco and a Pipes & Cigars database, this will be valuable to bars that promote smoking.

The entire Wine & Dine department is managed by Craig Goldwyn, President of the Beverage Tasting Institute, Inc. and the former wine columnist for the *Chicago Tribune* and *Washington Post*.

ELECTRONIC FOOD FOR THOUGHT

Restaurant owner Rick Knight, of Holmes & Watson, Ltd., Troy, New York, is a member of AOL and uses the Wine & Dine department to stay abreast of beverage trends and products.

"I have begun to explore the wine sections, where I am a real novice—but it has helped my knowledge base," says Knight. "I purchased a number of wines because of information found on AOL, and some of those wines will be making their way onto our lists. I often find myself making notes on a particular winery or vintage and checking in my distributor's books to see if it is available in our area. We carry over 60 single malt scotches, so I check there as well. I do a monthly cigar/pipe evening and I check in there also."

The Cooking Club's Wine Cellar

Selecting the **Go To** menu option on the main menu and entering "cooking" as a **Keyword** will take you to the Cooking Club. One of the folders, The Wine Cellar, is a beverage resource that should not be overlooked by professionals. It contains an area for beginners' comments, drink recipes, and reviews on not only wine varietals, but also spirits and brew.

COMPUSERVE

CompuServe offers comprehensive coverage of beverage issues with the Bacchus Wine & Beer Forum. The sections are paralleled by file libraries of similar subject matter.

Bacchus Wine & Beer Forum

To access Bacchus, select **Go To**... from the **Services** menu and enter "wine" or "bacchus." The forum contains the following message areas:

- News/Tools/Business
- Wine Tasting Notes
- General Wine
- Wine Shopping
- Wineries
- Cellars/Cellaring
- Wine Questions
- Winemaking & Grapes
- Food & Beverage
- Coffee/Tea/Etc.
- Spirits/Bartending
- Books & Periodicals
- Cigars & Pipes
- Dining/Travel/Events
- Soapbox
- Friends & Fun
- Beer & Breweries
- Beer Tasting Notes
- General Homebrew
- Technical Homebrew

For professionals, the Wine Tasting Notes will be valuable. During the California floods in January 1995, this section featured posts with updates on the effect of flooding on wineries in the Napa Valley.

Restaurants and bars with extensive cellars will find the Cellars/Cellaring section an important resource. Discussions of temperature control and various technical issues in cellaring wine are common.

The Food & Beverages section concerns itself with both the pairing of food and beverage and cooking with beverages such as wine and beer. This can be a catalyst for creativity or a way to reduce risk in planning menus with food and wine.

Spirits/Bartending is the online home for some bartenders. It is also full of tasting notes on liqueurs, single malt scotches, and other related beverages.

Most of the sections have a parallel subject library online with files and software for downloading. These include transcripts of online conferences and a number of databases on wineries and wine.

DELPHI

DELPHI features two resources focused on beverages: the Wine & Spirits Forum (343) and the Homebrew Forum (325).

Wine & Spirits Forum

To reach the Wine & Spirits Forum, type **go custom 343** from the main menu. The forum topics are as follows:

- General Discussion

- Recent Releases

- Spirits

- Sell/Trade Within the Law

- Retailers/Wholesalers

- SCH—Spirits Chatter

- Tasting Notes

- Wine Recipes

- Recipes for Spirits

- Industry Notes

- WCH—Wine Chatter

The beverage professional will be most interested in postings in the Retailers/Wholesalers and Industry Notes topic areas. However, currently very few messages are posted on these topics. As the professional membership grows, this will surely improve.

The Homebrew Forum

The Homebrew Forum can be accessed by typing **go custom 325** from the main menu prompt. Topics here include the following:

- General Discussion

- Micros and Brew-pubs

- Recipe Forum

- Database

- Brewing Forum

The most interesting topic to professionals will most likely be Micros and Brew-pubs. It features reviews of pubs and micro-breweries written by members of the forum. It will also include information on pub crawls nationwide.

If you are brewing beer on-premise, there is a database here that will be an important resource. You can search for recipes and information on techniques and processes using keywords that narrow or broaden your search.

PRODIGY

The Wine, Beer & Spirits BB is the sole beverage offering by PRODIGY, but it offers a wide variety of subject areas. Professionals will find ample opportunity to interact with beverage producers and marketers.

Beverage Resources on the Big Boards

Wine, Beer & Spirits BB

PRODIGY's beverage bulletin board has nearly 20 different subject areas that can be accessed by using the **Jump** word "wine" or selecting **Entertainment** from the main menu, then **Dining.**

The subjects, which include some constantly changing items to accommodate special guests online, are as follows:

- Graham

- Glenmorangie

- Rex Hill

- Jerry Cebe

- Beer Basics

- Beer Homebrew

- Beer Talk

- Breweries & Pubs

- Liqueurs

- Mead/Sake/Ciders

- Mixed Drinks

- Spirits

- Wine Basics

- Wine Talk

- Wine Talk Lounge

- Winemaking & Equipment

- Other

- Pierre Cellis

For the professional, the opportunity to interact with the special guests, such as the staff at Glenmorangie, a Scotch distillery, is a special attraction. Notes are posted by members for a period of a week or so with questions and comments. Then the special industry guest responds and comments in public messages. This gives operators the opportunity to acquire knowledge that will be of special interest to customers and enhance their knowledge of specific products.

The Breweries & Pubs topic will also be of interest to professionals. You can find comments about what others are doing around the world and stay current on trends.

Many of the forums feature tasting notes on the topic's beverage—beer tastings in Beer Talk, wine tasting notes in Wine Talk, and so on.

There are posts by industry professionals on occasion, and they are certainly welcome. The producers and manufacturers especially like hearing from the operators who serve their brands.

CONCLUSION

Just as beverage hobbyists dominate the Internet resources, they also are the majority on the commercial online service resources. However, an increasing number of wineries are represented on CompuServe, AOL, and PRODIGY. DELPHI continues the Internet tradition as an online home for mostly hobbyists. All of the services offer the food and beverage operator the opportunity to evaluate new trends, beverages, and attitudes.

Appendices

APPENDIX   A

PUBLIC ARCHIE SERVICES

To use any of the following Archie servers:

1. Telnet to the server.

2. Log in using `archie` as a user ID.

3. Enter commands to conduct a search
   (see Chapter 6 for details).

Canada	`archie.edvz.uni-linz.ac.at`
England	`archie.doc.ic.ac.uk`
Maryland, USA	`archie.sura.net`
Nebraska, USA	`archic.unl.edu`
New Jersey, USA	`archie.internic.net`
New York, USA	`archie.ans.net`

A P P E N D I X B

Lynx Commands

Movement:

Down arrow	Highlight next topic
Up arrow	Highlight previous topic
Right arrow	Jump to highlighted topic
Return	Enter
Left arrow	Return to previous topic

Scrolling:

+ (or space)	Scroll down to next page
- (or b)	Scroll up to previous page

Other:

? (or H)	Help (this screen)
a	Add the current link to your bookmark file
c	Send a comment to the document owner
d	Download the current link
e	Edit the current file
g	Go to a user-specified URL or file
i	Show an index of documents
m	Return to main screen
o	Set your options
p	Print to a file, mail, printers, or other
q	Quit (Capital 'Q' for quick quit)
/	Search for a string within the current document
s	Enter a search string for an external search
n	Go to the next search string
v	View your bookmark file
z	Cancel transfer in progress

Appendices

[backspace]	Go to the history page
=	Show file and link info
\	Toggle document source/rendered view
!	Spawn your default shell
CTRL-R	Reload current file and refresh the screen
CTRL-W	Refresh the screen
CTRL-U	Erase input line
CTRL-G	Cancel input or transfer

A P P E N D I X   C

GOPHER COMMANDS

Moving around Gopherspace

Use the arrow keys to move around.

Right, Return	"Enter"/display current item
Left, u	"Exit" current item/go up a level
Down	Move to next line
Up	Move to previous line
>, +, Pgdwn, Space	View next page
<, -, Pgup, b	View previous page
0-9	Go to a specific line
m	Go back to the main menu

Other Commands

q	Quit with prompt
Q	Quit unconditionally
s	Save current item to a file
S	Save current menu listing to a file
D	Download a file
r	Go to root menu of current item
R	Go to root menu of current menu
=	Display technical information about current item
^	Display technical information about current directory
o	Open a new Gopher server
O	Change options
/	Search for an item in the menu
n	Find next search item
g	"Gripe" via e-mail to administrator of current item

A P P E N D I X   D

COMMERCIAL ONLINE SERVICES

Restaurant Association Network
Information Inc.
7700 Old Georgetown Rd.
Bethesda, MD 20814-6100
301-215-4688

FoodNet
460 S. Arrowhead
San Bernadino, CA 92408-1309
1-800-366-3875
Fax 909-885-8286

CHRIE's HOSTEUR Network
PO Box 8440
Gaithersburg, MD 20898-8440
202-331-5990

America Online
8619 Westwood Center Drive
Vienna, VA 22182-2285
1-800-827-6364

CompuServe
5000 Arlington Centre Blvd.
Columbus, OH 43220
1-800-848-8990

DELPHI
GVC
1030 Massachusetts Ave.
Cambridge, MA 02138-5302
1-800-695-4005

PRODIGY
445 Hamilton Ave.
White Plains, NY 10601
1-800-PRODIGY

Glossary

Anonymous FTP: When a public Internet site lets you log in with no special clearance and transfer a file to yourself, it is call anonymous FTP.

ANSI: ANSI is an acronym that indicates a specific standard for communication.

Archie: Archie is a computer program that searches indexes of files that are available on public Internet servers.

Basic Services: Basic Services are those areas of interest on CompuServe that are included in the basic fee for membership. CompuServe offers unlimited access to the Basic Services.

BBS: A BBS is a dedicated computer that accepts dial-in access for the purpose of leaving private and public messages, transferring files, and chatting with other members.

Binary file: Software programs are written in special nonreadable language composed of 0s and 1s called binary code. A file that is written in this language is called a binary file.

Bits: The 0s and 1s that the computer uses to store information are known as bits. They are generally transmitted in groups that include eight data bits plus a start bit and a stop bit.

Bookmark: A link to a Web page that is saved for ready and direct access in the future is called a bookmark.

Case sensitive: When a computer program requires that uppercase and lowercase letters be used in specific instances, it is said to be case sensitive.

Chat: Chat services allow users to connect online with each other, instead of a database or message board. This allows for *real-time* communication as opposed to delayed response from, say, electronic mail.

Chat Rooms and Event Rooms: When a group of AOL members forms a regularly scheduled Chat Room, it may become an Event Room where discussions are more focused and have hosts. The schedule for Event Rooms is posted in the PC Studio.

Chat/teleconference: These two terms are often used interchangeably to indicate a conversation between users that is typed on a keyboard instead of spoken. In some online environments they may be two distinct forms of communication.

CIM: CIM is the CompuServe Information Manager software that lets you access and explore CompuServe.

Computer virus: When special computer language that will cause harm to hardware, software, or data is hidden in a computer file, it is called a computer virus.

Cross-post: When a Usenet message is posted to several newsgroups at once, it is called cross-posting.

Cyber*: When the term "cyber" is used it often implies the electronic transfer of information. Thus, cyberspace becomes the vast, almost tangible region of the online world where electronic communication takes place.

Dialing directory: A set of phone numbers that can be stored by modem software and accessed for later use is called a dialing directory.

Digital: Digital refers to information in the form of a series of 0s and 1s or digits.

Download: When you copy a file from a remote computer to your own, you download the file.

Echo: When a BBS exchanges messages with other BBSs on a regular basis, the network is called an echo network.

Electronic mail: The private messages that are sent from one computer to another are called electronic mail.

Electronic mall: An overtly commercial service online that seeks to match buyers and sellers is called an electronic mall.

E-mail address: Each user on the Internet has an e-mail address that specifies a unique place of delivery for all electronic communications.

Emoticon: A graphical symbol used to convey emotion and facial expression that is designed from keyboard letters and symbols is called an emoticon.

Emulate: When one type of computer terminal simulates the operation of another type of terminal it emulates the other terminal.

Executable file: When a computer file is a software program, it is considered to be executable. That is, it will execute commands as directed.

Extended Services: Extended Services are offered to CompuServe members for an additional cost.

Field: In an online message, there are several designated areas that are either manually or automatically filled with specific information. These designated areas are called fields.

File Transfer Protocol (FTP): On the Internet, FTP is a program that moves files from one computer to another. It is a fixed set of rules that determine how data is transmitted over a phone line.

Flaming: When a person attacks another person online with abusive and condemning language it is called flaming.

Folder: A folder on AOL is a menu selection that contains text files for reading. The folder is identified by an icon that looks like a file folder.

Gateway: A gateway is basically a connection from one computer system or application to another.

Gopher: The menu-driven, search tool created for use on the Internet is called Gopher.

Guides: On AOL, a guide is a specially designated helper identified by the word guide somewhere in his or her screen name.

Hotlink: A hotlink is a portion of text that, when selected, leads to another Web page.

Hypertext: Hypertext is a form of text where certain words are connected to more detailed information in other files across the Internet. The documents create a web-like information structure.

Initialization string: An initialization string is a set of predefined commands that your modem uses to send and receive data over telephone lines.

Glossary

Internet: The Internet is a vast, worldwide network of computer networks. Growing at an unimaginable rate, the actual size of the Internet is not really known. It is a tool for education, research, and, more recently, business and recreation.

Internet provider: A service that connects individuals or corporations to the Internet is an Internet provider.

Internet Relay Chat (IRC): IRC is the most popular chat facility on the Internet. It comprises hundreds of "channels" that are open only as long as a user is present. Each channel allows multiple users to chat simultaneously.

IRQ: An IRQ or interrupt number is a line the port uses to tell the computer that there is information to process. Each device *must* use a unique IRQ.

Jump words: On PRODIGY, the keywords that are entered manually by members to move to other screens are called Jump words.

Keyword: AOL names departments with words that can be entered with the keyboard. These words are called keywords, and their use gives quick access to various departments and services.

Kilobits: A kilobit is a unit of 1,000 bits.

Listserver: A listserver is like an electronic traffic cop, automatically handling memberships to the list, distributing messages, and sending information on the list when requested.

Log file: When you capture in a file the content of screens you see online, you create a log file. A log file serves as a record of an online session.

Lynx: Lynx is a text-based Web browser, as opposed to a graphical Web browser, that is available free from many Internet providers.

Mailing list: A mailing list is an automated mail distribution tool on the Internet for electronic mail. Messages sent to a "list server" are redistributed to all list members.

Main menu: On a BBS there is a screen that serves as the primary menu of services. It is from this menu that each service on the BBS can be reached. The main menu is the top of the BBS.

Majordomo: Majordomo is a specific type of listserver requiring its own unique set of commands.

Message board: A message board is an area where members can post public messages on a specific topic.

Mirror: When an Internet site carries the identical files of another site, it is said to be a mirror.

Modem: A modem is a device that converts (*mod*ulates and d*em*odulates) electronic signals from one form to another form.

Moderated: A newsgroup that has a person who filters and controls the messages posted to the group is called a moderated newsgroup.

Netscape: The fastest, most advanced browser available for traveling the Web is Netscape.

Newsgroup: An individual public message board on the Usenet is called a newsgroup.

Newsreader: A computer program that lets you navigate through the Usenet newsgroups and messages is called a newsreader.

Off-line: When the computer and modem are not transmitting data over the telephone lines, you are off-line.

Online services: Online services are computer-based information and communication resources that are accessed with a modem.

Point of sale (POS) system: A point of sales system is a business machine, usually computerized, that tracks sales transactions. In a restaurant, it generally tracks the sales of individual menu items. Often, such machines are connected to personal computers for sales analysis.

Ports: A port is the point at which a modem connects to a computer.

Post: When you place a public message on a Usenet group or BBS, it is called posting. The message itself is a post.

Quoting: When a section of the original message is included in a reply, it is called quoting. Many BBSs let you quote a message automatically so that you don't have to retype the original message.

Real time: The actual time in which a process under computer control occurs is called real time. When users communicate simultaneously online, the communication takes place in real time. When, as in e-mail, communication takes place in a delayed fashion, it takes place outside of real time.

RIP: Remote Image Protocol (RIP) lets you see graphical images and use your mouse to navigate through a BBS.

RIP*term:* The special modem software that lets you see the RIP screens on a BBS is called RIP*term*.

Screen name: On AOL, screen names are used for identification online and resemble CB "handles" or pseudonyms.

Server: A server is a computer that provides a specific tool or resource.

Shareware: Software that is offered on a "try before you buy" basis is called shareware. The user is obligated to pay a registration fee after a trial period if use of the software continues.

Signal-to-noise ratio: Public message forums have a certain amount of very targeted, pointed information (signal). They also have posts that are inane and off-subject (noise). The balance between the two is called the signal-to-noise ratio. If the ratio is high, the information is easier to find.

SLIP: The mode of connection to the Internet that allows complete access to all the tools and resources of the Internet with a telephone line, computer, modem, and appropriate software is called SLIP.

Special Interest Groups (SIGs): The public message areas on DELPHI, defined by subject, are called SIGs.

Subscriber: A subscriber is a person who chooses to belong to a mailing list by e-mailing a request to join. Unlike other subscriptions in our life, you do not pay to subscribe.

Sysop: A BBS's online manager, host, and sometimes bouncer is called a sysop.

Taglines: It is common for BBSs to add short advertisements to outgoing messages on an echo or Usenet message. The short advertisement is called a tagline and usually contains a quote and the BBS's modem number.

Telnet: Telnet has multiple meanings: (1) software that allows you to connect to a remote computer over the Internet; (2) a command used to start the telnet software; (3) a verb to describe executing the telnet command.

Thread: Messages that are related by a common subject are part of a message thread. Threads are an important way to group and organize messages online.

Glossary

Trumpet Winsock: Trumpet Winsock is software that allows the Web browser to interface with Microsoft Windows.

TTY: TTY is an emulation of a typewriter or teletype style keyboard. It is effective and sufficient for basic text communication.

UNIX: Many of the computers that act as hosts on the Internet run on a version of the UNIX operating system. While it is not necessary to understand UNIX commands to work on the Internet, the serious Net explorer may find it helpful. A classic text on UNIX is Harley Hahn's *A Student's Guide to UNIX*.

Upload: When you copy a file from your computer to a remote computer, you upload the file.

Usenet: The Internet resource that features over 7,000 special interest bulletin boards is called the Usenet. The individual boards within the Usenet are called newsgroups.

Viral detection software: A computer program that can examine the contents of a file and identify viral contamination is viral detection software.

Virtual: The term "virtual" is often used in describing aspects of electronically created environments. It refers to the existence of something in effect but not in actual form. So a virtual community is one that has many of the attributes of a community as we know it in the day-to-day world; however, it exists and expands electronically.

VT-100, VT-102: The emulations called VT-100 and VT-102 do not allow you to view graphics online. They are text-only emulations used by some Internet providers.

Web browser: The software that lets you travel across the World Wide Web and access Web documents is called a Web browser.

Web page: A Web document is called a page. It often includes not only multimedia but also links to other pages. By "clicking" on a link the Web user is effortlessly and transparently connected to another specified page on an entirely different computer, possibly on another continent!

World Wide Web (WWW): The World Wide Web is the fastest growing and most exciting aspect of the Internet. Able to display full-color graphics and photos in an easy-to-navigate manner, the Web has become a mecca for entrepreneurs. Some Web sites even provide sound and video clips for downloading.

ZMODEM, XMODEM, YMODEM: These are the most common sets of rules, or file transfer protocols, for uploading and downloading files online.

Index

@ (at symbol), 93
: (colon), 38
/ (slash), 124
<> (angle brackets), 45–46

A

Academic American Encyclopedia, 63
Academic Services, 156–157
accounting software, 148
Adams, Steve, 18, 148–151
addresses, e-mail, description of, 93, 273
advertisements
  classified, 42–43, 148
  employment, 148, 150–151
Agricultural Library Forum (ALF), 209–210
Agriculture and Food Page, 205
Aichlmayr, Michail, 223
AIDS, 76, 209
alt.beer, 249
alt.callahans, 247 248
alt.coffee, 248
alt.college.food, 168
alt.drugs.caffeine, 249
alt.creative_cooking, 166
alt.food, 166
alt.food.chocolate, 169
alt.food.cocacola, 249
alt.food.dennys, 169
alt.food.fat-free, 168
alt.food.historic, 153
alt.food.mcdonalds, 169

alt.food.professionals, 99–100, 107, 153, 161–162
alt.food.taco-bell, 169
alt.food.wine, 167, 249
alt.good.gourmand (moderated), 167
alt.gourmand, 167
alt.hangover, 248
alt.org.food-not-bombs, 167
alt.restaurants, 166
alt.waffle-house, 169
alt.zima, 248
American Culinary Federation, 9
Americans with Disabilities Act (ADA), 77, 110
America Online, 6–7, 42, 49, 93, 113. *See also* American Online (services listed by name)
address/phone number for, 269
beverage resources on, 261–263
cost of, 58, 59
customer service, 52
navigating, 57–58
overview of, 50–60, 218–222, 261–263
primary departments, 51
sample screens, 51–52
strengths/weaknesses of, 59–60
the Usenet and, 98

American Online (services listed by name). *See also* America Online
Back of the House Chat, 56, 59, 218
Computing & Software Department, 54
Cooking Club, 221–222
Cooking Club's Wine Cellar, 263
Culinary BBS, 54, 56
Event Rooms, 55
Gay & Lesbian Forum, 54
Internet Resources for Food and Beverage Professionals, 57
Learning & Reference Department, 54–55
Lifestyles & Interest Department, 54
News & Finance Department, 53
Newsstand, 55
People Connection Department, 55, 59
@times Message Board, 56–57
Wine & Dine Forum, 51–52, 54, 56, 219–220, 261–263
Anonymous FTP, 109, 113–117, 125, 271
ANSI (American National Standards Institute), 18, 19, 22, 271

285

International Cookbook
  (PRODIGY), 84
Internet
  access through America
    Online, 59–60
  access through DELPHI,
    77–78, 93
  access through PRODIGY, 79
  basic description of, 3, 89,
    275
  e-mail on, 93–98
  providers, definition of, 90,
    275
  tools, list of, 90–91
  using the, overview of,
    90–93
Internet Resources for Food
  and Beverage
  Professionals (AOL), 57
IRC (Internet Relay Chat),
  3, 40, 78, 251, 275
IRQ (interrupt number), 17,
  22, 275

J

Jackson, Kendall, 129–130,
  199
Janos Restaurant, 8
Japan, 3, 5, 178
Jenanyan, Gary, 67, 223,
  224–225
J-Food-L, 178
Job Search Employee
  Services, 150–151
Johnson & Wales BBS,
  156–157
Jones, Richard T., 38–39
jump words, 85, 275. *See also*
  keywords

K

Kendall College, 155
Kerr, Graham, 160
keywords
  definition of, 58, 275
  navigating America Online
    with, 58, 59
  navigating PRODIGY with,
    85

kilobit, definition of, 14, 276
Knight, Rick, 263
Knowledge Index
  (CompuServe), 68,
  225–226
Kurnit, Scott, 79

L

Lacto-Vegetarian Recipes,
  184
Lady Baltimore Foods, 72
Lambic Beer List, 245
LAUNCHpad BBS, 110
Lawn, John, 57
Learning & Reference
  Department (AOL),
  54–55
Le Cordon Bleu, 6, 129, 200
Lee, David Alexander, 171
Lewis, C. S., 68
Lewis, Jonathan, 77, 110
libraries, on the Internet,
  190–193
Lifestyles & Interest
  Department (AOL), 54
List of Recommended Cajun
  and Creole Cookbooks,
  192
listservers, definition of, 102,
  105, 276
Lockley, Jo Lynne, 3, 7, 20
Lodging, 150
Lodging Hospitality, 42, 150
log files, 20, 47, 276
L'Opera Bistro, 113
Louisiana, 4–5, 36–37, 132
lowercase/uppercase typing,
  46, 50
Low-Fat Vegetarian Recipes,
  185
"lurking," definition of, 38
Lynx, 140–141, 144, 145
  basic description of,
    137–138, 276
  commands, list of, 266–267

M

Macintosh
  America Online and, 57–58

CompuServe and, 60–61
file archives and, 112
magazines, electronic, 63,
  65, 148
mailing lists, 92, 140
  basic description of, 7, 91,
    101–107, 276
  lists of, 171–182, 241–246
  new, notification of,
    106–107
  subscribing to, 104–106
mail-order supplies, 148
mailto setting, 121
Maine, 84
Majordomo, 105–106, 276
Mariani, John, 83, 86
Maribor Food and Drinks,
  202, 258
Marketing Forum
  (CompuServe), 66, 69
marketing resources, 66, 69,
  148
Market News, 53
Marriott Foodservice, 227
MasterCook (mailing list),
  179
MasterCook II, 154–155,
  179
Matt Loew's Cafenet, 254
Mead-Lovers List, 244
Member Services
  (CompuServe), 67
menus, 28–35, 276
message(s), 89–107. *See also*
  e-mail; mailing lists
  basic components of,
    46–47
  boards, definition of, 52,
    276
  creating, 35
  cross-posting, 166, 272
  posting, 99–100, 106, 166,
    277
  private, 37, 38–39
  public, 35–37, 78–79
  reading, 30, 32, 33
  threads, 37, 38
  the Usenet and, 98, 107
Metabisulphite Club, 251

Index

Index

Your Name_____

Company Name_____

Street Address_____

City/State/Zip_____

Country_____

E-Mail_____

Phone_____

Fax_____

Thank you for your interest in Van Nostrand Reinhold publications. To enable us to keep you abreast of the latest developments in your field, please complete the following information.

WE WILL SEND YOU THE FOLLOWING UPON RECEIPT OF YOUR RESPONSE:

- Free exhibit pass(es) to select trade shows & updates about our forthcoming books.
- A catalog of titles.
- Information on becoming a VNR reviewer.

Holleman, Food and Wine Online

1. **How I first heard about this book:**
   a. bookstore (please specify)_____
   b. advertisement(please specify)_____
   c. book review (please specify)_____
   d. colleagues
   e. catalog
   f. other (please specify)_____

2. **Number of Culinary/Hospitality books I currently own:**
   a. 2-5
   b. 6-10
   c. 10+

3. **I purchased this book for my:**
   a. professional use
   b. personal use
   c. both

4. **I would be interested in new books on the following subject(s):**
   a. Internet for __users or __developers
   b. Catering
   c. Baking and Pastry
   d. Beverage Management
   e. Buffets
   f. Other (please specify)_____

5. **My business or profession:**
   a. Chef
   b. Caterer
   c. Restaurant Manager
   d. Restaurant Owner
   e. Food & Beverage Manager
   f. Student
   g. Manager, Non-Commercial Foodservice
   h. Education Research
   i. Government
   j. Information Industry
   k. Librarian
   l. Other (please specify)
   _____
   _____
   _____

6. **I use a PC at:**
   a. home
   b. work
   c. school
   d. other

7. **I have a CD-ROM player:**
   a. yes
   b. no

8. **I have access to the following online services:**
   a. America Online
   b. Compuserve
   c. Internet
   d. Prodigy
   e. World Wide Web
   f. other (please specify)_____

9. **I participate in the following online activities:**
   a. forums
   b. conferences
   c. new groups
   d. other (please specify)_____

10. **Name the top publication you read for information in your field:**
    _____

11. **Please name the professional organizations to which you belong**_____
    _____

CHEFNET Free Trial Offer for Food and Beverage Professionals 10 hours Free Trial PLUS an extra 5 hours when you e-mail your restaurant name and phone number with a mention of this book, Food and Wine Online, to the SYSOP.

To set up a Free Trial account, use your modem and modem software to dial **1-218-751-5149**, set your terminal emulation for **ANSI** and log in as **"NEW"**.

ChefNet is a bulletin board service for professional chefs, students and allied members of the industry. For more information, e-mail **info@chefnet.com**
Free electronic updates to Food and Wine Online !
To subscribe, send an e-mail message to:
majordomo@vnr.com and leave the subject line blank.
In the body of the message include only the following words: **subscribe vnr-cul**